NEVER TRUMP

NEVER TRUMP

THE REVOLT OF THE CONSERVATIVE ELITES

ROBERT P. SALDIN
AND
STEVEN M. TELES

OXFORD
UNIVERSITY PRESS

OXFORD
UNIVERSITY PRESS

Oxford University Press is a department of the University of Oxford. It furthers
the University's objective of excellence in research, scholarship, and education
by publishing worldwide. Oxford is a registered trade mark of Oxford University
Press in the UK and certain other countries.

Published in the United States of America by Oxford University Press
198 Madison Avenue, New York, NY 10016, United States of America.

Library of Congress Cataloging-in-Publication Data
Names: Saldin, Robert P., 1977– author. | Teles, Steven Michael, author.
Title: Never Trump : the revolt of the conservative elites /
Robert P. Saldin and Steven M. Teles.
Description: New York, NY : Oxford University Press, 2020. |
Includes bibliographical references and index.
Identifiers: LCCN 2019054913 (print) | LCCN 2019054914 (ebook) |
ISBN 9780190880446 (hardback) | ISBN 9780190880460 (epub) |
ISBN 9780190933173
Subjects: LCSH: Republican Party (U.S. : 1854–) |
Intra-party disagreements (Political parties)—United States. | Conservatism—United States. |
Presidents—United States—Election, 2016. | Trump, Donald, 1946– |
United States—Politics and government—2017–
Classification: LCC JK2356 .S277 2020 (print) | LCC JK2356 (ebook) |
DDC 324.973/0932—dc23
LC record available at https://lccn.loc.gov/2019054913
LC ebook record available at https://lccn.loc.gov/2019054914

1 3 5 7 9 8 6 4 2
Printed by LSC Communications, United States of America

CONTENTS

———⇒◆⇐———

PART IV: Lawyers and Economists

ACKNOWLEDGMENTS

We would like to thank the Hewlett Foundation, and especially its president Larry Kramer, for generous and timely financial support. We also received helpful feedback from a number of friends and colleagues: Melissa Bass, Dan DiSalvo, Dan Drezner, Heather Hurlburt, Geoffrey Kabaservice, David Karol, David Mayhew, Larry Mead, Patrick Ruffini, Reihan Salam, Danny Schlozman, Adam Sheingate, Jerry Taylor, and several anonymous reviewers arranged by Oxford University Press. This book never would have been possible without our interviewees, and we are grateful to them for sharing so openly and frankly their experiences and insights of what has been, for many, an unsettling—even traumatic—period in their lives. We are also indebted to Dave McBride and his team at OUP. Rob wishes to thank his family for their love, support, and patience, especially Erin, Sylvie, Frankie, and his parents. Steve would like to recognize the students in his spring 2019 Political Polarization class at Johns Hopkins, who helped him think through how the nation got in this mess, and all his friends and comrades at the Niskanen Center. Lastly, Steve thanks his wife, Fawzia, whose pessimism about the prospects of her adopted country under Trump has pushed him to think harder about how it might get better.

I

Introduction

PANIC HAD ALREADY SET in by the time #nevertrump became a viral sensation on Twitter. For over seven months, Republican elites had dismissed Donald Trump as a buffoonish, unserious candidate, reassuring themselves that he was destined to be laughed off the Republican stage. If his opera buffa-esque campaign kickoff event—highlighted by his assertion that Mexican immigrants "are rapists"—wouldn't do it, certainly his ridiculous "policies" like having Mexico pay for a border wall would. There was no way, they insisted, that Trump could survive his vulgar allegation that Fox News personality and debate moderator Megyn Kelly's tough line of questioning was the result of her menstrual cycle. At the very least, they were confident that Republican voters would instinctively recoil from his cruelty, so plainly on display in episodes like his mockery of party icon John McCain's POW status, his attack on primary opponent Carly Fiorina's appearance, and his imitation of a disabled reporter. And what about his childish rhetoric characterized by schoolyard insults and his reliance on simple, low-syllable-count words like "stupid"? Or those garish hats brandishing his provincial slogan, "Make America Great Again"? Admittedly, they counseled themselves, Republican primary voters sometimes flirt with outsider candidates, but they always eventually settle down with a clean, respectable suitor.

Yet, by late February it was clear to all but the most delusional observers that Trump was well on his way to securing the Republican presidential nomination. Not only had he decisively won the key early-cycle states of New Hampshire, South Carolina, and Nevada, he'd also just picked up the one thing that had eluded him thus far: endorsements from establishment Republicans in the form of a vanquished primary opponent (New Jersey Governor Chris Christie) and a US Senator (Alabama's Jeff Sessions). Republican primary voters were flocking to Trump's revolution, and the party elites' fortifications were crumbling. It was only at this point that the #nevertrump hashtag blew up. Like any meme, #nevertrump had a variety of meanings to those who deployed it. But for the elite Republicans and conservatives who embraced it, #nevertrump signaled horror and incomprehension at the rise of Donald Trump and how it had turned their political world upside down. #Nevertrump was also a way of signaling that Trump represented something more sinister than normal quadrennial Republican and conservative movement primary politics.

Once they recognized the threat, the strongest adherents to Never Trump[1] relentlessly and desperately searched for ways to frustrate Trump's takeover of the Republican Party. They organized letters in which a range of the party's top experts and former Republican luminaries declared their opposition to him. They tried and failed to coalesce behind a single primary challenger, and then schemed to deny Trump the party's nomination at the Republican National Convention. They searched for and eventually found a third-party candidate in the hopes that they could deadlock the Electoral College and throw the election to the House of Representatives. Shocking even themselves, a number of these lifelong Republicans, who had spent their careers battling Democrats, ended up voting for someone other than their party's nominee, up to and including their former nemesis, Hillary Clinton. Even after his election, a remnant of these Never Trumpers have kept up rearguard efforts to expose the perfidy of the Trump administration and to call their former allies away from the siren song of Trumpian populism.

It is hard not to look at these efforts, at least as of the spring of 2020, as having comprehensively failed. Donald Trump is as popular with Republican voters as any president in the modern era. The party's core coalition partners—from the National Rifle Association (NRA) to pro-lifers—have, with various degrees of enthusiasm, stuck by him. The ranks of Never Trump, meanwhile, have seen considerable attrition, with some of their foot soldiers slinking into the Trumpian fold while others defected to the Democrats or simply resigned themselves to being politically homeless. Nonetheless, a dedicated contingent have sought to keep the candle burning, hoping for a turn of fortune. They may yet provide, like St. Benedict in the catacombs, the foundation for an eventual return to the true church. All indications, however, point to a long struggle.

Why did these men and women, who had not long ago been party stalwarts, take the historically dramatic step of actively opposing their own nominee and then continuing to hound him in office? They did so not just because they thought they were *obligated* to do so as individuals based on their own, idiosyncratic moral conscience. They also opposed Trump so ferociously because they thought they were *authorized* to do so by their role in their party and—critically for our account—by their professional vocation.

Creating Their Own Enemies List

Supporters of the president have been positively gleeful at writing obituaries for the movement. David Azerrad of the Heritage Foundation wrote that, "NeverTrumpism is not dead, but it is on life support with no possibility of returning to the vitality it displayed in 2016. Were it not for the news media's eagerness to amplify the voices of those who hate the president, the movement would have long since been relegated to the more obscure corners of the internet. . . . Among conservatives, Never Trumpism is already a fringe and irrelevant movement." *Washington Post* columnist Henry Olsen declared that, "Never Trump Republicans must confront the fact that on issue after issue they are in the minority within their own party." Even Liz Mair, a political operative who led some of the most aggressive attacks on Trump, was ready by 2019 to throw dirt on its grave. "In most politically meaningful ways, the Never Trump movement has disintegrated. It's now the political equivalent of a doomed exotic species, attracting a lot of stares from bystanders, but no longer playing much of a role in the actual biosphere."[2]

While the Never Trumpers now hold little to no influence with the party's base or its core coalition partners, their impact on the actual composition of the Trump administration has been far from negligible.

There has never been a party in the Western world that was elected and sought to govern with such a wide range of intraparty opposition. As Pat Buchanan observed after the election, the Never Trumpers "[made] up their own enemies list"[3] for the incoming Trump administration—a list that those in charge of political appointments paid close attention to. Trump's picks for a wide range of positions, especially in the area of foreign policy, look vastly different than they would have in any other Republican administration, in large part because so many potential officeholders had declared themselves implacably opposed to Trump—both the man and, to the extent this term can be applied to Trump, his ideas. Even more profoundly, the administration found it very difficult—and in many cases impossible—to fill a wide range of positions because all of the plausible candidates for jobs that require technocratic as well as ideological credentials had signed on to Never Trump. The Trump administration has had to govern without most of the party's brain, leading it to make profound errors of basic domestic and foreign policy governance that helped contribute to the impression that Trump is overseeing a never-ending sequence of incompetence, corruption, and political self-subversion.

Most of the politicians who once denounced Trump turned out to be, at least in the minds of Never Trumpers, summer soldiers and sunshine patriots. Elected officials like Lindsey Graham and Ted Cruz—who had once denounced him as mentally unbalanced, ideologically unhygienic, and fundamentally authoritarian—eventually came to bend the knee. Given the intense negative partisanship of our times, and the fear among members of Congress that crossing Trump will lead to a humiliating Twitter attack and a primary challenge, this is not much of a surprise.[4] Yet the white-hot core of the resistance to Trump was never with elected officials but among the professionals, public intellectuals, political operatives, and once and future political appointees that all modern parties depend on to run the huge undertakings of modern campaigns and governance.

It is for this reason that the chapters to come focus primarily on these people, whom we refer to as the Republican extended party network, rather than elected officials or core party coalition partners like business, the Christian right, and the NRA. It is, perhaps, an irony that a party that has defined itself by its opposition to professionalism and the administrative state should have accumulated such a large cadre of professionals ready and eager to work for the government. A feature of modern politics and governance, however, is that acquiring and then deploying political power requires the participation of scores of individuals with technical, administrative, and persuasive skills. Those experts are more than just hired hands because, in exchange for their professional services, they claim "jurisdiction" over the vast scope of expert work involved in seeking office and governing the sprawling American state.[5] In the pages to come, we will discuss the jurisdictional claims made by networks of experts in national security, elections, law, economics, and the more diffuse category of public intellectuals. Until the election of Donald Trump, it was taken for granted that Republicans could not run a modern campaign, develop a serious policy agenda, or staff the modern state without building up and then deferring to an elite class of their own. To varying degrees, Trump challenged the jurisdiction of these elite Republican Party networks. That variation in Trump's own behavior helps explain the different responses of these professional groups to Trump. For example, while Trump ruthlessly attacked the jurisdictional claims of Republican national security experts and their ideas, if anything he actually expanded the jurisdictional claims of Republican lawyers when it came to judicial selection.

Party Elites and Liberal Democracy

A large segment of the individuals in this extended Republican Party network agreed that they had an obligation to help save their party and the country from what they saw as the worst instincts of their own base. That impulse is one carefully analyzed by political scientist Daniel Ziblatt, who has argued that the consolidation of democratic government depends critically upon whether parties of the right agree to play by the rules of democratic government and exercise discipline over extremists within their own tribe.[6] In particular, for Ziblatt, it is precisely the elite structure of conservative parties and their relative insulation from mass pressure—and with it, populist demagoguery and anti-institutionalism—that is a critical safeguard of democratic norms. This framework puts the Never Trump revolt in an interesting light. Many of the leaders of Never Trump had been pivotal in framing appeals to voters in ways that they thought were responsive to the public's "reasonable" concerns about thorny social issues like race and immigration. But they saw Trump, by "making the subtext, text," as overstepping the bounds of acceptable conservative politics precisely by giving the party's voters what they wanted rather than what party leaders thought acceptable to give them.

In addition, Ziblatt has argued in a more recent book with Steve Levitsky that the maintenance of democracy depends upon certain "norms of forbearance," in particular a willingness to publicly recognize the legitimacy of one's opponents and to accept the necessity of institutional rules and practices that mediate direct democracy.[7] What so concerned many of the actors around Never Trump is that Trump made it quite clear that he was not willing to recognize the democratic legitimacy of the opposition—most obviously by calling for his opponents to be "locked up" or "sent home"—suggesting that he might not accept the 2016 election result if he lost, and asking foreign leaders to dig up dirt on a domestic political rival.

Never Trumpers, understood this way, were engaging in the kind of system maintenance activity that a healthy liberal democracy requires. In some other systems, like Germany, this gatekeeper function is performed formally, by banning parties that are judged to violate fundamental constitutional norms. In the American system, where the question is not what to do about illiberal, extremist minor parties, the system maintenance function is less formal and has to occur within the two major parties themselves. In many cases, Never Trumpers were trying to perform this gatekeeper function more with the health of the GOP or the conservative movement in mind, rather than the health of the American political system as a whole. But regardless of their motivation, their actions can be seen as performing a critical role of party elites in a properly functioning liberal democracy. What so frustrated and confused many Never Trumpers is that their fellow Republicans did not see the same necessity for performing these gatekeeping functions.

Yet the behavior of Republican voters in 2016 is consistent with international trends: voters themselves cannot be counted on to engage in system maintenance, especially under conditions of political polarization. Recent work by political scientist Milan Svolic convincingly shows that voters in polarized countries care about democratic norms, but not if they are asked to sacrifice too many of their policy preferences.[8] Disturbingly, the more a political system polarizes the more there is at stake, in terms of public policy, for a voter placed in the position of deciding whether or not to vote for a demagogue or authoritarian of their own party. While voting on their democratic principles is not a big sacrifice for moderates, who are more indifferent to the ideology of the rival parties, it is a significant sacrifice for strong partisans.

This, of course, is precisely the situation that faced Republican voters in 2016. Many of them were repulsed by Trump, considered him a threat to democratic norms, and voted for other candidates in the primary. For many, Trump was their absolute last choice. But by the time the general election rolled around, the only viable tool at their disposal was a vote for one of conservatism's great hate figures of the last quarter century. It was Hillary Clinton, after all, who had breathlessly warned about "a vast right-wing conspiracy," whom conservatives had mocked for saying "it takes a village to raise a child," and who had, as they saw it, hypocritically covered for her sexually predatory husband. And just as important, in an election in which the fate of the Supreme Court was very much on the ballot, they were asked to defend democracy in a way that would hand the judiciary over to Democratic judges they considered to be a menace to their basic rights. It is precisely this kind of hard choice that is regularly faced by voters in such situations. And confronted with such a scenario, they understandably, if unfortunately, rarely default to protecting democracy.

If the mass of voters cannot be counted on to protect democratic norms, then it is hard to see who else could do so other than party elites. It is for that reason that we focus so intently in this book on the behavior of the elite conservatives who, facing the same paradox as Republican voters, chose to reject their own party's nominee, knowing that doing so could help elect Hillary Clinton. Their actions during the primary can be understood as an effort to save Republican voters from having to choose between upholding democratic norms or their policy preferences. But having failed, they took the even harder step of forgoing their desire for conservative policy outcomes in order to stop someone whom they sincerely believed was a dangerous demagogue.

That sort of system maintenance is becoming ever more of a sacrifice, as the Democratic Party moves sharply to the left and the Trump administration (surprisingly for some) delivers major policy victories to conservatives, from corporate tax cuts to conservative judges to deregulation. Conservatives disgusted with Trump are being asked to give up quite a lot in policy terms in opposing him—something that critics to the left rarely appreciate sufficiently.

The evenly matched competition between Democrats and Republicans in recent decades has compounded this problem by raising the stakes in American politics, thereby accentuating polarization and fueling apocalyptic thinking. As political scientist Frances Lee has shown, under conditions of intense, closely matched competition in which the control of Congress and the White House (and, by extension, the judiciary) is constantly up for grabs, the parties have been incentivized to abandon bipartisanship and adopt rhetorical messages focused on differentiating themselves.[9] The constant hunt for messaging schemes designed to burnish your own party's image and tarnish that of your opponent's encourages the kind of hysterical, end-of-days, "Flight 93" mode of thinking that we saw in 2016. When every election is viewed as a tipping point, and losing means being permanently defeated, democratic norms and niceties will inevitably suffer. Never Trumpers saw themselves as pushing back against these forces of illiberal extremism, hoping that the center would hold.

That Never Trumpers failed is important for understanding the capacity of American political parties to perform the informal constitutional role that liberal democracy requires of them. Trump's capture of the GOP will have consequences for the party—and for the republic—for years to come. But the cracks in the system that Trump exploited are not unique to the 2016 Republican Party. Indeed, there is no reason to think that Democratic Party elites, faced with a populist demagogue of the left, could exercise this gatekeeping function either. As the Never Trump experience demonstrates, the combined forces of a democratized process of selecting presidential candidates, ideological polarization, the rise of politics as theatrical blood sport, and the anti-elitist temper of our age has eaten away at the social preconditions of party gatekeeping. In the coming decades, our institutional antibodies to populist demagoguery will be unlikely to come from elected officials, the kind that proved all too willing to bend the knee to Trump. Instead, as we suggest in the conclusion, what safety we have will need to come from parties that, having broken into durable factions, are no longer willing to march in lockstep behind an illiberal chief executive of their own party.

The chapters to come are organized around the professional or quasi-professional groups that form the core of the Republican extended party network, and one of the key questions we ask is what explains the varying degrees of intensity of Never Trump sentiment among them. Some of the variation turns out to be due to the systems of belief that participants in these governing networks share, while others are shaped by their personal relationships. As social scientists, we are trained to look for structures—and we found them. But we would not be true to what our informants told us if we did not emphasize that there was also an irreducible element of individual choice. There had never been a candidate remotely like Donald Trump, a fact that rendered the choice of response to him only weakly subject to rational calculation. Some conservatives resolved the uncertainty surrounding Trump during the campaign by leaning heavily on the fact—as for many it seemed—that he would never be elected. Opposing Trump thus seemed like the path of least resistance, the one that would allow them to emerge from the rubble as part of the "clean team" that would help put the Republican Party back together again.

For others, the choice was much harder. They were faced with decisions about exactly how aggressively to criticize Trump and, at the same time, had to watch as colleagues and friends, with whom they had not long ago served in the political trenches, made different decisions. These decisions were informed by a combination of personal and professional relationships, temperament, professional advancement, and choice under severe uncertainty. We try to make sense, in the pages that follow, of these complex and often excruciating decisions.

We tell this story by allowing the participants to speak in their own words, often at length. We do that in part to allow the reader to get a sense of the personalities and voices of the participants, but also to provide the reader with the raw materials to come to different conclusions than we have.[10] We hope that even those who disagree deeply with the Never Trumpers will learn at least a little something about the very human motivations that caused them to make the choices they did.

PART I

National Security Professionals

2

Guardians

DURING DONALD TRUMP'S MUCH anticipated debut speech on American foreign policy at Washington's Mayflower Hotel in the spring of 2016, he uncharacteristically read from a prepared script: "Our foreign policy is a complete and total disaster. No vision. No purpose. No direction. No strategy." Trump traced the cause of this malady—as he did in various other areas of American public life—to the establishment. In this case, that meant the foreign policy establishment. As a remedy, Trump pledged to surround himself with new talent rather than the entrenched elites "who have perfect résumés but very little to brag about except responsibility for a long history of failed policies and continued losses at war. We have to look to new people. We have to look to new people because many of the old people frankly don't know what they're doing, even though they may look awfully good writing in The New York Times or being watched on television."[1]

Trump's critique wasn't limited to personnel. Throughout his campaign, he routinely attacked the principles most national security experts hold dear and have spent their careers supporting and defending. On virtually every foreign policy issue—from the importance of alliances and human rights, to promoting democratic norms and free trade—Trump staked out positions, or impulsively lurched in directions, that ran counter to Republican foreign policy orthodoxy.

He was also decidedly undiplomatic—as he had been throughout the campaign—in discussing the elephant in the room. The Iraq War remained a particularly sensitive subject in Republican foreign policy circles, as many GOP experts had served in the George W. Bush administration or publicly advocated for its policies. In his speech at the Mayflower, Trump once again ignored the party's unwritten rules of etiquette by gratuitously disparaging the Iraq War and its Republican architects. Much worse, he parroted a long-standing criticism, most popular in far-left and libertarian circles, that Washington's foreign policy network in general, and its Republicans members in particular, are warmongers. Drawing a clear contrast between himself and the foreign policy establishment, he emphasized that "war and aggression will not be my first instinct." He continued: "I was totally against the war in Iraq, very proudly, saying for many years that it would destabilize the Middle East. Sadly, I was correct."[2] While the historical record clearly contradicts Trump's assertions regarding his position on Iraq, he made the claim frequently during the campaign, citing his keen discernment as evidence of his foreign policy acumen.[3] At times, Trump would go even further in disparaging Bush 43 and his national security team. Iraq had been more than a simple mistake, he alleged, it was a treasonous conspiracy in which the administration—not just the president—was implicated. "They lied," Trump charged in a February debate as former Florida Governor Jeb Bush looked on. "They said there were weapons of mass destruction. There were none. And they knew there were none."[4]

Iraq was only one item on a nearly unending list of differences between Trump and the Republican foreign policy network, but it crystalized the divide. For many in this milieu, Trump's belligerent allegations and false statements about the war revealed the fundamental character flaws that—even more than his policy positions, such as they were—rendered him totally unacceptable as a president. At the same time, for those who had served in the Bush 43 administration, the likely Republican presidential nominee's contempt for them and his impertinent use of the Iraq issue was an unprecedented attack on their professional and personal standing. Their post-government careers, reputations, and identities were inextricably linked to their work in government. Like most who serve as political appointees, those positions had marked the high point of their careers and remained a badge of honor. That work in government had also led, in many cases, to lucrative and prestigious positions in the years that followed. Some retained hopes of going into government again, at higher levels, when the next Republican president was elected. But the clear GOP front runner was now suggesting that the party's foreign policy experts were at the center of the corrupt DC swamp and that their service to their country had been deeply flawed, even dishonorable. He was also, of course, making it clear that they wouldn't have the opportunity to go into government anytime soon.

The Foreign Policy Establishment

The *foreign policy establishment* is a somewhat amorphous term that is not infrequently greeted with eye-rolls from those associated with it and skepticism from those outside of it.[5] It is generally used to refer to the informal, bipartisan milieu of national security experts and former government officials who are engaged in debates over American foreign policy. Sometimes the term is used pejoratively. In a much discussed 2016 article in *The Atlantic*, Jeffrey Goldberg revealed that President Obama "secretly disdains" the foreign policy establishment. Several weeks later, the administration dropped any pretense of secrecy. In a *New York Times* profile, it was reported that Deputy National Security Advisor Ben Rhodes had "a healthy contempt for the American foreign-policy establishment," or as he preferred to call it, "the Blob," and that he thought its members were a bunch of "morons."[6] Trump's loathing for the group, then, isn't exactly a new feature of American politics.

Joining the Club

Though there's no secret handshake or initiation ritual to mark one's entry into the foreign policy establishment, the process isn't random.[7] A standard-issue foreign policy establishmentarian has a graduate degree in political science, international relations, history, or some related field. Often it will be a master's degree from Johns Hopkins University School of Advanced International Studies (SAIS) or a similar policy-based school, though doctorates are also common. An MFA in creative writing, as Ben Rhodes possesses, is decidedly nontraditional. After graduate school, a prospective member of the foreign policy establishment is highly likely to get his ticket punched at one or more of a set of venerable institutions. She might take a job at a think tank, with a committee or personal office on Capitol Hill, as an assistant professor at a university, or as a staffer at the State Department, the Pentagon, or with one of the agencies in the intelligence community. A somewhat less conventional track goes through the military hierarchy.

Within the think tank world, the Council on Foreign Relations (CFR) is the most establishmentarian of the foreign policy establishment's institutions. CFR was founded in 1921, has offices in Washington and New York, and publishes *Foreign Affairs* magazine. Other key think tanks focused on national security include the Center for Strategic and International Studies (CSIS) and the Woodrow Wilson International Center for Scholars. Comprehensive think tanks like the Brookings Institution and the American Enterprise Institute also house national security experts. And with the proliferation of boutique think tanks in recent decades, there are many other potential bases of operations.

Members of the foreign policy establishment are also likely to be writers or professors. Many jump back and forth between writing wonky policy reports or academic articles targeted to their professional network and general audience essays and op-eds in outlets like *Foreign Affairs, Foreign Policy*, and leading newspapers. Many also follow the path blazed by Republicans like Henry Kissinger, combining prestigious academic careers with posts in the administration when a president from their party occupies the White House, after which they return to positions at think tanks or universities. Others who have served in government take their Rolodexes to established law firms or open consulting agencies. Some do both.[8]

The Company Town

The foreign policy establishment's haunts are in close proximity. As Bryan McGrath, a central Never Trump organizer in the national security network, explains, Washington "is corporate headquarters and we don't have many satellite businesses. . . . All the action happens here or up at Turtle Bay [the Manhattan neighborhood housing the United Nations], and none of us go up there. It's all here."[9] Inside the city of Washington, most of the key institutions are within walking distance, and many are within shouting distance. The main nerve centers are within steps of a small handful of tightly concentrated DC landmarks: Dupont Circle, Farragut Square, the White House, and Foggy Bottom. For instance, amidst the embassies of Dupont Circle, Brookings, the Carnegie Endowment for International Peace, and the American Enterprise Institute occupy adjoining buildings. SAIS and the Peterson Institute for International Economics are across the street, and the Center for Strategic and International Studies is just around the corner. Less than a mile to the south, the Council on Foreign Relations sits between the White House and the State Department. An outlier to this tight proximity is the Pentagon, which necessitates a several-minute Metro ride. Of course, not all members of the foreign policy establishment are based in Washington, but the vast majority are. And those who aren't tend to visit frequently.

This high concentration of national security experts in Washington is unique relative to other policy areas such as healthcare or education, where experts are widely scattered. As Tom Nichols, a professor at the Naval War College and one of the rare national security experts based outside of Washington, explains, the reason for this distinction is that while states and localities are deeply engaged in a wide variety of policy issues, they don't conduct their own foreign policy. As a domestic policy expert, Nichols notes, "you can work around the country in the states because the states have those programs. You can be a leading light on welfare reform working in Michigan." In fact, prior to focusing on national security issues, Nichols himself worked on domestic policy in Massachusetts. At the state-level, "You can go to work every day and talk about really important policy stuff that has impact in Washington [and] you could have contacts with people and think tanks in DC . . . who were interested in the same thing. [But] nobody in the Massachusetts statehouse is doing foreign policy. . . . [And] if you're a nuclear weapons expert, you're not spending your time talking to the national security apparatus while you're also the state nuclear weapons expert for South Dakota. Foreign policy is a one-town industry."[10]

For Republicans in the foreign policy establishment, the centrality of Washington is even more pronounced because—relative to Democrats—fewer of them are based at universities. According to Nichols, for the GOP, "It's not even a hub and spoke [system], it's a center and outposts. . . . To get a critical mass of Republican foreign policy specialists, you have to get inside 495," the interstate highway that circles Washington and its closest suburbs. As a result, the national security wing of the Never Trump coalition "is really an inside the Beltway thing."[11]

Zealous Moderates, Reluctant Partisans

Most of political Washington defines itself in terms of partisan teams. But within the foreign policy establishment, party has customarily been a secondary consideration. In this milieu, the essential distinction has traditionally been between those who fall within the American foreign policy consensus and those who don't. That consensus isn't as strong as it was during the Cold War, but a basic understanding of the mission of American foreign policy nonetheless endures among elite-level foreign policy professionals. Eliot Cohen, a SAIS professor, Bush 43 State Department official, and leading Never Trumper, aptly articulated the centrality of this consensus for national security experts and explained how Trump stood outside its boundaries. "Trump can be seen as a talented demagogue, or as the manifestation of deep pathologies in the body politic," Cohen wrote in the spring of 2016, "but he is also the bearer of ideas—crudely framed and sometimes incoherent, but ideas nonetheless. Nowhere is this more true than on foreign policy." And those ideas, Cohen continued, pose a central threat to "the two-generation-old American foreign policy consensus. Even in this era of partisanship, there has been a large measure of agreement between the two parties, cemented by officials, experts, and academics who shared a common outlook. That outlook held that American interests were ineluctably intertwined with American values," like promoting liberty and human rights, "and that when possible, each should reinforce the other."[12] Most national security experts and leading politicians in the Democratic Party fall within this mainstream, as do their counterparts in the Republican Party.

To be sure, there are still discernible differences between Republicans and Democrats when it comes to foreign policy. Support for the Obama administration's Iran deal, for instance, split largely along partisan lines and was hotly contested. However, unlike the partisan rancor seen in other policy areas, debates within the foreign policy establishment occur within well-established bipartisan networks and institutions that foster considerable interaction between experts in both parties. Additionally, the differences that do exist between foreign policy experts from different parties are largely confined to a limited sphere defined by a shared understanding of America's place in the world, a commitment to internationalism, a belief in the importance of expertise, and a recognition that it would be bad if the judgments of non-specialists came to dominate American foreign policy. Conflict is contained, as it is in few other domains of American politics, both by ideas and institutions that generate cooperative, personal relationships between partisan adversaries.

Members of the foreign policy establishment also tend to be more moderate and less partisan when it comes to domestic politics relative to elites in other networks. Cohen explains:

> [The typical GOP foreign policy expert] is more moderate on domestic issues than a lot of the rest of the Republican Party. . . . Most of the Republican foreign policy, national security types that I know are very moderate conservatives. . . . [For instance, they'd] probably be a bit more liberal in terms of wishing that the Republican Party had some kind of plausible policy on healthcare. In that sense, a little bit more liberal. You wouldn't find many libertarians. You for sure wouldn't find Grover Norquistian, starve-the-beast kinds of people. They believe in fully funding the Park Service and the Library of Congress. It's fairly centrist.[13]

Foreign policy establishmentarians combine ideological centrism with a relatively tempered taste for partisanship. As a general rule and relative to other policy networks, most national security professionals pride themselves on doing "policy, not politics" and say things like "I don't consider myself an extremely partisan person."[14] They'll go out of their way to say that they are actually registered independents, aren't involved in party politics, or sometimes vote for Democrats, especially down ballot. For many, picking a team is more about the uncomfortable necessity of accommodating oneself to the American party system than it is about taking a principled stand between two organizations that have starkly opposed ideologies or policy preferences. When people come to Washington seeking Cohen's advice on these matters, he tells them: "Look, if you're going to be in government as a political appointee, understand there are the blues and the greens. You've got to pick one of them. You can have friends on the other side, but it's just the way it works."[15] This attitude used to be widely shared by Democrats and Republicans, although especially in the wake of the Iraq War, it's less common among Democrats now. Republicans—particularly those who went Never Trump—would still be open to working in a Democratic administration, but many Democrats have become increasingly convinced that they could never work in a Republican administration. As such, the stronger sense of cross-party solidarity among elite Republican foreign policy experts is an interesting departure from the usual story of today's "asymmetrical partisanship" in which Republicans are more ideological and polarized than Democrats.[16]

Mike Green's career path illustrates this traditional dynamic within the foreign policy network. An Asia expert and academic by training, Green's initial engagement with the political sphere came through Joe Lieberman, the Democratic senator from Connecticut and Al Gore's running mate in 2000. Yet several years later, Green found himself in the Bush 43 White House serving as Special Assistant to the President and on the National Security Council (NSC). Since then he's been considered part of the Republican foreign policy elite. As Green explains:

> I did not work on the George W. Bush campaign. In fact, I was at the Council on Foreign Relations and I ran projects trying to find bipartisan consensus on North Korea policy, Japan policy—things that were controversial in those days. So, I was actually approached during that sort of interregnum when the Florida tally was being re-done by both Gore's people and Bush's people for the same job, which I ended up getting, the Japan-Korea director in the NSC. And Bush won and so I went in and I worked there.[17]

Green would have happily worked for Gore, and in an ideal world, he says he'd be most comfortable with a Republican State Department and a Democratic Defense Department. A registered independent, Green has always voted Republican at the presidential level but he's often supported Democrats down-ballot. Among the Never Trump foreign policy experts, that's not unusual.

Others, like Cohen, may have been registered Republicans, but they didn't necessarily always vote that way. "I was never a gung-ho, particularly partisan Republican," Cohen recalls. "I've voted for Democrats for president. I have other tribal identities, but my partisan identity is not one of my tribal identities." Indeed, Cohen didn't even vote for George W. Bush in 2004, though he later served in 43's administration. "When they hired me, I told Condi [Rice], I said: 'I hate to tell you this, and I kind of regret having done it, but I voted for [John] Kerry.' She said, 'What?' I said, 'Well, my son was about to go off as an infantry officer to fight in this war, which I was in favor of. I think I just felt the administration was really fucking it up, and I was angry.' She said, 'Oh, Jesus. All right.'"[18]

The uneasiness about partisanship within the Republican foreign policy network was also evident when Never Trump activity got underway. As will be seen, this activity centered around two public letters denouncing Trump. The first of these included a controversial statement that its signers were "committed and loyal Republicans."[19] One prominent Never Trumper who declined to sign that letter on account of this wording emailed the letter's organizers, writing that "if you would say 'as officials who have served in national security positions in previous Republican Administrations,' I would be willing to sign it. I don't think it is relevant to say 'dedicated and loyal Republicans.' We want to show national security expertise, not partisan loyalty."[20] Several others, despite having worked in Republican administrations and being widely identified as members of the Republican foreign policy establishment, wrote back to say that they were registered independents, considered themselves as such, or simply felt uneasy about being identified as a Republican. Notably, the second Never Trump letter purposefully avoided branding its signers as Republicans, opting instead for the more innocuous phrasing that the "undersigned individuals have all served in senior national security and/or foreign policy positions in Republican Administrations."[21] Surely this fine distinction would be lost on the broader American public, but it was an important one for many members of the Republican foreign policy establishment.

One reason for this unusually low degree of partisanship within the foreign policy establishment is that there are many institutions and informal networks that bring people together across party lines. To be sure, products from left-of-center think tanks find their way into the hands of Democratic politicians, and the same is true on the other side. Yet even if politicians do not necessarily see foreign policy experts as nonpartisan, relative to experts in other fields, foreign policy experts know and interact with their counterparts in the other party and care more about how they are seen by them. As Green, who now holds positions at the CSIS and Georgetown University, explains, this is especially true at the most prominent think tanks. It is certainly true that Brookings and Carnegie have "a heavy Democratic flavor, whereas CSIS is considered a little more Republican." But these tendencies mask a commitment to cross-party relationships.

> [The think tanks] are all basically nonpartisan and try to encourage these sort of bipartisan and nonpartisan groups. And the Council on Foreign Relations creates task forces and study groups . . . that are designed to get people from across the aisle. And so the whole process is about breaking partisanship. . . . Then another important one that a lot of people who signed the letter are in is the Aspen Strategy Group. . . . It's 50 or 60 people from both sides of the aisle talking about arms control or Asia strategy or something. We spend a week together with our families, outside of Washington. So, there's lots of bonding there.[22]

Further, in some instances—such as whether America's future in Asia lies with the emerging power China or the traditional ally Japan—each party is internally split. As a result, foreign policy experts on either side of the issue are accustomed to looking for issue-specific allies across the aisle and have a stronger sense of commonality and purpose across party divides than within their own party.

Elections intrude on this bipartisan dynamic, but only partially. As Green describes:

> Election cycles come around and everyone gets tribal. And we all go to our teams. And then we secretly have coffee and sort of compare notes and do no harm. So, I worked for [2008 Republican nominee John] McCain and I was one of the leads on the foreign policy team. And I met with Jeff Bader, Obama's guy, all the time. Not to

talk about campaign strategy, but just: "Look, Ma Ying-jeou just got elected president of Taiwan. Let's not let our crazies in each party escalate. Let's kind of put out a reasonable response because it doesn't matter what happens in the election." . . . So, it gets very tribal around election time. And then, everyone goes back to being friends.[23]

Of course, foreign policy professionals would typically prefer that their party win presidential elections. They are, after all, more likely to agree on things with those on their partisan team. And some of the most coveted professional opportunities require their team winning the White House. But more so than in other policy areas, national security experts feel comfortable with people from the other party so long as they are within the consensus spectrum of American foreign policy.

The national security elite, whatever differences they have among themselves, share a common belief that responsible foreign policy requires insulating decision making from their own party's "crazies," as well as from those who simply do not understand or care about the world beyond the nation's borders. So even while they are pulled apart by their differences with experts in the other party, they are pulled together by a common fear of their own party's always-looming tendencies toward populism and isolationism.

Keeping the Crazies at Bay

Containing each party's "crazies," as Green puts it, has traditionally linked members of the foreign policy establishment in an elite, bipartisan project to defend their jurisdiction against non-experts. While this spirit of a bipartisan conspiracy against their respective bases has been on the decline among Democratic national security experts, it still runs very strong on the Republican side, particularly among those who opposed Donald Trump. The danger posed by foreign policy outsiders in the Republican and Democratic coalitions isn't identical, though both versions are grounded in opposition to the internationalism that is central to the American foreign policy establishment. As national security experts see it, the Republican variant of craziness is animated by a toxic and dangerous mix of isolationism and xenophobia, a strain of thinking with deep roots in the American right.

Indeed, particularly with the benefit of hindsight, it's obvious to those in the Republican foreign policy network that the Trump phenomenon didn't come out of nowhere. There were hints and premonitions of a dark undercurrent within the party. Eric Edelman, a GOP foreign policy veteran-turned-Never Trumper, remembers a prescient offhand remark made by his former boss, President George W. Bush: "You don't have to scratch very deep in the Republican Party to hit a pretty deep vein of xenophobia and protectionism and isolationism. My job as party leader is to push back against that."[24] Bush's understanding of his role in pushing back certain forces within the party can be understood as referring to two different, though sometimes overlapping, threats. The first is a disagreement over policy—namely, the dispute between mainstream internationalist Republicans and fringe elements of the American right. This schism is anything but new. Indeed, in the 1940s and 1950s, the isolationist strain wasn't even fringe. Embodied by Senator Robert Taft of Ohio, the Republican Party was home to a sizable contingent that sought to limit America's international engagement out of concern that such activity would bring excessive militarization, big government, imperialism, socialism, and, ultimately, totalitarianism. Taft attacked the bipartisan foreign policy consensus in the United States and its "tendency to interfere in the affairs of other nations, to assume that we are a kind of demigod and Santa Claus to solve the problems of the world."[25] He strongly opposed US engagement in World War II prior to Pearl Harbor and later opposed the establishment of the North Atlantic Treaty Organization (NATO) and the International Monetary Fund (IMF), while seeking to reduce funding for the Marshall Plan. Taft's anti-interventionist perspective never gained majority standing in the party, though it was a prominent minority view. The isolationist wing's influence declined following Dwight Eisenhower's defeat of Taft for the 1952 Republican presidential nomination.[26] The marginalized remnants of isolationism became increasingly associated with extreme elements of the American right as well as the American left that operated partially or entirely outside the two-party system. Gradually, isolationism on the right would be relegated to talk radio and associated with peripheral figures like Pat Buchanan, Phyllis Schlafly, and Ron Paul, who as often as not saw themselves as thorns in the side of the GOP.

The other, sometimes overlapping, threat that Bush pointed to in his comment to Edelman is one the Never Trumpers think is arguably more worrisome and that has a xenophobic lineage that can be traced back to the witch hunts and conspiracy theories of McCarthyism, the John Birch Society, and American dalliances with fascism. Philip Zelikow, a former State Department official under Secretary Condoleezza Rice and a professor at the University of Virginia, says that while he thinks Trump is personally "malevolent," perhaps the greater concern is the "significant faction underneath him that has no bottom." Zelikow continued:

> As a sometimes historian, what it reminds me of most is not so much [former Wisconsin Senator Joseph] McCarthy himself, but the claque of Republicans that were among the McCarthyites in the Senate. So, you have to think about people like [Indiana's William E.] Jenner or [Ohio's John] Bricker or, sometimes, [California's William] Knowland. There were about eight or nine of these guys. And if you actually went back and read their speeches, the kinds of things they say, you kind of see the abyss in them. The rhetoric [now] is very similar. . . . The alt-right today is actually not very different from the Birchers of 1958.[27]

Cohen traces the connection back a bit further, seeing in Trump's "America first" rhetoric an idea that clearly channels "the notorious movement before World War II that included not only traditional isolationists but also Nazi sympathizers."[28]

Yet going into the 2016 presidential cycle, despite being cognizant that these extreme forces still existed in some distant corners of the United States—and that they constituted some small element of the Republican electorate—GOP foreign policy professionals felt that this enduring challenge from the far right was contained and controlled. "The xenophobia," Edelman says, "while we were aware of it, I think most of us felt that had been a kind of minority current. You'd have [Colorado Representative] Tom Tancredo and other kind of xenophobes run in the past and go absolutely nowhere."[29] Nonetheless, a defining feature of the foreign policy establishment's thinking is grounded in the conviction that foreign policy is so important because the stakes are so high. And that means you can never rest easy. "It's the nature of the threat," explains Nichols. "You make a mistake in tax policy, you can rewrite the tax code next year. You make a mistake in North Korea, and a couple of million people are gonna die. . . . There's only so many times you can roll the dice before the game is over."[30]

One of the difficulties for those in the Republican national security network, however, was that the most prominent foreign policy engagement of the most recent GOP administration had gone disastrously. As a result, their claim to jurisdiction based on effectiveness had been damaged and made vulnerable to exploitation.[31]

Isolating the Isolationists

From the perspective of presidential candidates, engaging the foreign policy establishment has been one of the stations of the cross on the campaign circuit. Candidates ritualistically kiss the ring of the foreign policy establishment and receive the group's blessing as a means of demonstrating their status as a serious person—and thus a legitimate candidate—who can be trusted in the high-stakes enterprise of national security. The perception that engaging in this ceremony with the foreign policy mandarins was mandatory for candidates aspiring to be seen as viable presidential material granted this group an important structural source of power. Those understood to be within this establishment had a monopoly on the performance of this legitimation ritual, which also created significant pressure for experts to stay within the confines of approved behavior and beliefs.

At the top level of a campaign, foreign policy experts also provided important services to the candidates which, at least until 2016, were thought to be absolutely essential. These experts briefed candidates on the issues of the day, produced position papers, and imparted wisdom on everything from matters of policy to made-for-the-debate-stage one-liners. These eminent figures constituted a government in waiting that demonstrated to critical audiences that a campaign was serious and ready to govern. This was, in sum, a box that needed to be checked. As a result, the typical presidential campaign would involve courtships that often began two or three years prior to the election in which candidates would compete among one another to sweep up the best talent within the foreign policy establishment.

Yet there was also a clear and important distinction between the few top-tier foreign policy experts on a campaign and the many lower-ranking experts who nonetheless had an official role in the operation. Outside of the top staffers, the practical, day-to-day utility of the many mid- and lower-level foreign policy experts on a campaign was always rather dubious. Many did little or nothing. And the tasks that did get completed were often of a "make-work" nature. President Clinton's National Security Advisor Sandy Berger has described the process of campaigns engaging the foreign policy establishment as one of creating "the illusion of inclusion." Recounting his top-level foreign policy role in Bill Clinton's first presidential campaign, Berger describes the situation he faced:

> It's a process of engaging people, even though you don't have very much for them to do. You get some people digging holes and some people filling up holes. . . . You have hundreds of people who were part of the Democratic foreign policy establishment who want to feel like they're part of this campaign. There's only a little keyhole through which you're going to get to the candidate. So people did memos and people wrote talking points, and other people vetted them, and other people rewrote them. You keep moving this around so people feel as if they're involved.[32]

Beyond ego management, the exercise of sweeping up as many of the best foreign policy experts as possible was nonetheless seen as meaningful because it allowed a campaign to, at a minimum, demonstrate basic foreign policy competence and, ideally, create an impressive list of top talent. The point wasn't to put all of the best and the brightest to work fulfilling critical roles in a campaign. Rather, the value was in the signal it sent to the media and to competing campaigns. Berger illustrates the point with reference to the 1992 Clinton organization: "We were particularly interested in getting the neocons, who at that point still were Democrats. . . . Because of Clinton's war, Vietnam experience, or lack thereof, it was important for us that the more conservative, the Scoop Jackson Democrats, supported him. We made tremendous efforts to reach out to them and to include them in the campaign."[33] And even if they didn't actually "do" anything, having them assume a formal role was still seen as important for what it signaled to outside audiences.

One of Trump's critical insights—or fortuitous stumbles—was that from the purely political standpoint of winning a presidential election (not to be confused with actually being president), it turns out that it was not, in fact, necessary to go through the elaborate ritual of wooing the foreign policy establishment. Perhaps it is desirable for the sake of propriety to be able to point to some people—apparently anyone will do—whom you call advisors, but because the American public doesn't really know who most of the elite figures in the GOP national security network are in the first place, a committee of circus clowns might do the trick, so long as they are dressed up in suits and sporting lapel pins. Trump had discovered that the foreign policy establishment—unlike, say, the top echelon of social conservatism— simply doesn't command armies of voters and could be dismissed without electoral consequence.

The John Hay Initiative

Going into the 2016 presidential cycle, many Republican foreign policy elites had invested several years of time and energy building an institutional structure and articulating a clear vision for what the party's foreign policy was, where it needed to go, and how it would get there. The origins of this project dated to Mitt Romney's 2012 presidential campaign and the extensive preparations that had been undertaken for his potential administration. This groundwork marked the debut of an overhauled presidential transition system.

The handing of the baton from one administration to the next had been a growing concern for years. Traditionally, it had been considered bad form, bad public relations, and bad luck to begin measuring the drapes in the White House too early. Transition teams had often been composed of little more than a couple of the candidate's confidants brainstorming cabinet picks on cocktail napkins. And prior to the election, sitting administrations were in no hurry to coordinate with their potential replacements from the other party. But the September 11, 2001, terrorist attacks exposed serious vulnerabilities, and the 9/11

Commission had made recommendations that led to a new transition process that started earlier. The 2012 election was the first in which the new transition procedures were followed. The Romney Readiness Project, as it was known, was far more elaborate than any previous effort to plan for a transition.[34] Peter Feaver, a political scientist at Duke University who served in National Security Council positions during the Bill Clinton and George W. Bush administrations, was a part of that planning process and recalls that "every campaign experiences disappointment, but I think the psychological blow in 2012 was even greater because they had invested so much in planning."[35]

Yet out of that planning process emerged an ongoing, institutionalized effort to shape the future agenda for the Republican Party's approach to foreign policy and national security. After the 2012 campaign, Feaver says, the national security wing of the transition team "realized that they had a very good structure [in place]. They had great lists of great people who were mobilized and networked together, ready on day one to be Romney's national security team, and now they were unemployed."[36] There was a conviction that all of this work shouldn't simply be cast aside and a feeling that it would be wise to keep the group together in some kind of institutionalized form in order to articulate the consensus foreign policy position within the Republican Party and to lay the foundation for 2016.

Yet there was another reason, more defensive in nature, for building an institutional presence within the party. While the GOP's 2012 nominating process had ended with the sensible and seemingly inevitable choice of Romney, it had contained two warning signs of a nightmarish alternative version of the Republican Party. The first of these warning signs took the form of out-of-their-depth candidates like Minnesota Rep. Michelle Bachman and pizza mogul Herman Cain. As Feaver recounts, postmortems of the campaign "identified a number of Republican candidates who experienced a brief flutter of, if not front runner status, then at least a lot of buzz." With that attention came increased scrutiny of their positions, revealing an unsettling degree of ignorance on foreign policy issues that reflected poorly not only on those particular candidates but on the party as a whole. "Whatever their strengths in other areas, [these candidates] were really weak in foreign policy and national security. Not much of a background, and not much of a network of advisors." It made for some embarrassing moments on the campaign trail and detracted from the other candidates who knew what they were talking about. As a result, Feaver and others thought, "Couldn't we do a better job of prepping all of the primary candidates so that the caliber of the debate would be higher? . . . Next time around we really want to make sure that everybody can debate foreign policy well on our side."[37]

The other warning sign during the 2012 Republican primaries was the surprising performance of Ron Paul, the elderly and enigmatic Texas libertarian. Like Cain and Bachman, he was considered a fringe candidate by the foreign policy establishment and Republican regulars. But his campaign had generated more of a following than that status would seem to warrant. When it came to international affairs, he was way off conventional Republican talking points in promoting isolationism and conspiracy theories, and in suggesting that American foreign policy caused the 9/11 attacks. He had also been a strident critic of the Iraq War back in 2002 when it was being debated, and he was one of only seven Republicans in Congress who voted against it. During his presidential campaigns in 2008 and 2012 he routinely invoked Iraq as a prime example of the tendency for international entanglements to end badly and the general folly of the American foreign policy consensus. All told, Ron Paul's libertarian-influenced views on international affairs were diametrically opposed—both in terms of general philosophy and in a rundown of specific policy issues—to that of the Republican foreign policy network. This reawakened populist and isolationist strain of thought in the GOP was alarming to establishment Republicans.

Looking ahead to 2016, Republican foreign policy experts didn't perceive Ron Paul himself as a threat because it was widely assumed that 2012 marked the end of his days as a presidential candidate. However, he had a potentially far more formidable heir apparent in his son, Senator Rand Paul of Kentucky. As such, there was "a concern coming out of 2012 that Rand Paul and the neo-isolationist wing seemed to have the most buzz," Feaver recalls. "Ron Paul had done better than people thought he should have done, and Rand Paul seemed to be an even better politician and with more upside potential and with very fixed views that were out of the Republican mainstream. So, [the other] idea was, let's make sure that whoever is debating that wing in the party has the best background and knowledge base and talking points and understanding that they can have."[38] The goal, in other words, was to create a firewall around Rand Paul and ensure that his views didn't make any further inroads into the party.

Coming out of the 2012 cycle, then, the Republican foreign policy establishment was mobilized and looking to create some type of enduring institutional structure to lay the groundwork for 2016. On the supply side, there was already a large, established group of experts who had been mobilized by the Romney transition effort; on the demand side, there was a recognized need to boost the level of debate in 2016 among the mainstream Republican candidates, both to ensure that the party appeared more competent and to articulate and defend its mainstream foreign policy consensus against the latest challenge from the party's "crazies."

The John Hay Initiative was the institutional structure that emerged. Named after the storied scholar-diplomat who served as Abraham Lincoln's private secretary and later as Secretary of State under William McKinley and Theodore Roosevelt, the group described itself as "a network of foreign policy and national security experts who share a conservative internationalist tradition." The Hay Initiative was an augmented version of the Romney transition team, repositioned to articulate, promote, and defend mainstream Republican orthodoxy on foreign affairs with an eye toward the 2016 presidential campaign. Its stated mission was to counter "the neo-isolationist strains of thought in both of our major political parties" by emphasizing "the importance of self-confident American leadership to secure our country, foster international peace and economic prosperity, strengthen our friends, and uphold values of liberty and the rule of law."[39]

The Hay Initiative was structured like a larger version of the National Security Council, with an inner circle of principals and some 21 working groups focused on specific policy areas such as Russia, the Middle East, strategic planning, nuclear proliferation, and so on. At the top were Eliot Cohen, Eric Edelman, and Brian Hook, a trio of well-established figures in the Republican foreign policy establishment, all of whom had been top-tier advisors to the Romney campaign after serving in the George W. Bush administration. Cohen, as previously noted, is a longtime professor at SAIS and was Condoleezza Rice's top aide at the State Department. Edelman was a career foreign service officer and US Ambassador to Finland and Turkey prior to becoming Under Secretary for Policy at the Bush 43 Defense Department. Upon leaving government, Edelman assumed positions at SAIS—just several doors down the hall from Cohen—and at the Center for Strategic and Budgetary Assessments, a Washington think tank on Farragut Square specializing in defense. Hook had been Assistant Secretary of State at the end of the Bush administration. Cohen and Edelman would later be at the vanguard of the Never Trump movement, though Hook's name would never appear on any of the statements condemning candidate Trump, and in 2017 he would emerge as Secretary of State Rex Tillerson's leading deputy on policy and a finalist to replace John Bolton as National Security Advisor in 2019. The Hay Initiative eventually grew to include 250 foreign policy and national security experts, and its Advisory Council included Romney and Robert Kagan, a prominent scholar at the Brookings Institution and the Council on Foreign Relations. Other notable Hay Initiative figures included Bush 43 alums such as Elliott Abrams, Michael Chertoff, Michael Hayden, and Megan O'Sullivan.

With this structure in place, the Hay Initiative proceeded to churn out policy briefs, memos, analyses, talking points, and, in some cases, speeches for the party's presidential candidates. They also sponsored events featuring addresses by Florida Senator and likely presidential candidate Marco Rubio and House Majority Leader Kevin McCarthy.[40] Additionally, the Initiative produced a book, *Choosing to Lead: American Foreign Policy for a Disordered World*, that laid out a plan for the next president "to deal with the foreign policy mess [he or she] will inherit from [President Obama]."[41]

The centerpiece of the Hay Initiative's work was to brief potential presidential candidates and help them become conversant on the wide range of foreign policy issues. The presidential candidates sorted into three rough categories with regard to their interaction with the Hay Initiative. Those most engaged with Hay included Chris Christie, Carly Fiorina, Rubio, and Scott Walker. Less engaged but with some interaction were candidates like Jeb Bush, Ben Carson, Ted Cruz, Lindsey Graham, and John Kasich. The only two Republican candidates who had no interaction with Hay were Rand Paul and Trump.

It was no surprise that Paul and Trump kept their distance. The organization's reason for being was, after all, to defeat Paul and his isolationist vision for American foreign policy. And there was mutual contempt between Trump and the type of people—"pinstripe cookie pushers who are globalists"—associated with the Hay Initiative.[42] Feaver recalls:

> Our official position was we would talk to anybody who wanted to hear us. But probably most of the people involved in that organization felt like Donald Trump personified the problems of 2012: outrageous statements, not well-briefed, a stance of anti-expertise, as if knowing something about policy [and] having experience was a bad thing. . . . Donald Trump was personifying that, doubling down on it, tripling down on it. . . . It was like, everyone who's worked [in high levels of foreign policy], they screwed it all up and don't know anything.[43]

Somewhat surprisingly, the only other candidate who had a contentious relationship with the Initiative was Bush. In the very early stages of the campaign, Edelman recalls:

> The Jeb Bush campaign did not like what we were doing with John Hay. They signed up an impressive cast of characters early on. They put a lot of pressure on us and John Hay to sign up with Governor Bush. I told the people who were doing it: "We're going to be providing advice for all the candidates. Happy to provide advice for Governor Bush, but I won't sign up." [They replied:] "Well, the train is leaving the station. You're going to be really sorry." I'm like, "Well, okay. Fine. Whatever." . . . They were not very successful, actually.[44]

While Bush's attempt to woo the Hay Initiative at the very beginning of the 2016 cycle failed, he did eventually meet with Edelman and others.

Later in the campaign season, in the beginning of 2016, formal activities under the banner of the Hay Initiative slowed down because, as is the norm during presidential cycles, many of its members had signed on with one of the campaigns. But the plan remained the same. As Feaver describes, while Hay's team of experts temporarily went their separate ways, they did so "with the understanding that, whichever of these guys wins . . . we all Kumbaya, come back together, and now whoever it is will inherit an A-league national security advisory team, ready to go, already networked, already prepared. . . . That was the theory." And if things had gone slightly differently, the Hay Initiative may have worked to perfection. "If you look [at what we were trying to do], I think that succeeded, within the terms that we imagined them to be in 2015. If you set aside Donald Trump, the rest of the [candidates were] much higher caliber, and the debate was better than it had been in 2012."[45]

But, of course, Trump could not be set aside, and as the campaign wore on, the Hay Initiative's greatest strength—its high-powered and organized team of impeccably credentialed experts—was attacked as a weakness. The group's extensive links to George W. Bush had always presented something of a challenge. From the beginning, the group had to, at once, aggressively push back on what it saw as the dangerous, destabilizing, and amoral outlook of the "neo-isolationists" while, at the same time, doing what it could to avoid triggering memories of the Bush administration's most prominent foreign engagement, the Iraq War. Several leading figures at the Hay Initiative had previously been key figures in the Project for a New American Century (PNAC), a foreign policy think tank founded in 1997 by Kagan and William Kristol that was also intertwined with the Iraq War. Physically located in the same Dupont Circle building that housed the American Enterprise Institute and *The Weekly Standard*, the PNAC was widely considered a hub of "neoconservatism," as that term had come to be understood in the late 1990s and early 2000s. It produced several key publications and laid the intellectual groundwork for American global leadership, including the idea of regime change in Iraq that came to fruition following the attacks of September 11.[46]

Yet despite the Hay Initiative's sensitivity to the Iraq issue, by late 2015 some outside observers were quick to perceive a secret neocon conspiracy. Most of the criticism came from those outside the mainstream right. *Right Web* called the Hay Initiative "a who's who of prominent neoconservatives and avowed militarists." Similarly, Daniel Larison took to the pages of *The American Conservative* to lament the influence of the "hawks" at the Hay Initiative and their "embarrassing and outdated foreign policy agenda" which made it all but inevitable that the eventual Republican nominee would "repeatedly make a fool of himself during the general election." Because "there has been no serious rethinking inside the party on foreign policy," Larison argued, "hardly anyone inside the GOP thinks that they have a weakness that needs to be fixed, and so they blunder ahead with calls for more aggressive and confrontational policies."[47] Perhaps not surprisingly, the most vitriolic reaction came from the Ron Paul Institute for Peace, which called the Hay Initiative "the neocon Walmart of foreign policy" and charged that it was run by "crooks" and "the 'experts' who brought us the 2003 Iraq War and the Libya 'liberation.'" At the time, these critiques of the Hay Initiative appeared only in rather obscure corners of the Internet. And many of them echoed the conspiratorial hysteria common during the Bush era.[48] These lines of attack made them easy to ignore, but they would soon be adopted, wholesale, by Donald Trump.

Sources of Foreign Policy Never Trumpism

The John Hay Initiative was designed to create a firewall around the heresies of Rand Paul and to help the other Republican candidates competently defend their vision of conservative internationalism. But no one around the project imagined that their party would be tempted by a figure like Donald Trump. Trump's candidacy threw them into a world of uncertainty, in which all of their experience and strategies were suddenly rendered unhelpful or even counterproductive. They were forced into the darkness, stumbling around for a sense of how to respond to a threat that they had not anticipated, with few weapons at hand that they could confidently rely on to stop the march of a candidate who had targeted them specifically. In sharp contrast to most of the rest of the groups discussed in this book, the Republican foreign policy establishment responded to Trump with open, furious, and mostly unified opposition. They became the purest strain of Never Trumpism.

There were two primary reasons that people within the Republican national security network offer for having gone Never Trump. First, many were mortified at Trump's statements on foreign policy issues. The list of heresies was extensive. He praised dictators like Vladimir Putin and Kim Jong-un. He expressed admiration for brutal authoritarian crackdowns in North Korea and in Tiananmen Square. He accused George W. Bush of the treasonous offense of deliberately lying the country into the Iraq War. He habitually lied about his own position on the Iraq War. He was dismissive of key post–World War II alliances and international organizations. He was hostile to free trade. He displayed a fondness for torture and pledged to use it more aggressively. He expressed a reckless attitude about nuclear weapons. He advocated killing terrorists' family members. He attacked John McCain for being a prisoner of war. He demonstrated a disinterest in and disregard for human rights and democracy. As Green recalls, "The Trumpisms got worse and worse. . . . I mean, it was, basically, a string of actions that are the antithesis of everything I've worked on my whole career and believe in, in terms of real political values. It was just bam, bam, bam, bam, bam."[49]

Even so, most Never Trumpers in the foreign policy network say that their objections ran deeper than policy disputes; it was Trump's fundamental and unredeemable character flaws that constituted the core problem. During the campaign, Zelikow, the former aide to Rice at the State Department, said that he would support a randomly selected name from the phone book over Trump, and he maintains that the comment wasn't hyperbole.[50] "Actually, I meant that seriously. I actually do believe that you could pick anyone at random out of the phone book and that that would be better." And for Zelikow, the Never Trump objection "can't be superficially intellectualized as policy dispute." Partly this was a function of Trump's inability to engage with policy: "You can't have a policy disagreement with Donald Trump. . . . He doesn't function at that level. He doesn't know anything about policy. He is a culture warrior . . . and culture warriors don't debate with you how to solve problems. Culture warriors find litmus-test issues that signal an attitude in a culture that is resonant for them. It's an attitude. It's a posture. It's a signal of identity, and they look for hot-button ways of expressing these postures."[51]

For Zelikow and many national security Never Trumpers, some things are more important than policy and point to an important crosscutting identity that is a distinguishing feature of the national security network:

It's personal revulsion. It has to do with character and old-fashioned words like honor, which actually are important words. . . . I do think that people who represented their country, and especially people like me who've been involved, over the years, in a number of decisions that have to do with war and peace and life and death, maybe, on a good day, acquire a certain consciousness and responsibility and think a little bit harder about what that implies. They maybe tend to place a little more importance on the character of leadership and the responsibilities of leadership than someone whose job is just to cut up the distribution of a welfare package among three clients.[52]

Members of the American foreign policy establishment see themselves as "guardians" of the nation's security. While they are partisans to one degree or another, that identity is subordinate to their shared guardian identity. Central to their near-unanimous rejection of Trump was his pleasure in rejecting the underpinnings of this identity. Where foreign policy elites see themselves as honorable public servants, Trump denounced them as self-interested hacks. Whereas they see foreign policy as a noble and high-stakes arena for well-trained statesmen, Trump dismissed foreign policy as simply another realm for instinctive, transactional deal-making.

As part of the guardian identity—and reinforced for many by their participation in the rituals of life in foreign policy and national security—these experts take the recognition of and respect for inherited standards of appropriate behavior very seriously. As Zelikow says:

Ask yourself: "What do they read? What do they talk about?" Mainly they read history or about contemporary events, and they're very interested in a lot of issues in which issues of honor, behavior, propriety can matter a lot. You go back to the stories about whether it's Vietnam or Korea, World War II and the Civil War, and people who are marinated a lot in reading about things like this, you are kind of marinated in an intellectual environment that has a very high consciousness about propriety and character and integrity and honor and duty—very much duty—and that there's a certain consciousness when you're entrusted with certain responsibilities, the way you're supposed to behave. . . . In government, you're often in a world in which there are lots of different ceremonials associated with appropriate behavior, funerals, commemorations, and I think all of this just tends to maybe give a stronger consciousness of the expectations for an American president and what an American president represents that's more important than policy.[53]

As would become even clearer after he was elected president— for example, his highly inflammatory speech in front of the CIA's Memorial Wall—Trump relishes violating norms of appropriateness and the rituals associated with them. This aspect of Trump's character looms especially large for national security professionals who, across partisan lines, have a greater intensity of commitment to the symbols and practices of the state than are generated in other policy communities.

For many in the foreign policy establishment, then, the core objection to Trump wasn't over issues that were specific to foreign policy, but about the factor that cuts across the larger Never Trump universe. It was the lying, the cruelty, the narcissism, the flagrant norm-violations—all the central features of who Donald Trump is as a human being. As Cohen succinctly puts it: "This is such a completely despicable character. And character does matter."[54] And these sentiments aren't simply retrospective rationalizations for external consumption. Email exchanges at the time clearly demonstrate that this sentiment—a "rejection of this man," not simply his policy positions—was front and center in the thinking of foreign policy Never Trumpers during the campaign.[55] As one wrote in the spring of 2016, it wasn't "only Trump's crazy positions, but his outrageous personal behavior [that] made him totally unsuited for the post. His treatment of McCain, Mexicans, Muslims, on and on, is just full of hate and ignorance. His ignorance, egotism, insults, and buffoonery [are] a violation of all the norms of behavior of a leading American, much less a president."[56]

While character and policy were, by far, the primary reasons that people within the foreign policy establishment offered for going Never Trump, at least a couple of people who took Never Trump positions viewed the move as simply a normal tactical step in a normal campaign. As will be seen, in Chapter 3, they weren't particularly put off by Trump's behavior or statements. They saw him as just another candidate competing against the person they happened to be supporting at the time. As one such individual explained, he thought he was merely taking a "stand against Trump now to help my guy, but if [Trump] ends up winning," that action wouldn't close off the possibility of working in his administration because that is just how campaigns work.[57] In a typical campaign, the candidates and their staffers duke it out until someone emerges as the nominee. At that point, everyone unites and shifts gears for the general election campaign, leaving primary disputes in the past. A small handful of people thought that was all that was going on in the spring and summer of 2016. But that view was very much at odds with the core Never Trump contingent. They believed that the 2016 campaign had stepped out of normal politics and raised fundamental questions about the preservation of liberal democracy. This justified extra-normal responses in order to preserve the character of the regime that most of them had served over a number of years. That collective response is the subject of the next chapter.

3

Experts Gone Rogue

NONE OF THE REPUBLICAN foreign policy professionals identified in Chapter 2 could have imagined that, by the spring and summer of 2016, they would be in outright rebellion against their own party's nominee. They were prepared for a normal election cycle, fought between establishment-endorsed Democratic and Republican campaigns. What they were not prepared for was their party nominating a candidate they suspected of illicit relationships with America's adversaries. Their level of alarm not only far eclipsed that of other Trump skeptics, but their tight network structure and orientation toward collective action allowed them to act quickly, and in concert. They managed to put together two letters, one during the primary and the second after Donald Trump was nominated at the Republican National Convention in Cleveland, that denounced him in the strongest possible terms.

These letters, signed by a wide swath of the most senior members of the Republican foreign policy establishment, were aimed with martial intent. The signatories hoped that a warning this grave would alarm GOP primary voters, and then the electorate in the fall, causing them to turn away from the serious risk Trump posed for the nation's security. Later, having shot at Trump and missed, they were declared persona non grata as the president staffed his administration. These men and women could only stand by, appalled, as the president conducted a strangely cozy relationship with dictators in Russia and North Korea, sacrificed the nation's honor in Syria, and used the foreign policy of the United States as a tool for his reelection.

Despite the dire consequences of their actions, most of the signatories to these letters continue to believe, to this day, that they had no choice in 2016. Perhaps ironically, these practitioners of the calculating arts of foreign policy responded to Trump in surprisingly absolutist terms. They believed something like the nation's honor was on the ballot in 2016, a belief that most think has been vindicated by his record in office. They hoped at the time that, when Trump went down to defeat in November, their party would turn back to them to once again guard the nation's security. It turned out that the wait would be longer than they had anticipated.

Shots Across the Bow

For Republican foreign policy professionals, Never Trump activity centered around a series of public letters, two of which garnered substantial attention.[1] A clear reflection of the foreign policy establishment, the letters were grounded in the broadly shared, consensus viewpoint of the party's and the country's leading experts on foreign policy and national security. The key figures behind the letters were part of that tight, elite, Washington-centered network. They knew each other from having served together in previous Republican administrations and from the think tank circuit. Many of them had also been part of the Republican foreign policy establishment's most recent project, the John Hay Initiative. That effort had served many functions. It had been a platform for advancing the network's shared viewpoint. It had strengthened and given organizational structure to the network's already remarkably tight bonds. It had established the boundaries of respectable opinion with regard to foreign policy and national security. It had presented the party's hierarchy of experts and identified the appropriate figures to staff the next Republican administration. The letters were that network's response to what they thought was the greatest challenge to their stature and authority in their lifetimes.

March 2016: The Cohen–McGrath Letter

The first organized, public pushback from the Republican national security establishment came in the form of a letter that was the brain-child of Bryan McGrath, a former Naval officer and expert in military and defense policy at the Hudson Institute, a conservative think tank located a few blocks from the White House. The lifelong Republican had been an advisor to Romney's 2012 presidential campaign and had signed on with Marco Rubio's defense policy team for 2016. The letter emerged from a discarded essay McGrath had penned prior to Thanksgiving of 2015. McGrath said:

> It was going to be me making a statement like: "This is a problem; this man is unfit, and this party needs to exorcize him." I talked with some people in my network about printing this, and the response I essentially got in November 2015 was: "He's gonna crash and burn. He's gonna die. He may even drop out before the first primary. So, it's not worth it." So, I put it away . . . until late in February after Marco Rubio lit himself on fire on a debate stage in New Hampshire.[2]

Following that infamous Rubio–Christie exchange[3] in Manchester on February 6, McGrath reached out to Eliot Cohen, the SAIS professor and former aide to Secretary Rice. The two were acquaintances from the Romney campaign and crossed paths occasionally in Washington. McGrath recognized a kindred spirit in Cohen after following him on Twitter. As Cohen recalls his thinking at the time:

> As soon as [Trump] became a visible figure on the campaign trail, I thought, first, he was just a horrible human being and utterly un-qualified to be president. I also just had this sinking feeling that he could end up going all the way. I didn't think it was likely, but I did not think it was inconceivable. I thought it was possible, oddly enough, because of my low opinion of both Obama and Hillary. I thought, first, she was such a terrible politician and a completely artificial human being. And Obama embodied so much of the ar-rogance and cultural condescension of the left that there would be

an opening for somebody like this who could connect with average Americans.[4]

Another factor for Cohen was his assessment of the Republican field. As a leader of the Hay Initiative, he'd spent significant time meeting with and advising many of the candidates, and he'd left that experience feeling underwhelmed. While many would have been perfectly acceptable, Cohen "didn't think any of them had the magic." By contrast, he worried that Trump had some significant strengths. "I've always thought it's really important to acknowledge your adversaries' strengths for what they are. This guy, I thought, okay, he does have a certain roguish charm, and he can connect with people, and he has a certain kind of feral set of instincts, which will appeal to a lot of people. [And] he's coming at a time when a lot of people were just furious with cultural condescension."[5] When McGrath floated the idea of putting together a group letter to Cohen, he found an eager comrade-in-arms, and one who was at the center of the Republican national security network.

Following a heavy edit of McGrath's original essay, the pair settled on a final draft. The letter adopts the form of the Declaration of Independence. A brief introduction is followed by a list of grievances. A short, final section draws conclusions from the listed objections and forms the basis for a shared commitment. The list of signatories follows. The introduction states that the signers are all members of the Republican national security community and that they represent a broad range of opinion, noting in particular disagreements on the wars in Iraq and Syria. The letter asserts that whatever differences may exist within the group of signers, they are united in opposing Trump's candidacy. The letter then provides a list of the group's "core objections" to Trump:

- his inconsistency and lack of principles—"He swings from isolationism to military adventurism within the space of one sentence";
- his advocacy for trade wars;
- his enthusiasm for torture;
- his counterproductive, alienating, and dangerous anti-Muslim bigotry;

- his inflammatory and contemptuous rhetoric concerning the wall on the Mexican border;
- his dismissive attitude toward key post–World War II alliances and demand for protection payments from allies—"the sentiment of a racketeer";
- his admiration of dictators like Vladimir Putin;
- his dishonesty;
- his false equation of business and foreign policy expertise.

The letter concludes by stating that if Trump is elected president, he would make the country less safe, diminish its global standing, and pose a threat to civil liberties. "Therefore, as committed and loyal Republicans, we are unable to support a Party ticket with Mr. Trump at its head. We commit ourselves to working energetically to prevent the election of someone so utterly unfitted to the office."[6]

Once they settled on a final draft, McGrath and Cohen sent out an email to their networks asking that they join them in an "effort to inform the American people of our concerns about Mr. Trump's candidacy and our resolve not to support him." Because they felt time was of the essence and didn't want to get bogged down in endless rounds of edits, Cohen and McGrath stipulated that there would be no consideration of proposed revisions; this was a take-it–or-leave-it proposition. People wishing to sign the letter had just 72 hours to do so.[7] The letter was published on the national security website *War on the Rocks* on March 2, the day after Trump's Super Tuesday primary triumph.

August 2016: The Bellinger Letter

An even higher-impact letter, by an even more prestigious group of signatories, came out at the end of the summer. It was organized by John Bellinger, who had served in the Bush 43 administration as Legal Advisor to the National Security Council in the White House and in the same role at the State Department under Secretary Rice. Early in the 2016 cycle, he had been an advisor to Jeb Bush's campaign. That summer—long after his candidate had dropped out—Bellinger says, "I was debating internally what more I could do other than watch the car go into the ditch. I had written a blog post, and considered writing another blog post but wondered who's going to really listen to me? I felt an obligation to do something more if I really considered him to be a danger to our national security. I knew I would kick myself later if he won and I had done nothing to raise the alarm."[8] There was a key difference between the letter Bellinger had in mind and the Cohen–McGrath letter that had preceded it by five months. The first letter was signed by foreign policy people at all levels—from the most senior level all the way down to people who were not well known. It had strength in numbers. But Bellinger's idea was to include only the most senior people who had served in Republican administrations. The goal was to say that these were the people who have been closest to the center of power in Republican administrations and know the traits necessary in a president, and they are united in the conclusion that this Republican nominee is below the bar and will not be receiving their votes. Bellinger put together the first draft. Cohen and Robert Blackwill (a former diplomat and NSC Deputy for Iraq in 2003 and 2004) then edited it before Bellinger began asking people to sign on.

The letter opens by stating that the signers have worked on national security and foreign policy at the very top levels of Republican administrations from Richard Nixon to George W. Bush. It then states: "None of us will vote for Donald Trump." Trump, the letter continues, "would be a dangerous President and would put at risk our country's national security and well-being."[9]

The letter then describes three critical presidential qualities that Trump lacks. First, and "most fundamentally," he "lacks the character, values, and experience to be President." These failures would undermine the country's "moral authority as the leader of the free world." Additionally, he lacks "basic knowledge" about the Constitution, laws, and institutions. Second, and more specifically, the letter alleges that Trump "displays an alarming ignorance" of international affairs that will do active harm to American foreign policy. He lacks elementary information about the country's national interests, diplomatic challenges, alliances, and the role of democratic values in American foreign policy. He is friendly to America's enemies and belligerent toward her allies. And "unlike previous Presidents who had limited experience in foreign affairs, Mr. Trump has shown no interest in educating himself." Finally, Trump's temperament is disqualifying. Based on their experience, the signers wrote that presidents have to listen to advisors, consider a range of views, acknowledge and learn from mistakes, and comport themselves in a disciplined, emotionally controlled, reflective, and deliberative manner. And presidents have to be able to gain the respect and trust of world leaders. "In our judgment," the signers wrote, "Mr. Trump has none of these critical qualities." The letter concludes by acknowledging that there is widespread frustration with the federal government's failure to address problems at home and abroad and notes that many Americans—including many of the signers—"have doubts" about Clinton. "But Donald Trump is not the answer to America's daunting challenges. . . . We are convinced that in the Oval Office, he would be the most reckless President in American history."[10] The Bellinger letter was released on August 8.

Who's With Us?

The strategic calculations behind these collective statements were the same. While one letter came out in March toward the end of the primary season and the other in August following the failed effort to deprive Trump of the nomination on the floor of the GOP National Convention, in both cases some signers hoped that it was still possible to avert disaster and that their activities might make a difference in the election's outcome. Bellinger held out hope that it could hurt Trump: "The one thing we can do . . . is to come together as a group and say to the American people: 'We have worked with Republican presidents. We know what it takes to be president. Please listen to us that this guy doesn't have the qualifications to be president in the foreign policy/national security area.'"[11]

Others expressed no hope of influencing the outcome of the election. One reason for this had to do with the defining feature of Trump supporters. As one signer argued in an email shortly before the March letter was released: "I think we have basically no chance of influencing any voters. Any. The things that drive Trump are not susceptible [to] rational discussion, and his potential supporters are not interested in having one."[12] Additionally, many thought Trump had effectively already secured the nomination by the time the first letter came out. "Amongst us, I think the chances of Rubio making it are minimal, although I'm quite willing to have my name out there associated with him. Cruz's chances [are] infinitesimally better, but that's not much. At the barest minimum, Trump romps to the convention with a very large plurality of delegates and the momentum, at which point the process of capitulation that has begun already continues."[13] Likewise, Zelikow recounts thinking that the August letter "would have all the effect of hitting them with a feather pillow . . . because he had already positioned himself as the enemy of the elites."[14]

But even for those who didn't expect the letters to influence the outcome of the election, there were still compelling reasons to forge ahead, the most common of which was personal integrity. One signer explained his rationale in those terms. "The reasons for the letter are pretty straightforward," he wrote. "It's like the small band of French soldiers joining de Gaulle in 1940—no immediate prospects of success, the scorn of those who stay behind, but we're saving our country's honor, and not insignificantly our own as individuals."[15] As Cohen recalls: "My answer was always so that when my granddaughter comes back from spring break in 15 years and she's taking a course on contemporary American politics, and they're looking at the 2016 election, and she says, 'Well, Grandpa, you were around then. What did you do about all this?' I can say, 'Well, at least I did that.' "[16] This sense of having to do something as a matter of personal integrity, even if it wasn't going to be successful, is a particularly distinctive feature of Never Trumpers in the national security realm.

Many also expressed an interest in positioning themselves for the future. Numerous signers were hoping for an opportunity to rebuild the Republican Party after Clinton's inevitable victory in the general election. As one expert wrote:

After enjoying Trump's crushing defeat this November, I plan to keep working inside the Republican Party for a sane version of conservatism on issues foreign and domestic. Yes—I would never have imagined that over 10 million Americans would vote Trump for president. I thought more of Republican voters. My mistake! But he'll still need to get something like 65 million to beat Clinton. And I really can't see that happening. In any case, as Bryan suggests, we're finding out who you can trust in a foxhole. Damn few, as it turns out. But certainly, Cohen and McGrath.[17]

That email reflects the sense of many signatories that they had to stick together as a matter of unit cohesion, something largely missing from the other professional groups that we will discuss in subsequent chapters. But it also shows that, at the time, these experts believed that Trump would go down to a crushing defeat. Consequently, those who were forcefully on the record repudiating Trump prior to his defeat would be in a much stronger position to put the pieces back together and refashion the party in their image. Others thought the Republican Party as they had known it was finished but that a new party could emerge. "We're probably headed for a realignment which will lead to a new party in which I suspect all of us will play a role on the foreign/security policy side. That will be a necessary thing, and an important thing."[18] But regardless of whether the Republican Party would survive or a third party would emerge, the March letter was worthwhile. One signer wrote: "I see nothing counterproductive about laying down our position now. Moods and time change, and if we come out of this with our heads held high, having taken out a position of principle and having been shown to be right, we'll be in a position to do some good."[19]

One sensitive issue that the leading figures behind both letters had to deal with was a concern that their statements could be interpreted as comeback attempts by "neoconservatives" seeking to reclaim their natural position directing American foreign policy after their post-Iraq wilderness years. The issue had received attention in the press. For instance, Jacob Heilbrunn, editor of *The National Interest*, had written: "There they go again. The neocons who led the George W. Bush administration into Iraq are now touting a fresh crusade to save American democracy—and the Republican Party—from an authoritarian foe: Donald Trump."[20] The clear implication was that the neoconservatives were frantically mobilizing against Trump—even threatening to go so far as to vote for Clinton—because he was directly challenging their "moralistic, crusading Wilsonian mission" to impose freedom and democracy on unwilling parts of the world. Those affiliated with the Never Trump letters were well aware of this storyline and were concerned about it. In compiling his list of signatories, Bellinger made a conscious effort to avoid falling into the neocons-are-back trap. As Bellinger says, "I didn't want them to just say, 'Well, these are all the people who brought you the Iraq War.' Because one of [Trump's] lies was, 'I was always against the Iraq War.' So, to be candid, I was careful in who I asked so that really there's very few people on the letter who were architects of the Iraq War."[21] Those involved with the Cohen–McGrath letter were also well aware of the Iraq minefield. One signer emphasized the need "to make sure we are careful not to make it look like a neocon conspiracy."[22] Another urged the lead authors to revise the letter as a means of achieving that goal: "I would strongly urge you to move up and expand on the threat he clearly poses to democracy and civil liberties at home. The 'neocons bailing on Trump because he doesn't want more wars and they do' trope is out there already. . . . Maybe your list of signatories will be broad enough to discourage such an interpretation of this statement. But I think raising the non–foreign policy critique is just as important."[23] Cohen and McGrath ultimately held firm on refusing to engage in rewrites. But the figures most associated with the Iraq War and the term neoconservative as it was popularly used and understood during that era—such as Dick Cheney, Richard Perle, Donald Rumsfeld, and Paul Wolfowitz—did not appear as signatories.

Among those who were asked to sign one or both of the letters, most enthusiastically added their names to the list. Illustrative responses to Cohen and McGrath's solicitations included: "Damn right!" "I'm in. Gotta side with the good guys regardless of the odds." "I would be honored to sign the letter. Thanks for doing this; our party and our country are in your debt." "Happy to sign. The statement is, if anything, not strong enough. But it gets the point across." "I've thought a lot about this, and while I'm fully aware that there may be blowback [from my employer], I can't in good conscience do anything other than join up."[24]

Once the initial rounds of emails to potential signers went out, both letters gained a momentum of their own. After the first letter was published, Cohen and McGrath fielded requests from people looking to have their names added to the list. They agreed to do so and eventually their statement grew from the original 60 signatories to 122. Several months later, a similar phenomenon occurred with the Bellinger letter. "I really was surprised at how quickly" the positive responses came in, he recalls. "I was at about 35 to 38 before I'd even batted an eye, and then I thought, well, I'm really not going for numbers here." But word had circulated that Bellinger had a letter he was shopping around, and people began contacting him asking if they could sign. Some of them had held somewhat lower positions than he initially had in mind. "I didn't want to say no to people, but I was trying to emphasize that these were people who had literally worked for the president and watched a president, knew what it took to be president. . . . I was really going for seniority and name. But people had all signed up so quickly that I thought I'll see if I could get to a nice round number."[25] The letter was released with 50 signatories.

Unintended Consequences?

For various reasons, some declined to sign on. A small minority refused to sign the Cohen–McGrath letter because they thought it was too late to deprive Trump of the nomination and that the letter would therefore only serve to help Clinton. One person replied to Cohen and McGrath: "This is simply too little, too late to make a difference. . . . Where were you on August 7 [2015] after the first presidential debate? After all [the] candidates pledged to support the Republican nominee INCLUDING DONALD TRUMP? This will simply not matter in the least in the outcome of the primaries at this point." And given that Trump was going to be the nominee, this non-signer argued that it was incumbent upon good Republicans to support him. "I, for one, will give no aid or comfort to Hillary . . . and will work for her defeat with all my power. We will need a strong national security advisory team for our nominee. As Lyndon Johnson said, 'It is better to have you inside the tent pissing out, than outside the tent pissing in.' "[26] But this sentiment was not widespread.

By far, the most prominent objections raised were tactical in nature and focused on the potential for unintended consequences. There were three variations on this theme. One argument was that a public letter from Republican members of the foreign policy establishment could backfire and actually end up *helping* Trump. Some non-signers replied to Cohen and McGrath by saying that while they agreed with the content of the letter, they nonetheless thought it was a bad idea for strategic reasons. One wrote: "I fear that Trump will use this as just another talking point about how Washington insiders really oppose him and need to go."[27] Similarly, another non-signer replied, "Instead of cautioning voters, it can become one more tool in Trump's arsenal. I do not want to give him this ammunition."[28] Plenty of others pointed out this problem as well, but nonetheless agreed to sign. In the words of one: "I worry that this may just be one more prop for Trump to wave around. But it is also the right thing to do."[29] Yet among the hard core Never Trump national security crowd, there is no indication that they ever had second thoughts about moving forward. One stalwart wrote: "When I've heard friends second guessing the messenger or the timing I say, 'Look, this is the close-in fight. You empty every magazine and then reach for the entrenching tool. No longer time to fret about the finer points of tactics.' "[30] Others were long past the point of reasoning with the holdouts who refused to endorse the statement on these grounds. One prominent signer emailed his colleagues with a curt one-liner regarding the hand-wringing holdouts: "I have to say this is self-serving cowardly garbage. Silence = consent."[31]

A second objection over the potential for the letters to backfire centered on the help it might provide to the Clinton campaign. From this perspective, opposing Trump in the primary was one thing, but the Cohen–McGrath letter's assertion that "we are unable to support a Party ticket with Mr. Trump at its head [and] commit ourselves to working energetically to prevent [Trump's] election" went too far.[32] That line clearly implied that if Trump was the GOP nominee, the signers were pledging to either vote for Clinton or to throw their votes away on a third-party candidate with no chance of winning. As one prominent veteran of past Republican administrations replied: "You had me until the last line. Working energetically to prevent his nomination, sure, but working energetically to prevent his election requires knowing what the options are. . . . The final line comes close to saying we will work to elect Hillary, which I cannot do because she is in my view a criminal."[33] And in what must have been a tough note to receive, an individual who had been a friend and mentor to one of the lead authors sent the following response:

I urge you not to send this letter. You are handing Hillary strong ammunition. While I share your concerns and strongly support Rubio
and Kasich, it now appears that it is too late to stop Trump, although
I for one will continue to work and hope for a brokered convention.
But that is a very long shot. So what you are saying in the letter is
that you prefer Hillary and all her likely appointees to Trump and
his Republican appointees. If that occurs we will lose the Senate,
the Supreme Court, governors, state legislatures, and possibly even
the House. That outcome will end the United States as we know
it. A Trump nomination may of course bring that about, but it is
also a possibility that he will preside very differently than he has
campaigned. He did not become a billionaire by being stupid. That
is what we must pray for. If that happens you both are going to be
very much needed. It would be unpatriotic, childish and irresponsible to put yourselves on a blacklist by such a hostile negative letter.
Think about it.[34]

In these circles, being called unpatriotic is no small thing. However,
others had no reservations whatsoever about abandoning the
Republican Party and considered "the implicit promise never to vote
for Trump under any circumstance" as part of the letter's appeal. One
signer replied: "If Trump wins the nomination, please count me the
first volunteer for the reborn Federalist Party and the campaign to draft
Robert Gates for the presidency."[35]

For some signers, part of the reason for shrugging off these objections
is that they never had expectations that the letter would sway the public
in the first place and were therefore dismissive of electoral considerations.
And, in any event, from this perspective, focusing on campaign strategy
missed the larger reasons for going public. "Tactically it won't make a
particle of difference to the outcome, which I fully accept," wrote one
signer. "Mind you, I think either way we're headed to a pretty massive
crackup, including possibly the formation of a new party. Which again
pushes me in the direction of laying down some very clear markers."[36]
In an environment in which it was still widely believed that Trump
would lose, Never Trump was conceived of as a kind of party in exile
which, free of the stench of Trump's failure, could rebuild the party in
his wake.

But there was a final way in which the letter could backfire. This third major argument against the letter—and against Never Trump activity among national security experts in general—was that, in the highly unlikely event that Trump won the presidency, those who participated would be blackballed from playing any role in the administration. Within this space there was a critical distinction that separated the real Never Trumpers from those who opposed Trump due only to the conventional political necessity of picking a candidate as part of normal primary politics. The principled Never Trump variation of this concern centered on—without overstating it—the worry that this deplorable individual posed an existential threat to American democracy and the post-1945 world order that, in one way or another, most foreign policy establishmentarians thought they had spent their careers defending. For Never Trumpers in the national security network, this understanding of what their role is—and what the role of the United States is in the world—is essential to understanding their reaction to Trump. As Cohen explains:

> [The Republican foreign policy establishment] is genuinely conservative in that it doesn't really believe in turning the world upside down, and it doesn't believe in radical change, and is basically content with the world order that we had helped devise and thought that our main job is preserving it. They're not a big gang of revolutionaries, and they're not going to feel comfortable with the Newt Gingrichs of this world, quite apart from Trump, because they're not bomb throwers. Plus, I don't know if you'd quite put it this way, but they'd all been sobered up by Iraq.[37]

Yet, while this view of Trump as an existential threat was widespread within the Republican foreign policy establishment, not all who held it agreed with Cohen and McGrath's scorched-earth tactics. For some who held a dystopian view of what a Trump presidency could mean, the obvious corollary was that, if the awful scenario became reality, it would be essential to do everything possible to surround Trump with responsible people. From this perspective, the best people had a duty to their country to serve in a Trump administration in order to restrain a crazy and impulsive man from doing harm. The concern here, then, wasn't that potential signers would be disappointed to miss out on the opportunity to go into government and advance their careers, but that it would be vital to the national interest that they not disqualify themselves. As one non-signer put it: "If he does win the nomination or—heaven forbid—the presidency—he is going to need good advice and good advisors. I don't think it is smart to take the brightest lights in foreign policy today (your distribution list) and make them *a priori* people Trump will never listen to. Maybe he will never listen to anyone. But I'd hate to rule out the best people."[38] It was imperative, the thinking went, to err on the side of caution and be in a position to prevent the worst if the unthinkable happened and Trump managed to go all the way. "To be clear," a non-signer wrote, "I would never work in a Trump administration and I don't know anyone who would. But if there is a chance of influencing things for the better later on—concerning specific policies—that may be better for our country than a shot across the bow today that will likely have little positive impact and could potentially even help Trump."[39]

Notably, it wasn't only people within the foreign policy establishment who worried about the ramifications of putting together an enemies list for Trump; some international leaders did too, and they were urging their American contacts to stay on the sidelines. Mike Green received such requests, including one directly from the Japanese Prime Minister Shinzo Abe:

My main thing is allies. Due to my research and my previous time in government, I'm pretty close to Shinzo Abe in Japan and know the Australian government at very senior levels. And Abe personally, and senior officials in the Australian government and Korean government, came to see me petrified about what Trump was saying, of course, about allies. And then with—I would not say an official *demarche*—but with a strong request that I not sign any letters. And they were telling this to other alliance people. And I don't know if this is true on the Europe side, but I know it was true on the Asia side. Because they were really terrified of Trump, and if he won they wanted people who would go in and sort of protect the alliances. And in my case, I was personally asked by the Prime Minister of Japan. And finally, I signed the letter. And I saw him, and I had to explain that just on a personal level I couldn't. I just personally could not serve for someone who said what he said.[40]

Green thinks others made a different choice, declining to sign for precisely this reason.

For committed Never Trumpers in the foreign policy network, this objection—that the best people should avoid going public because they'd be blackballed and therefore unable to work within the administration and mitigate the damage of a Trump presidency—was well known and well considered. They just didn't find it compelling. In response to such objections, one letter signer wrote: "It's not a question of better foreign policy advisors. You could surround Donald Trump with ten Henry Kissingers, and it wouldn't matter, because Trump does not have the personal qualities to be a good, serious commander-in-chief. That isn't going to change. When I said Never Trump, I meant it."[41] In short, the true Never Trumpers recognized the blackball risk but concluded that it must nevertheless be taken.

By contrast, some, albeit a small minority of the letter signers, were motivated more by the usual politicking of presidential campaigns and didn't share the zeal of their colleagues. And in another contrast with their colleagues, they apparently failed to fully recognize that by signing the letter, they were adding their name to a blacklist. For leading public policy experts, the chance to work in an administration as a political appointee is usually a long-pursued dream. Achieving that dream typically requires, among many other things, a president from your party. And there is never any guarantee that that is going to happen anytime soon. Going into 2016, this worry had to be all the more troubling for potential Republican appointees because Democrats had won the popular vote for the presidency in five of the previous six presidential elections, and there was a cottage industry of political experts trotting out demographic data suggesting that it would be less and less plausible for a Republican to win the White House in the future.[42] At least a couple of people who signed the Never Trump letters did so only because they preferred, or were working for, a different Republican presidential candidate. They thought they were operating within the informal rules of a normal primary process. Typically, when a candidate drops out, his or her staff are free to then sign on with another candidate. This happens routinely, and there is often a competition among surviving campaigns to pick up displaced staffers associated with candidates who depart the stage. Some foreign policy experts viewed the 2016 campaign through this lens and would have been happy to sign on with Trump once their preferred candidate dropped out.

Perhaps most emblematic of this small contingent was Matthew Kroenig, a Berkeley-trained political scientist and professor at Georgetown University who had also previously served at the CIA and the Pentagon and had worked on the Romney 2012 campaign. Kroenig was young, but he had all the hallmarks of a rising star in the Republican national security network, including the résumé, connections, and ambition to be in line for a low-level political appointment in the next GOP administration. When the 2016 presidential election cycle got underway, it appeared as though the standard process of policy experts sorting and resorting themselves—sometimes formally, sometimes not—would play out, and Kroenig's experience is illustrative of that process. Early in the cycle, Kroenig had encouraged his friend (and future Congressman from Wisconsin) Mike Gallagher to return to his home state to accept a position as Wisconsin Governor Scott Walker's top foreign policy advisor on his expected campaign for president. "I said, 'Oh, I think it makes a lot of sense,'" recalls Kroenig. "'It's your home state.'" Plus, Walker "was leading in the polls at the time. And I said, 'He's the leading candidate, you might as well.'" When Gallagher accepted the job, he got back in touch with Kroenig to see if he'd come aboard with Walker, too. But Kroenig was hesitant to commit. So, as Kroenig recalls, Gallagher responded: "'Well, how about this: You don't have to exclusively work for us. But I'd just like to be able to call you and get your thoughts on things, maybe have you come give some briefings in Madison. But you don't have to commit to us. You can work for another candidate later if you want.'" Kroenig agreed. Soon enough, the call from Madison came, and Kroenig joined Gallagher and Walker in the basement of the governor's mansion. "[Walker] spent a lot of time with us. We were probably down there three hours or so. And so at that point I was kind of pumped. It was kind of cool to get that much direct personal interaction with the candidate who is leading in the polls." Kroenig was officially on board.[43]

Alas, the Walker campaign was short-lived. Kroenig first learned that his candidate had dropped out when he simultaneously received emails from the top foreign policy advisors on the Bush and Rubio campaigns saying they wanted to speak with him immediately. Both offered him jobs. As Kroenig recounts: "I kind of agonized over it for several weeks. Again, I still thought Bush would eventually win because of the name recognition and the money, but I just liked Rubio better because he was more charismatic." And so he ultimately decided to sign on with Rubio. Several months later when Bush dropped out after the South Carolina primary, Kroenig was certain he had picked the right horse. He and the Rubio team "were so convinced by this 'party decides' thesis that we essentially thought we had it wrapped up at that point. We thought there were three establishment candidates: Rubio, Bush, and Walker. Now Bush is out; Walker is out; this is Rubio's election."[44]

It was at this time that Cohen reached out asking Kroenig if he'd like to sign the first Never Trump letter. Kroenig explains:

I didn't agree with every sentence in the letter, but I basically signed up because I saw it as part of primary politics. I was working for Rubio. I wanted Rubio to win. We were gonna take down the other guy who was doing well. So I signed on for that reason. So, I know some of my other colleagues . . . for them it was more personal and they were emotionally offended by things that Trump was doing. And I guess I'm more pragmatic or too rational or something. I wasn't really personally offended by anything that Trump was doing. I like Rubio better and was working for Rubio. I saw this as part of the campaign, trying to help my candidate and take out the other ones. . . . I mean, personally, I've always been interested in serving in government and working for politicians, not because I think they're perfect but because I think they could use the help. So some of the sentences that were more personal about Trump's character or anything, I wasn't really thrilled by those parts of it because I think you could say things about a lot of politicians' character.[45]

Kroenig recalls thinking carefully about what he perceived to be the unlikely scenario in which Trump became president, but he says he was comforted by the letter's language: "It didn't say anything about what would happen after he's elected. And so I did take note of that before I decided to sign. I said, 'Oh, well this is just about the election. After the election's over, anything goes. . . . This is just the way it works. You fight hard in the primary but then everybody comes together eventually.' "[46]

With the benefit of hindsight, Kroenig clearly regrets signing the letter. "I guess in the future, I think I'll probably be a little more judicious and way more careful signing up to do big group letters like that [and] more judicious about what I really believe in and do I believe in every word before signing up for things like that in the future."[47] Kroenig isn't the only one with regrets. Two days after the election, the *New York Times* reported that Mary Beth Long, a former Assistant Secretary of Defense in the Bush 43 administration and a signer of both the Cohen–McGrath letter in March and the Bellinger letter in August, had "reversed her position on Mr. Trump at a campaign rally in Charlotte, NC, about a month ago." She was quoted as saying that she had abandoned her Never Trump views because Trump had "matured" between the August letter and the Charlotte rally on October 14 (which occurred one week after the release of the *Access Hollywood* tape). The *Times* story also reported that if "experienced, respected Republican national security figures like [Stephen] Hadley . . . were offered jobs and accepted them, it would provide cover and comfort to other Republicans who might otherwise balk at joining the Trump team."[48] Kroenig waited a bit longer to publicly reverse his position on Trump. But a few months after the inauguration, he took to the pages of *Foreign Affairs* to offer "The Case for Trump's Foreign Policy," noting that the administration's "critics have gotten a lot wrong and failed to give credit where credit is due," particularly with regard to what he asserted was an A-list team of appointees. While acknowledging a few missteps that are typical of any new administration, Kroenig observed that "taking a step back reveals that Trump has gotten much of the big picture right."[49]

Kroenig and Long were atypical and were coming from a starkly different place than those who played a leading role in writing and organizing the letter, as well as most of those who signed. Indeed, within the national security Never Trump contingent, there is palpable anger that Kroenig and Long signed onto a principled and honor-bound letter and then "repented of it almost immediately." Many of the other signers express disbelief that someone could have failed to understand the pledge they were making. According to Kori Schake, who has served on the National Security Council and in the Pentagon and the State Department: "There's a lot of uncharitable assessment about that in the group right now. I think almost everybody who signed the letters understood that we were signing a pledge not to work in the administration."[50]

McGrath and Cohen were careful to avoid having their letter state that directly. As McGrath recalls, "What I thought was, putting it in explicitly—if it keeps people from signing the letter—is a bad thing. But if you sign this letter, you damn sure better know that that's what you're signing up to. Because who would hire somebody like that?"[51] Says Cohen: "I think there were some people who didn't consider that there might be a cost associated with this. I suspect that if they had to do it all over again, we'd probably have somewhat fewer signatories."[52] Part of the reason people didn't consider the cost associated with signing the letters is the widespread assumption that Clinton would easily win the election.

Another reason some cited in declining to sign was that they held jobs or affiliations that prohibited such activity, though in many instances McGrath and Cohen saw this as a convenient excuse. "Some of them sent me weasel-grams," Cohen recalls. Some "clearly didn't want me to think they were in favor of Trump and didn't want me to be offended" but ultimately decided to hedge their bets to preserve the possibility of going into the administration should Trump manage to win.[53] Listing organizational affiliations on politically charged, public letters of this sort is always somewhat dicey. Indeed, that is why McGrath and Cohen made the early decision to just list names and eschew mention of any current affiliations. Nonetheless, the line between what is and isn't permissible is rather murky. One signer initially agreed, then emailed later that day to say she couldn't, only to send McGrath another note the following day asking to have her name put back on the list, explaining that she had decided that she was "willing to risk being reprimanded for this."[54]

Yet some of the most senior figures in the Republican national security network weren't willing to take the risk. While several prominent individuals, such as Robert Blackwill, Michael Chertoff, Eric

Edelman, Frances Townsend, Dov Zakheim, and Robert Zoellick did sign the letter, others were notably absent, some having cited professional obligations that prohibited their participation. As one wrote: "I need to pass because of some organizational positions I currently hold that necessitate my staying out of the political fray at this point."[55] These rejections from friends, colleagues, and mentors prompted disappointment, bemusement, frustration, and, at times, anger. One signer expressed faux surprise, for instance, with Condoleezza Rice's "thunderous silence" and noted: "I'm fascinated by some of our more chicken-hearted friends and former colleagues."[56] And one signer quipped that the group should "release a black list of those refusing to sign so they can be shunned."[57]

But more than anyone else, it was Stephen Hadley who provoked contempt when he declined to sign. Hadley is a lynchpin in the GOP national security community, having served every Republican president beginning with Gerald Ford. For all eight years of the George W. Bush administration he was in the inner circle of the president's foreign policy team, serving first as Deputy National Security Advisor under Rice and then taking over her role as National Security Advisor when she went to Foggy Bottom. When Hadley said that his positions at various organizations prevented him from signing the letter, several of his former colleagues were clearly indignant. Upon learning of Hadley's position, one wrote, "This is such bullshit. His positions didn't stop him from endorsing Mitt four years [ago] (after the point where it didn't matter in the primaries any more)."[58] Another noted, "This is why we always referred to him as 'Heave Sadly.'"[59] Yet others were more generous to Rice and Hadley. Bellinger insists that in discussions about the August letter, Hadley raised all the right questions and pushed everyone involved to avoid rushing into something dramatic without thinking it through. Schake notes: "Of all of the conversations I've been a part of, Steve Hadley's admonition still rings most strongly, which is to be kind to each other because this is a hard choice for everybody. And not to be hairshirty towards others because the line's going to fall in different places for all of us, and yet we are all people who admire each other and respect each other's work."[60] In a similar vein, Mike Green observes that there has been a real upside to some staying above the fray. "People criticize Condi and Steve or Gates, but I think they felt a responsibility.

Maybe there were some personal or professional reasons, but I think they felt a responsibility to . . . retain access to the candidate. Any candidate who won . . . . They wanted to preserve their position as stewards of Republican foreign policy. And, frankly, it's a good thing they did because they were the ones who suggested [Rex] Tillerson [for Secretary of State] and so forth."[61] What seemed reassuring in 2017, when we spoke to Green, seems less so in the light of the turnover in the president's foreign policy seen since then.

Putting "the Vichy Wing of the Party" on Notice

Those involved with the Cohen–McGrath letter were generally pleased with its reception. The letter was featured on Fox News, CNN, and MSNBC, and generated articles in the *New York Times, Washington Post, Politico*, and many other domestic and international papers. McGrath and Cohen also both gave numerous interviews. Over email, one individual called the letter "a stunning success" and proclaimed that "we blew up the internet." Another wrote: "Can't tell you how pleased I am with the outcome of all this. Not only an enormous amount of play, but some genuine pressure on Trump: his retreat on torture, for example, probably had something to do with the letter." However, within a week, the American press had moved on, and what interest remained was from abroad (one signer suggested that unlike many Americans, foreigners "see what's going on and are terrified"). Still, one signer emailed his colleagues, "This has been a good thing. Among others, it puts the Vichy wing of the party foreign policy establishment on notice. . . . Two important results, I think are (a) finally getting people worried about Trump; (b) laying down a marker with members of the national security community who will be tempted to sign up to some fictitious advisory committee for him. I think we've made a contribution on both counts."[62]

The day after the Cohen–McGrath letter's release, the national security Never Trumpers received some welcome support from the Republican Party's two most recent presidential nominees. On May 3, Mitt Romney delivered the most full-throated, broad-based anti-Trump speech of any GOP politician of national stature.[63] Later that day, Arizona Senator and 2008 presidential nominee John McCain issued a statement expressing his support of both Romney's speech and the Cohen–McGrath letter:

> I share the concerns about Donald Trump that my friend and former Republican nominee, Mitt Romney, described in his speech today. I would also echo the many concerns about Mr. Trump's uninformed and indeed dangerous statements on national security issues that have been raised by 65 Republican defense and foreign policy leaders. . . . I want Republican voters to pay close attention to what our party's most respected and knowledgeable leaders and national security experts are saying about Mr. Trump, and to think long and hard about who they want to be our next Commander-in-Chief and leader of the free world.[64]

Some of the ringleaders of the Cohen–McGrath letter were notified ahead of time by a Capitol Hill source that the McCain statement was forthcoming. The note they received served as a courtesy heads-up, a thank-you note, and as evidence that the letter played a key role in convincing McCain to go public with his own criticism of Trump: "This will go out after Romney speaks. Thank you so much for what you did. Needed to be said. And it prompted McCain's statement. I've been urging him to smack Trump, regardless of his primary issues in AZ. Thanks for enabling that. Wish I could have signed too!"[65]

Yet for all the positive reinforcement they received, the letter signers also clearly realized that their effort to deny Trump the Republican nomination was extremely unlikely to succeed. "I'm pretty fearful, honestly," one wrote in an email. "I hope Rubio can hang on." The only plausible scenario at this late stage of the nominating process was for Kasich to carry Ohio (which he did) and for Rubio to pull off a win in Florida (which he didn't). They hoped that if those two shoes dropped, Trump might enter the GOP convention just short of the requisite 1,237 delegates, albeit with a still overwhelming advantage. By this point there was also talk of secretive efforts to convince a prominent Republican to launch an independent bid for the presidency (as will be discussed in Chapter 5). And while those engaged in the email chain were generally pleased with the attention their letter had received, there was also significant pushback which was not necessarily unexpected but nonetheless mystifying. "We continue to get a fair amount of play, much of it abusive, but so it is," wrote one signer. "What is very striking to me is how many people who presumably dislike Trump are taking their shots at us instead. It's quite insane."[66]

Indeed, reactions from the left were far from universally embracing. Illustrative of these reactions were two progressive *New York Times* columnists who, despite sharing the Never Trumpers' loathing of the likely Republican nominee, nonetheless chose to use the Cohen–McGrath letter to attack the band of GOP dissidents rather than Trump. Maureen Dowd relished the Never Trumpers' anguish:

> The most enjoyable thing about the Trump phenomenon has been watching him make monkeys out of a lot of people who had it coming. . . . It's delicious watching the neocon men who tricked the country and gulled the naïve W. into the Iraq invasion go ballistic trying to stop the Gotham con man. . . . It's amazing, having been tainted by the worst foreign policy disaster in American history, that the Republican national security intelligentsia would unite against a Trump presidency in an open letter, charging that he would "make America less safe" and "diminish our standing in the world." Sort of like the Iraq invasion?[67]

Paul Krugman was similarly unmoved by the Never Trump effort. Two days after the Cohen–McGrath letter ran, he wrote: "Establishment Republicans denounce Mr. Trump as a fraud, which he is. But is he more fraudulent than the establishment trying to stop him? Not really." Krugman continued: "Then there's foreign policy, where Mr. Trump is, if anything, more reasonable—or more accurately, less unreasonable—than his rivals. . . . He's even said what everyone knows but nobody on the right is supposed to admit, that the Bush administration deliberately misled America into that disastrous war." Krugman ended his piece with a prediction that turned out to be only half right. "If Mr. Trump is the nominee, pundits and others who claim to be thoughtful conservatives will stroke their chins and declare, after a great show of careful deliberation, that he's the better choice given Hillary's character flaws, or something."[68] Krugman accurately foresaw the path that many Republicans would go down in the months to follow, but he failed to recognize that an unprecedented number of others—especially in the area of foreign policy—were quite determined in their resistance to Trump. Perplexed at these reactions from Trump's opponents on the left, one letter signer lamented that "They have to believe it's warmongers trying to pull a fast one over them. They are like the dwarves in C.S. Lewis' *Last Battle*."[69]

The Bellinger letter's release several months later yielded a similar round of media attention as well as a direct response from Trump himself. In a Facebook statement issued hours after the letter was made public, Trump went on the attack using the same themes that had characterized his earlier denunciations of the Republican foreign policy establishment: "The names on this letter are the ones the American people should look to for answers on why the world is a mess, and we thank them for coming forward so everyone in the country knows who deserves the blame for making the world such a dangerous place. They are nothing more than the failed Washington elite looking to hold onto their power." He went on to conflate the letter signers with Hillary Clinton and the Obama administration: "These insiders," Trump continued, "are the owners of the disastrous decisions to invade Iraq, allow Americans to die in Benghazi, and they are the ones who allowed the rise of ISIS." Trump's statement continued: "Yet despite these failures, they think they are entitled to use their favor trading to land taxpayer-funded government contracts and speaking fees. It's time we put our foot down and declare that their gravy train is over: no longer will Crooked Hillary Clinton and the other disasters in Washington get rich at our expense." The statement concluded with standard Trump rhetoric about his "America first vision" of foreign policy which "stands up to foreign dictators instead of taking money from them . . . makes other countries pay their fair share for their protection," and dispatches "the rigged system" currently in place and based around "a ruling family dynasty."[70]

The Men Who Failed to Kill the King

As of the spring of 2020, the Republican foreign policy experts who organized the effort to deny Donald Trump the presidency remained defiant but, on the whole, pessimistic. This was in spite of the fact that, as they saw it, everything that had occurred since Trump took the Oath of Office had vindicated their warnings. The president's first National Security Advisor resigned just weeks into the administration and was subsequently convicted of lying to the FBI. The administration left dozens of foreign policy positions open, and those they filled were often occupied by men and women they considered far inferior to those left on the sidelines. Trump cozied up to Russia and North Korea while bullying America's traditional allies. He precipitated various trade wars with no obvious strategy for prevailing. He impulsively abandoned the Kurds in northern Syria after a phone call with the Turkish president, betraying a key ally and allowing ISIS prisoners to escape from captivity in the predictable chaos that followed. And, of course, his casual, self-serving and anti-institutional conduct of foreign policy culminated in the Ukraine call that precipitated his impeachment. Yet the organizers of the most disciplined network of Never Trumpers remained on the sidelines, only able to watch as almost all Republican elected officials showered the president with acclaim, seemingly unable to see what they considered the obvious truth.

The organizers of the letters remained convinced that they had done the only thing that their honor permitted. Eliot Cohen reflects: "I'm very proud of the national security community for being willing to sort of step up and talk about that, and talk about the centrality of character." Bryan McGrath observes that his wife "Catherine still loves me, and I know that when I have grandchildren someday I can say, 'Yeah, I did that. I did that.'" John Bellinger believes that their work was not without consequence, but more importantly he still believes he had to do something. "I would never forgive myself if the election were as close as it was or even closer, and I felt that, rather than simply casting one vote, I had not engaged in some collective action to warn the country of the national security danger that I and others felt that he posed." All that said, none of these men has any illusions about the consequences of their actions. McGrath notes that, "I sit here and I think, 'We called it.' We made our stand. We told everybody what was coming, and we lost the argument. . . . I don't know what [more] we could have done. We shot our wad in 2016. And we did it first and we did it strongest, and there's very little that we said that hasn't come to fruition, but the bottom line is the party that we were talking to stopped listening to us." For Bellinger, the lesson is simple: "If you aim for the king, you better not miss."[71]

These men had aimed for the king, and in the years afterward they were hard put to figure out what more, if anything, they could do after having missed. While Bellinger, for instance, played a role in the creation of the conservative lawyers' organization Checks and Balances (discussed in Chapter 8), no similar new organization emerged in the foreign policy space to counter the president. Bellinger has not seen "any sort of organized pushback. It doesn't mean acquiescence or certainly falling into line like Republicans on the Hill. I think it's been more simply depression and a feeling of there's not too much that one can do about it."[72] Cohen agrees, arguing that there was little that the Republican foreign policy establishment could do given the nature of their policy area.

> I don't think anybody really saw the point in trying to forge a new organization. What would it do? We always thought that this guy was terrible. We continue to think this guy is terrible. . . . Lawyers are different. There are a lot of points of purchase in our system on domestic politics. . . . There are the state legislatures. There're the two houses of Congress. There's the bureaucracy. When it comes to foreign affairs, we are really an executive branch–driven system. And that's just about it.

Moreover, because the national security network is relatively small and so Washington-focused, it's not necessary to create new structures to forge cohesion.

> The thing is, there isn't really a need for that. I mean, here again, there's a bit of a difference. The foreign policy–national security community is actually pretty strong. One of the deep dark secrets is it's actually fairly bipartisan, and so therefore there was no particular reason to create a new forum or new organization. You know, I see many of the people who signed those letters a lot. . . . You create structures when the structures are needed. You don't create them for the sake of creating structures.[73]

The experience of seeing where the Republican Party has been led under Trump has convinced McGrath that it may never again be a vehicle for the kind of foreign policy he believes in. "The political party that was the instrument through which all of these people had political relevance, that political party has dissolved. It no longer exists in the shape that it did when they made themselves known in 2016. What would be the appropriate channel for that? Because it's certainly not the Republican Party." Similarly, Cohen worries that the GOP may be too far gone to ever reconcile with the people who used to govern the nation's security. "If what it's essentially morphing into is this sort of populist, ethno-nationalist, neo-isolationist party, they're not really going to have any real foreign policy establishment to speak of."[74]

In the end, the organizers of the foreign policy letters are convinced that, having done what they could in the election, they have little option but to put their future in the hands of fate. McGrath sums this attitude up when he notes that, "We got our asses handed to us. And to some extent, I'm content to just be right at this point and watch everyone else kind of get on the bandwagon of where we were in late February of 2016." In his optimistic moments, McGrath is hopeful that it might be possible to return to the pre-Trump status quo. "Maybe a right-of-center Republican Party will reemerge where I am welcome and where his vocal defenders are not welcome. . . . The most effective thing to do right now is to let the President be his own worst enemy, and limit his damage to four years, at which point most, if not all, the people on those lists will be happy to get back in the game." But McGrath also knows that his ship may have sailed. "It's a race against time. I'm 54 years old. I am not without a reasonable retirement plan. At some point, I'm going to say, 'Fuck it' and just be a gentleman farmer." The president's own foibles may yet give him and his Never Trump comrades an alternative to plowing.

PART II

Political Operatives

4

Pack Animals

THE BEGINNING OF THE 2016 campaign cycle was a heady time in Republican circles. By the end of the Obama years, the GOP was stronger than it had been in nearly a century. The party had gained control of the House in 2010 and the Senate in 2014. It had also been running circles around Democrats in statehouses across the country. And now the presidency looked ripe for the taking. For one thing, voters have a natural tendency to shake things up after one party has had two consecutive terms in the White House. Additionally, Republicans thought Hillary Clinton, already assumed to be the presumptive Democratic nominee, had a likeability problem and was hobbled by personal baggage from decades in the public spotlight. But as much as anything, it was Republicans' own deep bench of outstanding candidates that caused such optimism. The crop of potential Republican standard-bearers included high-profile, successful governors like Jeb Bush, Chris Christie, John Kasich, and Scott Walker, as well as celebrated Tea Party insurgents like Senators Marco Rubio, Ted Cruz, and Rand Paul. Surely, with riches like this available to the Republican primary electorate, a white knight would emerge to put the party back in control of the White House. Helping them get there would be the party's band of political operatives.

Political operatives are the professional campaign consultants, pollsters, media experts, fundraisers, and staffers who make a living by providing key services to their party and its candidates. Unlike the GOP national security experts or the conservative movement's intelligentsia,

Republican operatives who were publicly Never Trump cut against the grain of their professional network. Despite near-universal, albeit largely silent, opposition to Trump initially, most operatives dutifully fell in line once he became the presumptive nominee. Yet the small minority within the political operative world that refused to make their peace with him emerged as one of the brightest constellations in the Never Trump universe.

Many factors—professional, financial, ethical, and a complicated set of crosscutting attachments, tribal identities, and loyalties—were in play for Republican political professionals when they were forced to grapple with Trump's candidacy. However, three factors do a lot of work in sorting the Never Trumpers from the herd. The first is their association with a particular idea for reforming the GOP, one that long predated the 2016 campaign. In their professional assessment, demographic trends were a ticking time bomb for the party. As the country became increasingly diverse, they maintained, the Republican coalition would inevitably shrink, making it progressively harder for the party to win national majorities. In response, they felt a profound sense of urgency to diversify the party through aggressive outreach to new demographic groups that the party struggled with but that had the potential to be brought into the fold. This effort was not understood to be a rejection of conservatism or a painstaking reevaluation of party orthodoxy. In essence, the idea was to basically keep the same menu of Republican ideological offerings but to start sending out dinner invitations to electorally important demographic groups. Indeed, the plan fortuitously dovetailed with the preexisting wishes of the party's donor class.

This vision of the GOP's future was given its clearest and most prominent articulation in the "Growth and Opportunity Project." "The Autopsy," as it was colloquially known, was an initiative undertaken by the Republican National Committee in the wake of the disappointing 2012 election. The project and the idea animating it were far from universally embraced among the party's operatives, and some instead supported a version of what would become Trump's basic strategy of going downscale and beating the bushes for more white working-class voters.[1] But most of the political operatives who ended up as Never Trumpers had prominently associated themselves with the Autopsy or the ideas underpinning it. They had made a bet on an entrepreneurial theory of the GOP's future, based on the idea that there was no way to squeeze more electoral blood from the existing Republican coalition's stone.

The second key factor in differentiating the Never Trumpers from the rest of the party's operatives is the unique nature of their work. Political operatives' livelihoods depend on the party's continued ability to win elections, and their ability to stay in the good graces of the party organization. Yet despite that pressure, some operatives opted for the nuclear option of opposing their party's nominee. In addition to personal and ethical considerations, two factors related to operatives' dependency on the party help explain their atypical behavior. For some, their concern over the demographic issues addressed in the Autopsy made diversifying the party not simply an intellectually desirable goal but a matter of great urgency for their professional futures. If the party tanked, so would their bank accounts. The other factor was that some of the operatives who went Never Trump had achieved a degree of professional success that inoculated them from the financial and career concerns that most operatives confronted. Many of the Never Trump operatives were older, had already made a lot of money in politics, and had achieved a level of fame that provided other lucrative and fulfilling professional opportunities as, for instance, media commentators. In other words, they could afford it.

Finally, a large chunk of the operative class is relatively ideologically moderate, particularly on social issues and diversity. The most determined Never Trumpers were drawn from this segment of the party's operative class. While their professional judgment told them that the party needed to be more racially diverse to be electorally successful, they were also ideologically committed to such a vision of the party. Some of those associated with the Autopsy—including Ari Fleischer, Reince Priebus, and Sean Spicer—later morphed into high-profile Trump boosters once he secured the nomination. Yet others who embraced the Autopsy theory of the party's future doubled down, insisting that going hard after "missing white voters" in 2016 came at the cost of the party's ability to appeal to a diversifying electorate in the future. Even more important than electoral strategy was their fear that Trump's approach meant abandoning any hope of forging the kind of multiracial, economically and socially open Republican Party that they associated with the tradition of Ronald Reagan and Jack Kemp. It was those ideas that had drawn them to the party in the first place. The realization that their former compatriots seemingly had no qualms with the GOP morphing into a European-style party of populist, ethnic nationalism was and continues to be disorientating and, in many cases, personally traumatic, even among this hard-boiled and jaded class of politicos.

As the 2016 election cycle got underway, the possibility of Trump taking over the party and remaking it in his own vision was unthinkable. Trump's operation was a laughingstock or an object of scorn among Republican campaign professionals, and they expected it to collapse in short order. Even after he emerged as the front runner for the nomination, the other presidential campaigns—wedded to an outdated model of how Republican nominees are selected—were obsessively training their fire on one another rather than trying to confront Trump. When the resistance, including the #nevertrump hashtag, finally emerged, it came not from the principals that the party's professionals are accustomed to serving but from among those party professionals themselves. Even then, they realized it was almost certainly too late.

Just Business

Understanding how Republican political operatives navigated the rise of Trump requires understanding their professional world and their role within the party.[2] To a much greater extent than other elements of extended party networks, party operatives think and talk about their work as a "business." This reveals a critical and distinguishing characteristic of the operative class: They are dependent on—and inseparable from—their parties. Because they earn their living by providing services to the party, their personal livelihoods are almost always entirely dependent on being in good standing with its formal organization. Other partisan professional networks, by contrast, are less tethered to the formal party apparatus. Foreign policy experts, economists, and public intellectuals receive pay checks and have prestigious institutional homes in a variety of settings including academia, think tanks, magazines, and newspapers. If, for whatever reason, these individuals find themselves crosswise with their party, they have other ways of making ends meet financially. As we saw in Part I, it was a difficult, disorienting, and often personally traumatic experience for Republican foreign policy experts to find themselves at odds with their party over its choice of nominee. Yet it wasn't something that threatened to ruin their careers or prevent them from paying their mortgages. In many cases, it certainly narrowed their horizons and dashed their hopes of landing jobs in the next administration (which often translates into lucrative future opportunities). But they had other sources of income and professional fulfillment.

For operatives, however, breaking with their party meant leaving their professional network. Of course, there are exceptions to this rule. The most successful, high-profile consultants—like the top advisors on presidential campaigns—are often able to leverage their relative fame into other opportunities, especially as pundits on TV. But for the vast majority of operatives, those kinds of outside options are not realistic alternatives to their day jobs.

The Workplace Environment

"It's a secret world," says Mike Murphy, who ran Jeb Bush's 2016 Super PAC, of the loose and competitive network of campaign consultants, an elite group within the operative world. "It's a scrappy, self-made thing, and so they tend to be interesting people."[3] That characterization may not necessarily fit the average political operative, but it's a fairly apt description of the most high-profile consultants who lead double lives as cable news pundits. Murphy previously worked for, among many others, John McCain, Arnold Schwarzenegger, and many of the party's most successful moderate governors. But he is perhaps more well known for his many media appearances which highlight his sharp wit and, at least in his younger days, flamboyant hair. He sits at a very small table atop the GOP consulting class. His longtime rival Stuart Stevens joins him there. Stevens worked for George W. Bush's presidential campaigns and was Mitt Romney's top strategist in 2012. On the side, Stevens is a prolific writer of fiction, nonfiction, and TV dramas. He also once famously chronicled his use of performance-enhancing drugs to aid his amateur cycling hobby in *Outside* magazine.[4]

Political operatives have their own internal hierarchies, with their professional stature ultimately measured by their win-loss record. Those who rack up wins move up the food chain. Internally, the campaign consultant network is characterized by rivalries and a well-defined pecking order. Murphy describes the upper echelon of the consulting world this way:

> The phone book is full of people who say they're political consultants. But the elite group has been around for a while and have run a lot of successful races as chief strategists or consultants. . . . We all carry our records along. It's kind of like being a Big Ten or professional football coach: "Alright, Stuart did eight years and two championships in the Big Ten and then five years and two playoff championships in the pros; Murphy's done a Superbowl, he did these eighteen things." . . . And after you've been at it a couple decades, if you keep winning, you stay at the top and you become one of the A-list consultants. And it's a fairly small group.

Below that top group, the Republican operative network balloons in numbers. As Murphy explains:

> There's a ton of people at the mid-level, where it's really kind of an industry. I mean, somebody's got to do all those state senate races; there's money to make there. So as campaign spending has gone up and the independent groups have become better funded and more prevalent, it's become kind of an industry. And I would say, of the so-called consulting class—which would be the A-list people, the B-list people, the C-list people, the people around the [House and Senate campaign] committees, the state capitol people, the state people who are in the smaller markets—you're talking thousands of people now in the Republican Party.[5]

These operatives are geographically and professionally distinct from lobbyists. Even for those ostensibly based in Washington, many operatives don't spend much time there. "People think we're all hanging around Washington drinking martinis," Murphy says. But "most real campaign consultants are on the road, out where the elections are. And that leads to a different sociology between the Washington lobbyists"—who may say they're political consultants, but generally aren't—"and the actual campaign operative types who can tell you about every Marriott from here to the end of the world."[6] Among the most visible Never Trump political operatives, many are based outside of Washington. Murphy and Tim Miller live in California; Stevens in Mississippi; Sally Bradshaw, Joel Searby, and Rick Wilson in Florida; Steve Schmidt in Utah; and John Weaver in Texas.

In contrast to some other professional networks in the extended party, most operatives do not think of themselves primarily as advocates, but—like lawyers—as hired guns who provide services to paying clients. As Stevens explains:

> What counts is not what your opinion is, it's what your client believes. I don't think people should hire me to remind them of their deeply held beliefs. Consultants are just mechanics. . . . We're people that serve a function. We're like orthopedic surgeons for Olympic athletes. We're not making them better athletes, we're just sort of like, "We'll fix the knee. We'll get this." I don't think it's the role of consultants to [push a political or policy agenda].[7]

Because they are so exposed to the ruthless logic of the market and the need to make payroll, political consultants—despite widespread consultant revulsion for Trump—were relatively scarce among those who made their objections public and went Never Trump.

Yet despite their hired-gun roles, as their careers advance, operatives come to be associated with certain segments of the party. Going into 2016, there was a long-standing ideological split within the Republican operative class. "There's two basic business models," explains Patrick Ruffini, a Republican political strategist and vocal Never Trumper.

> One is the Republican establishment business model, which is every kind of consultant who became Never Trump. . . . There is this strain of Republican consultants who are generally pretty moderate on social policy, and generally more center-right—certainly much more centrist than the voters that they have to talk to. [They're]

people who are educated, who are urban dwellers, who have more tolerant views on social issues, have more tolerant views on gay marriage, who have more tolerant views on a lot of these things, who are not as motivated by what you might call the grievance-style politics.[8]

The other group, Ruffini says, consists of "a very professional conservative class of consultants and conservative class of operatives that views this as: it's the litmus test, it's the Freedom Caucus, it's everything that was embodied by the Ted Cruz campaign, which is, I'm gonna be down-the-line conservative on every single policy issue." Notably, this internal split among GOP consultants does not have analogous counterparts across the aisle. Democratic consultants have, at least until recently, fewer internal ideological divisions, and fewer awkward points of departure between themselves and their voters. "That's a key difference between us and the left," Ruffini says. "Professional operatives on the left are much more generally in line with their base on a lot of policy issues—on choice, generally on all the economic policy issues for the most part. That difference is not as fractious and tribal among [Democratic] consultants."[9]

The operative experience of the 2016 election can be helpfully illustrated by thinking about the Republican Party as a whole in terms of a grid with quadrants. On one side is the ideological spectrum running from moderate to conservative, on the other is a low information–high information scale. For years leading up to 2016, the political consultant class was engaged in a war within the high-information quadrants of the Republican Party. As it played out in 2016, the pure uncut version of that divide was encapsulated by the moderate candidacy of John Kasich and the conservative candidacy of Ted Cruz, each of whom presented a discrete worldview and a formulation of where the Republican Party should go. The moderate high-information wing of the party represented by Kasich thought Republicans needed to be more entrepreneurial in seeking out new voters who weren't currently buying the GOP product line. The obvious way to do that was to moderate on social issues, thereby allowing voters who "should be" Republicans but were put off by the party's social conservatism to come home. The competing theory offered from the conservative high-information wing of the party represented by Cruz argued that Republicans lose because, as Ruffini explains the thinking, "we aren't aggressive enough in just taking it to the Democrats in terms of just punching their face in." Notably, and despite this persistent divide within the high-information quadrants, moderates and conservatives were actually unified in their Never Trumpism in the fall of 2015 and through the 2016 primaries. However, as Ruffini explains, while one set of Republicans—including the party's operatives—were fighting it out in the high-information quadrants, Trump was cleaning up in the low-information quadrants, which turns out to be half the party's actual voters. "You have high-information voters who care about principles one way or the other, but a majority or a plurality don't care. They want to win and they want someone who reflects their basic cultural worldview, which Trump tapped into perfectly."[10] This breakdown of the Republican Party illuminates the fact that Never Trumpers in the operative class were focused on the high-information quadrants. They were unified in being Never Trump but were blind to the way Trump was successfully targeting an entirely different set of voters whom they were not focused on.

This way of thinking about the party also helps to explain developments to come. The conservative operatives largely dropped their Never Trumpism when Cruz finally endorsed Trump (noting in his announcement that he'd "always been #NeverHillary") six weeks before the general election or, at the latest, once the votes were tallied.[11] The operatives who have remained steadfast Never Trumpers weren't randomly selected; they all came out of the moderate wing. To be sure, not all of the operatives associated with that part of the GOP went Never Trump. But those who did emerged from that milieu and shared a set of preestablished views that were grounded in both their professional analysis and their personal ideological and policy preferences.

"White Boat Sinking:" The Case for a Republican Reformation

Just hours after the 2008 election, Ruffini and Mindy Finn, a then–27-year-old Republican political operative who specializes in digital media, launched "Rebuild the Party." The reform initiative featured tactical plans to help the GOP catch up to Democrats' ground game, but it was also crystal clear about the need for the party to appeal to a new generation of conservatives. Part of the reason the Obama campaign had been able to run circles around Republicans on the nuts and bolts of campaign tactics was the GOP's failure to adapt to changing times and embrace a younger, Internet-friendly generation at the grassroots level. Rebuild the Party's founding manifesto proclaimed: "We don't need a slight tweak here or there. We need transformation [to bring] the Republican Party into the future." In a press interview, Finn was blunter about the type of transformation they sought: "The Republican Party cannot reboot if it's viewed only as a party of old, crusty white guys."[12]

Similarly, Murphy took to the pages of *TIME* with a warning: "I've made a career out of counting votes, and the numbers tell a clear story; the demographics of America are changing in a way that is deadly for the Republican Party as it exists today. A GOP ice age is on the way. Demographic change is irritating to politicos, since it works on elections much as rigged dice do on a Las Vegas craps table: it is a game changer." Notably, Murphy maintained that his plan for saving the party wasn't "about diluting conservatism but about modernizing it to reflect the country it inhabits instead of an America that no longer exists." The only road to salvation was to be found by broadening the character of the party's appeal and initiating "a Republican reformation right now."[13]

Two specific areas of party dogma had to be addressed to attract new demographic groups. First, revamping the party's approach to social policy could bring in more young people. Murphy argued that young voters would never get past first base with the GOP unless it lightened up on social issues, especially gay rights. For Murphy and others who shared his view, these matters were not central to their own personal identities as conservatives and what they thought the Republican Party stood for. "With changing demographics come changing attitudes, and aping the grim town elders from *Footloose* is not the path back to a Republican White House." Murphy made a partial exception for abortion, which differed in the crucial respect that pro-life sentiment wasn't polarized by age group; its supporters were evenly distributed across the generations. Yet even so, "the overall GOP view on abortion must aggressively embrace the big tent," which meant accepting a diversity of views within the party and abandoning the GOP's outdated and off-putting litmus-test approach to the issue. Second, Murphy counseled wooing Latinos by reassuring them that the party was not hostile to immigration. As Murphy wrote, "Latinos need to see a quick end to the Republican congressional jihad on immigration. . . . The GOP should support practical immigration reform that includes a path to citizenship." Murphy was channeling that element of the American tradition that celebrated welcoming and assimilating immigrants (and that was consistent with the interests of the party's business wing), although his advice ended with a grave warning: "Illegal immigrants can't vote. Their children will."[14] The electoral calculation behind Murphy's argument—and later that of the Autopsy—was always presented as being at the center of the case.

Murphy attributes his "white boat sinking" warnings to his unusually extensive experience running Republican campaigns in unfriendly territory. Most GOP operatives came up in much more Republican-friendly environments and were therefore less concerned about, or even aware of, the problem the party was facing:

A lot of the operative play book that we have in the Republican party has been in bad decline. I came up doing the blue states in the '90s and early 2000s—the Michigans, the Wisconsins, the Massachusetts, California. I did the Schwarzenegger race out here. I did Romney's governor races, New Jersey governor races—[places] where Republican governors could win swing or tilt-blue states. So we were always very creative in our politics. We wanted to fight the whole campaign on Democratic turf, to break the Dem vote to add to the Republican [vote] that we got for free, which was a minority vote in those states. But that was very much out the window by the mid-2000s. The party had gone to this base strategy of whip up our voters and turn them out, which was a wonderful way to win Texas. But we started losing the Great Lakes swing states and other places. And so, having come up in that tradition, I was a big alarm bell guy.[15]

Consultants like Murphy were pushing for a party coalition that looked different than it had in the past, one that broadened its appeal by including the educated, cosmopolitan middle class, and ethnic minorities. As we will see in Chapter 6, there were other Republicans who were also pulling the alarm bell but with a class- rather than race-based theory of the problems with the party's electoral coalition.

Ruffini, Finn, and Murphy had the same starting point as Democrats John Judis and Ruy Teixeira in 2002's *The Emerging Democratic Majority*, which foresaw an unstoppable, demographic-driven triumph over Republicans.[16] However, they thought that a Democratic majority was not inevitable if Republicans took steps to reshuffle the demographic deck. Their attempt to play the canary in the coal mine fell largely on deaf ears, at least initially. Kristen Soltis Anderson, a prominent operative with ties to Jeb Bush and who is also now a regular media commentator, was among those issuing stern warnings about the need to reach out to new groups of voters. The polling and focus group expert was especially attuned to young voters. As Anderson explains, the advice she and others were offering "wasn't fashionable. It's still not fashionable to be the Republican who is saying that you think doom is coming to your own party. Nobody really likes the person who's the skunk at the garden party."[17] Even so, the massive disappointment of the 2012 campaign, a campaign that many Republicans believed was winnable, provided the opportunity that these political operatives needed to force the party to take a serious look at the country's changing demographic profile and its implications for the GOP.

The Autopsy

A month after Barack Obama defeated Mitt Romney, Republican National Committee (RNC) Chairman Reince Priebus announced a major initiative that would "dig deep to provide an honest review" of the party's 2012 failure and devise "a plan to grow the Party and improve

Republican campaigns." Over the next three months, five volunteer co-chairs and a small band of RNC staffers spoke with 2,600 people ranging from party members and elected officials to voters and technical experts, convened focus groups with voters who had abandoned the party, conducted a poll of Hispanic Republicans, consulted pollsters and Republican operatives, and administered an online poll generating 36,000 responses.[18] As Autopsy co-chair and longtime Jeb Bush confidante Sally Bradshaw recounts, "every stone we could turn over, we did, to build that report."[19]

The RNC released its findings in March 2013. There were two components. As communications expert Tim Miller—then an RNC staffer working on the Autopsy who later rose to prominence as communications director for Jeb Bush's presidential campaign and an informal Never Trump spokesman on "Pod Save America"—recalls, one part was "what I just call the blocking and tackling" fundamentals of campaigns and "looking at things Democrats did well that we weren't doing as well," including data analytics, tactics, field staffing, shaping news cycles, voter contact, the presidential primary process, and so on. "Frankly, I think a greater share and effort went into that part. Most of that stuff pretty much holds up," and much of it was adopted by the party for the 2016 campaign cycle. In fact, Miller suspects the tactical changes drawn from Autopsy recommendations helped the party in 2016 and may have even "been one of the reasons Trump ended up winning." Ruffini, who was also engaged with the Autopsy, agrees, noting that the group's work on establishing an RNC-based digital and data team later provided the foundation for Trump's campaign. Ruffini explains:

> Normally this kind of team would end up being sidelined in a general election because the campaigns do their own thing, but the thought was that the RNC would at least provide a desperately needed talent pipeline for the campaigns to hire from. But then Trump ends up winning the nomination with zero infrastructure, so the RNC team morphed into the Trump digital team and is basically singlehandedly responsible for the fact that he had any money for the general. So, while I did my part to fight Trump, the irony is that these recommendations by me and some other Never Trump people

were responsible for the fact that he had any campaign at all in the general election.[20]

Yet it was the other part of the RNC report, calling for the party to reach out to new demographic groups, that received the most attention. It was also featured most prominently in the report itself, comprising the document's first two substantive chapters. The first chapter, titled "Messaging," was intended to be a hard dose of reality: "Public perception of the Party is at record lows. Young voters are increasingly rolling their eyes at what the Party represents, and many minorities wrongly think that Republicans do not like them or want them in the country." A subsection titled "Some People Say, 'Republicans Don't Care,'" noted that focus groups conducted for the Autopsy revealed that voters who had recently left the party found the GOP to be "'scary,' 'narrow minded,' and 'out of touch' and that we were a Party of 'stuffy old men.'" The Autopsy lamented that, however unfair and perplexing these critiques might be, the sentiment behind them was nonetheless widespread, as polling of the general public made clear. Moreover, the report ominously asserted that "unless changes are made, it will be increasingly difficult for Republicans to win another presidential election in the near future." The next subsection—"America Looks Different"—channeled the demographic decline narrative, arguing that "the nation's demographic changes add to the urgency of recognizing how precarious our position has become," and "if we want ethnic minority voters to support Republicans, we have to engage them and show our sincerity."[21]

The second substantive chapter identified specific ways to do just that. "Demographic Partners" began by asserting that the party "must focus its efforts to earn new supporters and voters in the following demographic communities: Hispanic, Asian and Pacific Islanders, African Americans, Indian Americans, Native Americans, women, and youth." The chapter then systematically outlined a strategy and set of recommendations for appealing to each of these groups.[22] "The pervasive mentality of writing off blocks of states or demographic votes for the Republican Party must be completely forgotten. The Republican Party must compete on every playing field."[23] Yet it was also clear from the Autopsy itself, as well as subsequent media commentary and interviews with the report's authors, that the Hispanic, women, and youth playing fields received much higher priority, with Hispanics in particular garnering far more mentions than the other groups.

"A No-Brainer": Comprehensive Immigration Reform

The Autopsy is remembered most for its endorsement of comprehensive immigration reform. The following language appeared three times, verbatim, in the report:

> We are not a policy committee, but among the steps Republicans take in the Hispanic community and beyond, we must embrace and champion comprehensive immigration reform. If we do not, our Party's appeal will continue to shrink to its core constituencies only. We also believe that comprehensive immigration reform is consistent with Republican economic policies that promote job growth and opportunity for all.[24]

This policy endorsement stood out because it is the only one in a document designed to focus on campaigning, not governing. Yet they made an exception, repeatedly, for immigration. Bradshaw says that the immigration exception, as well as a more general commitment to reaching out to minorities, reflected the Autopsy team's assessment that those efforts were particularly essential to the party's future and therefore fell within the scope of the Autopsy's charge:

> It was limited in scope. There was not a lot of policy, by choice, that we looked at as part of that report because it was really an RNC-driven report, and it was about the role of the national committee and the campaign committees. But there were some comments that we made on, for instance, the issue of immigration and being a party that would be more representative of the public at large and would reach out to a more diverse group of voters.[25]

Bradshaw maintains that the decision to include the immigration statements was uncontested at the RNC:

I don't recall any significant pushback. I recall a lot of people—whether it was the donor class or the grassroots class—that said: "If we've gotten too small, we've got to get bigger." The country is changing significantly and particularly with respect to Hispanics. The percentage of eligible Hispanic voters continues to grow astronomically, and you don't have to be a rocket scientist to see that unless we had a real effort to reach out to Hispanics and really made a point of producing substantive policy that impacted Hispanics in a positive way, the party was going to have a very tough go of it. . . . At the time, this was just a no-brainer.[26]

Miller similarly recalls that the decision to make comprehensive immigration reform "a key part" of the Autopsy was not particularly controversial:

Among the people who were involved, at least a good portion of them just felt like immigration reform is the right policy. It was something that obviously [George W.] Bush had been supportive of, the last Republican president. And he did better among Hispanic voters than Romney. It was something that, at the time, rising stars in the party were proposing, with Marco [Rubio]. So, I think that there was an ideological feeling that this is the right thing to do. This issue needs to be resolved. But there's also this electoral mandate to be able to talk to Hispanic voters. For a number of groups, they're not even listening to us when we talk about other issues because of the harsh tone that's being used around immigration and, just in general, the harsh policy proposals that were being put forth by a large segment of the party. . . . And so, if you're looking at it from a 2013 mindset that we've maxed out the white voters, how are we going to expand the pie? Hispanic voters are the obvious place to go.[27]

In other words, a key assumption behind the Autopsy's embrace of immigration reform was that the Republican Party's economic agenda was sound and had broad appeal. The problem was that a significant swath of the American public that should be voting GOP—in no small part because of that appealing economic agenda—refused to even consider doing so because they were put off by the party's intolerance.

When the Autopsy was released, it was met with a range of criticisms. As we will see in the discussion of the Reformocons in Chapter 6, there were some in the party with a very different account of the GOP's dilemma. They opposed the Autopsy's call for immigration reform both as a matter of electoral tactics and on the merits, and accused the report's authors of focusing on demography in order to avoid confronting the party's increasingly unpopular, donor-driven economic message grounded in tax cuts for the rich. The party's real problem, they argued, was plutocracy more than intolerance.

The Autopsy was also dismissed as a meaningless and cynical gesture by some, like Murphy. Bradshaw had consulted Murphy regularly during her work on the project, both because they were friends and because he was well known in the party as "a demography modernizer." Yet despite his engagement and a final product that mirrored his own long-standing assessment, Murphy emphasizes that the rationale for performing the Autopsy wasn't really as introspective and earnest as RNC press releases made it seem. "The RNC was under donor pressure," Murphy insists, so it produced a shiny report with bells and whistles "to buy off donors and the media." He recalls his reaction to the project:

I thought the Autopsy was kind of a bullshit document, although it got at real problems we had. What it identified as a threat, I totally agree with. That was obvious. [But] I don't think the Autopsy was a serious effort to do anything because that'd mean getting into policy. . . . It was just a cover-our-ass document to try to show the party had self-diagnosed some of its problems. But there was not the will under the surface—by Reince or anybody else—to actually act on it and do real things. Because doing real things means changing policy, which is where all the resistance is. It's one thing to say, "Alright, we gotta do something about Latinos. Let's make sure we hire a Mariachi band at every rally in Denver." That doesn't mean anything. What you have to do is look at changing policy on immigration, which the electeds in D.C., most of them, had very little interest in doing, because they were all the products of Republican primaries. There aren't many swing seats left with redistricting. And

those primaries were old, grumpy, and white, and they had no damn
interest in immigration reform.[28]

Ultimately, for many of those who would later end up in the Never
Trump camp, the Autopsy's call for immigration reform reflected
more than just hard-nosed, data-driven conclusions about optimal
campaign tactics. It was also a moral statement about what the
Republican Party's future ought to be, grounded in their interpretation of the Republican Party's history and guiding philosophy. As
Miller explains, "In addition to seeming like smart politics and in
addition to feeling it was the right thing to do, it was also how most
of the people who were involved saw the Republican Party that they
loved." He emphasizes formative political moments that shaped the
thinking of him and those who gravitated toward the Autopsy theory
of the party's future. For instance, there was the famous 1980 primary
debate in which presidential candidate George H.W. Bush described
immigrants as "honorable, decent, family-loving people" while his
opponent, Ronald Reagan, proposed that "rather than talking about
putting up a fence, why don't we work out" a legal mechanism to
"open the border both ways" that would allow Mexicans to legally
work in the United States.[29] Another generational touchstone was
President Reagan's immigrant-friendly metaphor of the country as a
"Shining City on a Hill," a line he had adapted from John Winthrop's
description of the Pilgrims' hopes for a new home. In Reagan's 1989
farewell address, he explained that this City was "teeming with people
of all kinds living in harmony and peace" and that "if there had to
be city walls, the walls had doors and the doors were open to anyone
with the will and the heart to get here." Reagan closed his speech by
expressing pride that after eight years in office, that City was "still
a beacon, still a magnet for all who must have freedom, for all the
pilgrims from all the lost places who are hurtling through the darkness,
toward home."[30] Miller also points to other key orienting experiences,
including siding with Elian Gonzalez against the Clinton administration and supporting George W. Bush's plan for comprehensive
immigration reform. "It was really the Democrats," he emphasizes,
"during a lot of our formative years, who had tougher things to say

about immigration because of unions—this old hardline union line that immigrants would threaten wages."[31]

At the time of the Autopsy, it was still possible to conceive of the GOP as a predominantly pro-immigration party. To be sure, the issue had long been contested by the likes of Pat Buchanan and Tom Tancredo, but they could casually be dismissed as fringe figures. In early 2013, Republican operatives like Miller were still convinced that the pro-immigrant tradition within the Republican Party remained strong, and Reagan's Shining City on a Hill "didn't seem as distant as it does now."[32]

Staffing Up for 2016 and the Overlooked Trump Threat

As the 2016 election cycle commenced, Republican political operatives did what they always do: They signed on with campaigns. Jeb Bush quickly cornered much of the market on A-list campaign talent. Senior Advisor Sally Bradshaw was a veteran Bush loyalist in Tallahassee. Another longtime confidant, Mike Murphy, headed Bush's Super PAC, Right to Rise. Campaign Manager Danny Diaz and Chief Strategist David Kochel had been leading figures in Mitt Romney's presidential runs. There was also lots of money. When Bush formally announced his candidacy, he had raised more cash than all the other candidates combined. (By the time he dropped out following the South Carolina primary in February, his campaign and Super PAC had brought in a massive haul of $155 million; only Clinton raised more in the 2016 cycle.) These early victories were part of a mystifyingly named "shock and awe" initiative—an inauspicious term given its connection to his brother's Iraq War. The strategy of the Bush campaign was to scare off other potential candidates by raising an overwhelming amount of money and locking down key donors, campaign professionals, and policy experts—a mission that was not accomplished. Other top-tier candidates declared and went through the standard competition for top staff, and were able to cobble together their own respectable operations by conventional standards. Nonetheless, Bush's candidacy appeared especially formidable by all the standard measurements used to gauge the early stages of a campaign.

In contrast to the professional organizations supporting these candidates, Donald Trump's campaign hired a decidedly less accomplished team of misfits and oddballs. Relative to normal presidential operations, Trump's staff—largely based in Trump Tower in Manhattan—was tiny and inexperienced, his fundraising operation was anemic, and his ground game was nearly nonexistent. At one point, a significant chunk of staffers quit because they never got paid, which is usually a sign of a campaign that is about to flatline.[33] The bizarre cast of characters included his first campaign manager, Corey Lewandowski, who had once been arrested for bringing a gun to work when he was a Capitol Hill staffer. He'd worked for Rep. Bob Ney (R-OH), who went to prison as part of the Abramoff scandal, and served as campaign manager for Senator Bob Smith's (R-NH) 2002 reelection campaign. In that race, the perennial thorn in the side of establishment party leaders became the first senator in a decade who failed to get re-nominated. Ensuing years saw Lewandowski work as a lobbyist, police officer, and in various capacities for the Koch network. Paul Manafort briefly replaced Lewandowski before departing the campaign less than three months later. Manafort never could have worked for another 2016 campaign in that capacity, or probably any capacity, due to his long record of shady international lobbying clients and political activity that had linked him to dubious figures, including Russian President Vladimir Putin. Since his time on the Trump campaign, Manafort has been sentenced to several years in prison for a series of financial crimes. Another key figure from the Trump campaign, Roger Stone, was convicted of several felonies as part of Special Counsel Robert Mueller's investigation of Russian interference in the 2016 election. Hope Hicks was hired to lead the Trump campaign's communications shop. Prior to that, the 27-year-old had worked in public relations for the Trump organization but lacked any political experience.[34]

The Republican operative class viewed Trump's campaign team as a ridiculous band of degenerates and professional failures, untouchables who couldn't find work in respectable Republican circles. As Juleanna Glover—a veteran Republican operative who has worked for George W. Bush, McCain, William Kristol, and conservative activist Phyllis

Schlafly—notes: "Is it a recognizable trend that people who weren't really able to cut it professionally ended up supporting Trump as an opportunity to really make it? Yes, absolutely." Ruffini similarly notes that the only people who were initially enthusiastic about Trump were opportunists who felt that they'd been unjustly shut out, and that everyone else was opposed to Trump: "The Never Trump movement [encompassed] a broad swath of official Washington and a broad swath of the campaign operative class in the sense of when Trump was going out and asking people to go to work on his campaign, everyone was turning him down. Everybody thought this was a joke." But for those who had no other options, Trump offered one last chance—however low-percentage it may have been—to desperate people who had been passed over and were bitter about it. Ruffini explains that by 2016, "Paul Manafort was nobody in terms of domestic politics, right? So Trump is his ticket back to relevancy. Corey Lewandowski is not going to get a job managing any other presidential campaign. Hope Hicks is not going to be communications director for any other campaign." As Glover puts it: "Do you feel like you've never gotten what you deserved, and this is your way to pop it to the man? That was very much the mentality."[35] It was impossible for political professionals like this to imagine that someone surrounded by grifters and yesterday's men could possibly pose a threat to serious candidates taking advice from people like themselves.

The absurd staffing choices reinforced the consensus among operatives that Trump's campaign was just a publicity stunt. Mindy Finn, who would later leave the GOP to run for vice president on Evan McMullin's independent ticket, recalls her thinking in 2015: "He was too much of an outsider-type candidate to have any kind of real shot, and too much of a clown to have a real shot." Glover similarly remembers dismissing Trump out of hand. "I didn't take him seriously. At that point in time, I was supporting Jeb, and [our] energy was focused on Rubio. [Trump was] sort of a sideshow." Even when Trump's poll numbers were strong, she was convinced it would pass. "The expectation was when he first popped up [in the polls], they would deflate the more people saw" of him. As Ruffini explains, Republicans "have that model of, in the end, the nice, respectable guy wins."[36] That model was rooted in the 2008 and 2012 cycles in which John McCain and Mitt Romney eventually emerged as the nominees but not before the party base flirted with a number of other candidates, including off-the-wall figures like Herman Cain or Newt Gingrich. For that reason, the assumption that Trump would inevitably collapse was conventional wisdom among Republican operatives.

Yet even as they waited for his inevitable collapse, the distaste for Trump among the GOP's stable of political operatives in good standing ran deep, and some of them thought his campaign was doing serious long-term damage to the party's brand. Ruffini explains:

> [The Never Trump movement] actually was very big. The sort of people that it drew from were the people who would have been in line to run the presidential campaigns—all the people who thought it was a great opportunity to go down to Miami to work for Jeb Bush. That's sort of the standard pathway that everyone pretty much was following. And it's not to say those people all became vocal Trump critics, a lot of people kind of just stayed quiet on the sidelines. But nobody was really happy about it.[37]

Least happy were those who were heavily invested in the idea of diversifying the party. Prior to the 2016 cycle, Finn had worked on three presidential campaigns and in senior positions at the RNC. She had created a niche for herself within the party as a leader on reform efforts designed to detoxify the Republican brand and make the party more appealing to African Americans, Hispanics, and especially women. She took Trump's candidacy more seriously than most, not because she thought that he could win but because of his offensive and divisive rhetoric. Thus, when Trump came onto the scene in August 2015, declared himself a Republican, trashed all the demographic groups she had been courting, and sucked up all the media attention, Finn quickly recognized that even if Trump flamed out as a presidential candidate, he threatened to do tremendous harm to the party. As Finn recalls, "Everything he's doing is anathema to what I've been working on for years."[38]

She wasn't alone in that assessment. Throughout the fall of 2015, Finn was part of an informal network largely composed of 45-and-under Capitol Hill staffers who were troubled by Trump because, among other things, he was messing up their rebranding effort. They commiserated about the urgent need to get him off the stage and hoped for the best. But it was not until Trump won the New Hampshire primary in February that they organized any kind of formal resistance. By that point, however, it was evident to most Republican operatives that the political sands were shifting.

Deer in the Headlights

Their competitive professional culture makes political operatives less than naturally suited to collective action efforts, and in the 2016 cycle they also misunderstood the situation they were in. Even as Trump became increasingly difficult to laugh off, Republican operatives—like the principals they worked for—were frozen in place. If the party's politicians and operatives started the cycle waiting for Trump to crash and burn, once it became clear that he posed a serious threat to capture the nomination, they waited for someone else to do something about it.

The campaigns ignored Trump because they were relying on flawed models of how the campaign would play out. As Murphy recounts, the conventional wisdom in general and within Bush world was that the contest for the nomination would eventually be reduced to one candidate emerging from the "regular" lane—Bush, Rubio, Kasich, or Christie—and another from the "grievance" lane, presumably Cruz. Thus, those vying for the regular slot were focused on knocking out one another so they could make it to the final round against Cruz. Bush and Murphy have been widely criticized for failing to go after Trump given that their Super PAC had, by far, the most money. Yet from their understanding of the 2016 landscape, that was not where the real action was. As Murphy explains:

> The problem with that was . . . that only at most 55% of the primary voters had any interest in ever voting for a Jeb Bush, or a Rubio, or a Kasich. So persuading a grievance voter who's leaning toward Cruz or Trump to switch over and become a Jeb voter was pretty much wasted money. We had a much bigger threat from Kasich and Christie in New Hampshire and Rubio in South Carolina and, to

some extent, New Hampshire. So everybody kind of followed their naked interest, which was compete with the competition they had for the voters they were able to get. And that was one reason Trump was able to survive more or less unmolested.[39]

The other campaigns vying for the mainstream slot saw things the same way. Murphy says that he'd "bet everything I own" that if he'd suggested to the Rubio, Kasich, and Christie campaigns that they work together to take out Trump—even if Bush and Murphy offered to chip in over half the cash—he would have been rebuffed because they all saw Bush, not Trump, as their primary competitor and assumed that Cruz would dispatch Trump.[40] This turned out to be a fundamental mis-assessment of both Trump's and Cruz's appeal.

Meanwhile, the mainstream campaigns were initially pleased to see Trump enter the race because he had the potential to draw blood from Cruz before his showdown with the last normal candidate standing. As Murphy recounts, "We thought, alright, we know that Cruz has the grievance issue ray gun, and we know it cuts steel, and we know he's going to use it on Trump, who's very vulnerable." They assumed that "when Cruz uncorked on Trump with ideological messaging— Trump is for gun control, he loves Chuck Schumer, he's not pro-life— it would be quite effective on Trump, and it would take the air out of the bubble." It came as a surprise that Trump not only quickly eclipsed Cruz in the grievance silo but also managed to attract some voters from the regular pool. And these developments altered Cruz's incentives. Instead of going after Trump, he bided his time drafting behind him as the populist wave grew. But at some point, without anyone fully realizing it, it became too late. "They waited too long and did too little," Murphy says of Cruz. "They thought their weapons would work, too."[41] Many of Trump's supporters just didn't care about his ideological heresies, since for voters in the low-information quadrants of the Republican Party, ideology as conventionally understood simply doesn't matter.

The campaigns also failed to recognize that elections now operate by what Murphy calls "reality show rules." While the other candidates were out doing traditional rubber chicken fundraisers to finance their ads, the media was rewarding Trump for his theatrics and insults with massive amounts of free media. Murphy observes that, "We're all from a culture where we learn through pattern recognition. And antics like Trump's had been tried on a lesser level in statewide campaigns and had always failed. And you're managing risk in one of these campaigns, so the idea of, 'Hey, let's go do a clown show because this is the year it's going to work,' is a risky bet to make because most of the time when people have tried clownish campaigns, it doesn't work."[42] Generally speaking, consultants of all sorts traffic in conventional wisdom, recycling strategies demonstrated by experiences with previous clients rather than proposing innovations based on unproven hunches or instincts.[43] Political consultants are no different. By the time Republican operatives realized that Trump's clown show was in fact a disruptive innovation—and that he was a real threat to win the nomination—it was too late. The party's political consultant class then faced a moment of choosing.

With few exceptions, they ended up choosing Trump.

Never Trump! . . . err, Never Mind

Perhaps more than any other professional cohort in American politics, political operatives like a winner. Unlike other segments of the extended party, such as policy experts and intellectuals who can find soft landings in academia or at think tanks or magazines, political professionals' careers and livelihoods depend to a much greater extent on being attached to electoral winners. As the plausibility of Trump's candidacy grew over time, political operatives recalibrated. While their ranks had once been full of anti-Trumpers, when it became clear who was going to be the Republican nominee, dissenting political operatives became scarce; once he became president, Never Trump operatives had become an endangered species.

On February 9, the night Trump won the New Hampshire primary, Finn's small, informal band of mostly young Capitol Hill staffers had finally decided to do something beyond consoling one another. She explains the thinking of her loose network at that time:

> The theory was that, first of all, by having a national and public counter movement to the Trump movement, we would at least be resisting this snowball that it felt like nobody was pushing back on.

Then, tactically on the ground, we decided the digital media was the piece that we could do efficiently and target in the right places. We would be doing a traditional counter campaign against [Trump] because no other primary candidate was doing so effectively.[44]

Finn and her group were not alone in viewing this period as a turning point in the campaign and perhaps the last opportunity to stop Trump from getting the nomination. It was at roughly the same time that Bryan McGrath and Eliot Cohen had begun planning the first anti-Trump letter of national security experts. But these efforts weren't coordinated. "It was desperate," Finn recalls. "These were spontaneous efforts among different tribes or groups of people."

They had good reason to worry. By the end of the month, after primary victories in the key early contests of New Hampshire, South Carolina, and Nevada, Trump had clearly emerged as the odds-on favorite to be the nominee. There were a series of other notable events. On February 20, Jeb Bush ended his campaign. Several days later, former Mexican President Vicente Fox garnered attention for publicly saying that Trump reminded him of Hitler. In a national TV appearance on February 28, Trump repeatedly declined to condemn the Ku Klux Klan and David Duke, the former Louisiana politician, American Nazi Party member, and KKK Grand Dragon. Later that afternoon at a massive rally in Alabama, Trump picked up his second major endorsement from Senator Jeff Sessions. Coming on the heels of Chris Christie's shocking endorsement two days earlier, it was a clear indication that Trump was now all of a sudden making major headway in winning over establishment figures within the party.[45]

With the situation increasingly getting out of hand, Finn's network attempted to rally anti-Trump Republicans and to put some formal structure behind the effort. It was their group that launched the "Never Trump movement," started a small Super PAC to support its digital and grassroots organizing, and popularized the term "Never Trump" and the Twitter hashtag "#nevertrump." It was the start of what, at least by conservative standards, would become a genuinely hip, if ultimately fleeting, "Never Trump" trend. Finn recounts, "A lot of people credit our effort with creating the hashtag. I actually can't tell you with certainty that we did. . . . It may have already existed somewhat but was not something that had been popularized. And then, when we organized different bloggers or people who have large Twitter followings and others who are influential on Twitter" it took on a life of its own. Our own analysis found that the hashtag appeared on Twitter as early as June 2015 but had only been used a few dozen times through late February 2016. It was only on February 26, once Finn's group had begun pushing #nevertrump, that it turned into a cultural phenomenon. February 27 was #nevertrump's biggest day with over 275,000 uses, making it the top worldwide trend on Twitter. It would exceed 5.3 million uses by September. By comparison, other greatest hits of the 2016 campaign included: #lockherup (476,000), #basketofdeplorables (995,000), #crookedhillary (3.6 million), #imwithher (6.2 million), #feelthebern (7.3 million), and #makeamericagreatagain or its acronym #MAGA (11.4 million).[46]

Yet as the months went by in 2016, the Republican operatives who stood their ground or became more vocal increasingly found themselves alone as their longtime allies began quietly gravitating toward Trump. Glover was surprised to find herself increasingly isolated: "I was frequently not just disappointed, but stunned that people who I thought would instinctually oppose this, did not." A deep sense of abandonment is universal among the political operatives who stayed Never Trump. They had been ready to defend their party and take the fight to Trump only to discover that their allies had become traitors to the cause, some reluctantly but others enthusiastically. In this sense, the Never Trump political operatives are similar to the beleaguered social conservatives and evangelicals who traveled their own lonely path to oppose Trump. By contrast, some other hubs of Never Trumpism never had to grapple with this feeling of being abandoned on the battlefield. In Republican foreign policy circles, especially, the opposite dynamic was at work: the social pressure to stay in the Never Trump fold was intense; in that orbit, crossing the picket line to go in with Trump was the stigmatizing and trauma-inducing choice.

The tale of Our Principles PAC offers an illustrative example of the operative class's brazen flip-flop on Trump. Unlike most PACs, Our Principles wasn't geared toward helping a particular candidate but instead had the explicit purpose of preventing Trump from getting the

Republican nomination. Any other candidate would be acceptable. Launched in January 2016, Our Principles was founded and led by Katie Packer, who had been Romney's deputy campaign manager in 2012. Tim Miller later signed on to run the organization's communications operation after Bush dropped out. The Ricketts family, the PAC's largest donors and the owners of the Chicago Cubs, contributed $5.5 million while Paul Singer chipped in another $2.5 million. Combined, they were responsible for over 40 percent of Our Principles' funding.[47] As the high-minded name implies, the PAC asserted that it was boldly standing against Trump on principle. Its mission statement piously recounted that "As Thomas Jefferson said, 'In matters of style, swim with the current. In matters of principle, stand like a rock.'" And just in case anyone failed to get the message, the organization's website prominently featured a full dictionary definition of "principle," explaining that the word referred to "A fundamental truth or proposition that serves as the foundation for a system of belief or behavior or for a chain of reasoning."[48] Trump was such an affront to what the GOP stood for that someone had to take a noble stand and draw a line in the sand. The organization's strategy was to boost different candidates in different locations—anything to hurt Trump. They ran ads supporting Cruz in Wisconsin, Rubio in Florida, and Kasich in Ohio. Following Trump's dominant May 5 Indiana victory, however, Our Principles ran out of steam and was out of money.[49]

After Trump was officially nominated at the convention a few months later, the staffers who had worked for Our Principles were offered jobs at Future45, a pro-Trump PAC. All but three promptly put their services to work in the effort to elect Donald Trump president.[50] Likewise, the donors who had financed Our Principles' Never Trump crusade—including the Ricketts and Singer—also gravitated to Future45.[51] Their principles, it turned out, were actually pretty malleable.

Miller and Packer were two of the three holdouts who opted against joining the pro-Trump PAC. Miller emphasizes that his former colleagues at Our Principles who shifted their allegiance to Trump once the game was up "are truly just a microcosm of the entire Republican Party consulting class."

With the exception of the people that actually worked for Trump and maybe just a tiny handful of other conservatives who are particularly immigration-hawk types and people who are just really radicalized against the left—so I'd call that 15% of the consultant class, and by "consultant class," I include anybody who is a political operative in a Republican campaign—I would say that 15% of them wanted Donald Trump to be the president. Everybody was Never Trump. Everybody was anti-Trump who worked on campaigns; the overwhelming, overwhelming majority. You can't find people that left campaigns over this, though! Think about the people that work on the Senate campaigns, that work at the RNC now, that work at the national committees: All of these people were anti-Trump. Everybody. 85% plus. In the [current Trump] White House, everybody was anti-Trump. And, you just can't find anybody that quit over it. There just aren't that many people [who stayed Never Trump]. There's a handful. Some of them, you would know from TV or Twitter, like the Rick Wilsons of the world. But a step down from that or over from that, people who are behind the scenes, people who have cut ads, or field people or data people, everybody just went with it. For some, this is a career thing and I get it. Some people got kids, they got dinner to put on the table, college to pay for, so some of it is that. But a lot of the people are single people in their 20s that could just go get another job, go do something else. . . . All these people have just convinced themselves that, "Well, everybody else is doing it, so it's okay, and we're going to make the best of it, and it's better than Hillary," and whatever other reasons they have to justify it.[52]

For Miller, no episode from the 2016 campaign better highlights the shamelessness of his fellow Republican operatives than his former Our Principles comrades-in-arms who ditched their principles immediately after Trump secured the nomination.

The decision by most Republican consultants to work for Trump made sense in crass business terms. Because political consultants are running businesses that depend on the support of the party, the costs of opposing the likely nominee are far higher for them than they are for, say, foreign policy experts comfortably ensconced in universities and think tanks. Additionally, by the time the party's anti-Trump operatives had organized a formal resistance—Our Principles in January and Finn's "Never Trump movement" after the New Hampshire primary in February—it was a day late and a dollar short. Finn says she recognized that her effort was a long shot but still felt compelled to do something. "Really, when he won New Hampshire, if I was just a betting person, I would bet on it being too late," she says. "But I felt that we had to try to stop him because no one else was. No one had run an effective counter campaign to his campaigns against them. Jeb didn't. Rubio didn't. Cruz didn't."[53] And yet, here again, there was a logic, flawed and self-defeating though it may have been, to the campaigns' failure to confront Trump. None of them took him seriously, assuming, based on past experience, that he would self-destruct. Trump was inaccurately perceived to be the wildcard candidate who Republican voters might flirt with before settling down with the sensible, serious, respectable candidate. However, as Trump was belatedly recognized as a formidable threat, a different strategic scenario quickly unfolded: To the extent that any of the campaigns used their ammunition against Trump, the benefit would be dispersed. That is, a dollar spent by, say, Bush to attack Trump would work to the benefit of not just Bush but also Rubio, Cruz, and Kasich. Even when everyone desperately wants investment in a public good, they still hope that someone else picks up the bill. In the end, few did. As a result, with the Trump juggernaut on its way to becoming unstoppable, the remaining Never Trump political operatives were forced to embrace an increasingly desperate set of alternatives. Those included, as we will see in Chapter 5, the previously unthinkable option of running a presidential candidate against their own party's nominee.

5

The Kamikaze Mission: The Last-Ditch Efforts to Sink the Trump Campaign

IN A CAMPAIGN WITH more than enough bizarre twists and turns, one of the strangest was the fact that a former CIA operations officer and House staffer—whom no more than a handful of Washington insiders had ever heard of three months before election day—captured 21.5 percent of the presidential vote in Utah. Equally peculiar, his vice-presidential running mate was a "digital media strategist" who had also toiled in obscurity for the Republican National Committee and the campaigns of Mitt Romney and George W. Bush.

Once the GOP made its decision—Trump for president—a horrified team of the party's political professionals who were eager to put their skills to work on behalf of a client they could believe in, led a frantic and flailing search to find a statesman willing to launch an independent run for the presidency. After soliciting some of the Republican Party's luminaries to take on the job of providing an alternative to Donald Trump and Hillary Clinton, the party's political professionals simply did it themselves.

Hi, Will You Please Run for President?

Joel Searby, a mid-level political consultant based in Florida, and William Kristol were at the center of the effort to run a "Real Republican" against Trump. Searby, a devout Christian, founded Data Targeting, Inc., a Republican consulting firm in Gainesville that eventually became one of the largest in the South and employed 22 operatives. His firm worked a level or two below the national heavy hitters like Mike Murphy and Stuart Stevens, focusing mostly on local and state legislative races with a smattering of congressional campaigns. Yet early 2016, it became apparent to Searby that Americans would likely be faced with a choice between two terrible presidential candidates. He thought there had to be space for another option.

Out of curiosity and to a degree that would eventually compromise his ability to run his own consulting firm, Searby started to research what, exactly, it would take to run an independent candidate. The most obvious hurdle was ballot access—meeting the requirements to get the candidate's name to appear on ballots. There was no single-answer formula; each state has its own rules. Soon, Searby had embarked on a what amounted to "a PhD-level ballot access course" crammed into two weeks. "I was just totally consuming it," he recalls. "And to be quite honest, even at that [early] moment, it began to have a real effect on running the company. I was really consumed by it." Among other things, he had conversations with several lawyers and operatives who had worked on ballot access for Ross Perot's third-party presidential campaigns in 1992 and 1996. At the end of his crash course, Searby reached the conclusion that the logistics and financial requirements of gaining ballot access were not the insurmountable hurdles that many claimed. The late start was definitely not ideal, and deadlines were rapidly approaching in some states. Yet even so, with something in the neighborhood of $6 million and a couple of court challenges in states with rules that were particularly hostile to independent candidates in legally questionable ways, it would be plausible to get a candidate on the ballot in nearly every state.[1]

The Dream Candidate

At roughly the same time, Searby commissioned a poll on potential independent candidates. As he recounts, "One of the names we put on there was Condoleezza Rice, and she polled astronomically well. And I thought, 'Hmm, that's interesting. I wonder if I could get in touch with her.'" But as a political professional operating below the national level, Searby did not have the kind of network in Republican

Party circles to facilitate an introduction, nor did he know anyone at the Hoover Institution, the Stanford-based think tank where Rice is based.

So, he took to Google, sent several emails to her chief of staff, and, failing to elicit a response, followed those up with several phone calls. Eventually, Searby received "a rather frustrated response from her chief stating in no uncertain terms that Dr. Rice would not be running for president and I should leave them alone." Not quite ready to give up, Searby attempted to stoke some interest by emailing Rice a memo he'd put together summarizing the research he'd done on ballot access, the polling data he'd compiled, and a rationale for her candidacy.[2] Searby's memo acknowledged his previous attempts to contact Rice and generously characterized her thoughts on the matter as "reluctant." The seemingly hastily drafted memo noted that based upon Searby's research, "There is only one viable independent candidate: Condoleezza Rice. No other candidate tested even comes close. . . . The reality of the matter is that we will have President Trump or President Clinton—if we do not have President Rice." Notably, the memo stated that the objective wasn't to simply stop Trump and throw the election to Hillary; the goal was to win an Electoral College victory or fracture the vote enough to prevent any candidate from getting a majority and thereby send the decision to the House of Representatives.[3] Searby followed up his memo with two new requests that Rice run for president. Those elicited a definitive reply: "Hell no."[4]

The quixotic pursuit of Rice had, however, fortuitously opened another door. "I was sitting in my office one day, and I got a call from a 202 number," Searby recounts. "It was Bill." William Kristol, a fixture of establishment Washington, has long maintained a foot in the Republican operative network as well as in conservative intellectual circles. He is the son of prominent first-generation neoconservatives Irving Kristol and Gertrude Himmelfarb. As editor of *The Public Interest*, his father had become the archetypal example of the intellectual and political transition from Democrat to Republican after, in his words, being "mugged by reality." A political scientist by training, Bill Kristol earned a Ph.D. in political philosophy at Harvard as a student of Harvey Mansfield. After a brief stint as a professor at the University of Pennsylvania and Harvard Kennedy School of Government, he left the academy for Washington where he worked in President Reagan's Department of Education before serving as Vice President Dan Quayle's chief of staff in the first Bush administration. He then was founding editor of *The Weekly Standard*, the neoconservative magazine shuttered in 2018 by its owner in a move widely seen by its supporters as a vindictive consequence of its prominent—and, by the standards of Trump-era conservative media, out of step—stance toward the president.[5] After Trump's attacks on John McCain in the summer of 2015, Kristol arguably became the most prominent anti-Trump Republican. He had become aware of Searby's efforts from a *Politico* article based on a leaked copy of Searby's memo to Rice.[6] "That was the first time we'd ever talked," notes Searby of Kristol's cold call. "He said, 'I read the memo. I'm interested in what you're doing. There're a couple other people out here talking about this stuff. Can you tell me about the work you've done?'"[7] As the unofficial leader of the growing Never Trump movement, Kristol was surrounded by Republicans who loathed their presumptive presidential nominee. Yet Searby had something no one else did: he had actually done the grunt work of systematically figuring out the details of getting a candidate on the ballot and thinking through what an actual candidacy would require. From that point forward, Searby and Kristol worked together in pursuit of an independent candidate. Rounding out the inner circle was another Florida operative, Rick Wilson, who knew Searby through the Sunshine State's Republican Party network, and John Kingston, a Massachusetts businessman and Republican donor who was part of the Romney network.

The Top Target: General Jim Mattis

The first serious discussion with a potential candidate occurred on April 22 with General Jim Mattis. The celebrated four-star Marine Corps general and former Commander of US Central Command overseeing American military forces in the Middle East had recently retired, trading in his fatigues for a scholar's cap at Stanford's Hoover Institution. After delivering a policy speech on Iran at the Center for Strategic and International Studies in the Dupont Circle neighborhood of Northwest Washington, Mattis walked across the street to the Beacon Hotel, which Kristol describes as "slightly dumpy."[8] There he met Kristol, Searby, and

Wilson for most of the afternoon. As Searby recalls, he found that Mattis approached the issue from a similar position as he did: "Where are the patriots and people of principle standing up? I think it really was about that for him. I think he was looking at what can I do that will best serve my country right now? And I'm gonna listen to all the options." And for three hours he did just that. Searby recounts:

> I did most of the talking in terms of the mechanics of it and how it would work to be an independent candidate [while] Rick and Bill talked about the political environment, the dynamics, and why they thought it was important. Twenty percent of the conversation was about a potential campaign; 80 percent of it was about mechanics, understanding the background, the environment. . . . It was obvious to me that he is a man who is a deep patriot, and what he saw was a moment in our history where there were significant risks to the future of the country, depending on how this election played out. . . . [He] asked all of the right questions and demonstrated a high grasp of the politics of the matter. He never once indicated that he was going to do it or not going to do it. . . . He never once mentioned Donald Trump. He never once mentioned Hillary Clinton. I have no context for this, but it certainly sounded like a general trying to get a sense of the battlefield.[9]

There were two major hang-ups. The first, and the one that plagued the entire search for an independent candidate, was that everyone assumed Hillary Clinton was going to win, reducing the perceived need to derail Trump. The second, unique to Mattis, was the Eisenhower analogy. While American history is full of generals who found their way to the White House, it's a frontloaded lineage. Had Mattis emerged as a serious candidate for the presidency, he would have been the first career military man and the first general to be in such a position since Dwight Eisenhower in 1952. And when Ike ran, World War II was still a fresh memory. But America was very different in 2016 than it was in 1952. "He wasn't scared of it, he wasn't scared of being president, he wasn't scared of taking on Trump or Clinton," Kristol explains. However, "he was worried about the things we couldn't reassure him about. Was there a military–civil relations issue? Would it look like he was trying to be

Eisenhower?" Mattis wondered if he would look presumptuous and whether his candidacy would end up hurting him or hurting the military, especially if he ended up not being competitive.[10]

For Kristol and many other Never Trumpers, there were still reasons to go all out in opposing Trump because he represented a direct assault on key institutions they cared deeply about and had played a role in developing. As Kristol puts it, "The urgency, for me, was what could happen to the Republican Party, to conservatism, etc. I've been vindicated in that sense, incidentally. But, obviously, Jim Mattis, I mean, he cared about that, but it wasn't his thing."[11]

Mattis took a week to consider the independent run. The day after the meeting at the Beacon Hotel, he departed for the Middle East, though communications continued during his trip. Ultimately, however, the General emailed the group to let them know that he'd decided against it. "Do I wish he'd taken the shot?," asks Wilson. "Of course I do. I think it would've changed the race. But, you know, we are what we are in this world, and you can't lead a person to want to do politics unless they want to do it. It's this proverbial fire in the belly question. And if you don't feel it, you don't feel it. You can't fake it. It's like being in love."[12]

Because rumors had started to circulate, Mattis asked the search party to "just close it down for me." Kristol and Searby both communicated that message to Alex Burns at the *New York Times,* who ran a piece making it clear that a Mattis run was a no-go. However, Burns's article included a quote from a defiant Kristol: "Of course, the fight to help the country do better than a choice between Donald Trump and Hillary Clinton goes on."[13]

The Second Target: Senator Ben Sasse

The next target was Nebraska's junior senator. Ben Sasse holds a Ph.D. in history from Yale University and, in addition to several stints in Washington, had been a professor at the University of Texas and the president of a small college in his home state. His literary background and clever, jovial manner quickly gained him an enthusiastic following among conservative public intellectuals when he emerged on the national scene in 2014 during his first political campaign.

By the end of April, the Cruz and Kasich campaigns were in their death throes, and Trump was clearly on his way to the Republican nomination. The project to recruit Sasse for the independent run culminated with a private breakfast in Paul Singer's New York apartment. Sasse and a top aide succeeded in slipping into the early morning gathering without drawing any press attention. Upon arriving, Sasse found the billionaire businessman and Republican donor along with several of his confidants. Over the next two hours, the group had a hard-nosed discussion of Sasse's potential run. The key point conveyed by Singer and those encouraging the run was that launching a viable candidacy was entirely within the realm of possibility. Ballot access was one issue. While deadlines had passed in a couple states, almost all the others were still doable. The other big issue, of course, was money. That's where Singer stepped in. He pledged to Sasse: "I will fund you." On this most critical of points, Sasse asked specifically how much Singer was willing to commit. Singer replied: "Don't you understand what I'm telling you? I will fund you."[14] He was pledging to make Sasse's candidacy the real deal. In addition to his own money, Singer had the ability to facilitate Super PAC funding to support a Sasse for President bid.

Despite taking the meeting, the relatively clear path to getting his name on the ballot in nearly every state, and Singer's pledge of major funding, Sasse was skeptical. A couple of days later he told those encouraging him to run that he'd decided against it.

The Third Target: Governor Mitt Romney

The next stop in Kristol's increasingly desperate effort to find a challenger to Trump was the previous Republican nominee, Mitt Romney. Over glasses of water in Romney's room at the J.W. Marriott Hotel near the White House, Kristol made the same, now-familiar pitch to the former Massachusetts Governor. There was good reason to think he might be persuadable. Just two days before, Romney had made the definitive Never Trump statement of the 2016 campaign. It was the kind of full-throated denunciation of the front runner that Trump's primary opponents had shied away from making until it was too late. Speaking at the University of Utah's Hinckley Institute, Romney issued a blistering 17-minute critique of Trump, denouncing him as "a con man," a "fake," a "phony," and a "fraud." He asserted that "dishonesty is Donald Trump's hallmark" and that he is "very, very not smart." Romney pleaded with Republicans to "think of Donald Trump's personal qualities: the bullying, the greed, the showing off, the misogyny, the absurd third grade theatrics," and warned that "Mr. Trump is directing our anger for less than noble purposes." Invoking the words of Reagan, Romney closed by saying that the country once again faced "a time for choosing." Trump, he insisted, "has neither the temperament nor the judgment to be president," and his nomination for that office by one of the country's great political parties "would mean that America would cease to be a shining city on the hill. . . . God, bless us to choose a nominee who will make that vision a reality."[15] Romney gave every indication that his level of alarm was such that—for the good of the party and the good of the country, not to mention his long-standing interest in being president—he was open to being drafted at this historically pivotal moment.

Kristol recounts that Romney "was very cordial, and we met in his hotel for about 45 minutes or an hour." The Governor's entourage, however, was decidedly unenthusiastic:

> Mitt was intrigued. Mitt and I were not close, though, and I'd been a critic of his in 2012, and a lot of his people thought I was a pain in the neck. I didn't think it was a well-run campaign [in 2012], and said so at times. . . . His people were very much against [a 2016 independent campaign]—Spencer Zwick and, I think, Beth Myers. I know Zwick really thought, "Kristol's trying to use you for his own purposes. This will ruin you." And I was like, "What's to ruin?" He's run twice, like, what was the risk? But they were surprisingly hostile to it. This is what I generally found. People were not pro-Trump, but they really didn't like the idea of doing this. I guess maybe they thought correctly that, at the end of the day, maybe he would get 5% of the vote, and a guy who had got 60 million votes and lost a respectable race to an incumbent president would now go down in history as a kind of John Anderson or Harold Stassen. . . . That was their attitude, so far as I could tell.[16]

However, despite the strong opposition from his advisors, Romney didn't give Kristol an answer one way or the other.

That night, Romney and Kristol crossed paths again as honorees at an event hosted by American Friends of the Hebrew University, and the Governor's comments sparked further speculation about his plans. During a Q&A session at the gala, Romney was asked about an independent presidential run. He dismissed the idea, but then made comments that sounded like those of an independent candidate, or at least one who was seriously considering the possibility:

> I don't intend on supporting either of the major-party candidates at this point. . . . This is a critical time for freedom, a critical time for America. I think it happens to be an inflection point in our history. . . . I am dismayed at where we are now, I wish we had better choices, and I keep hoping that somehow things will get better.[17]

Romney did ruminate on the possibility for a few weeks, but on May 26, he emailed Kristol: "I'm just not going to do it."[18] With that, Kristol's most promising targets had been exhausted. Condoleezza Rice and Jim Mattis, who might have had enough cross-party support to win a three-candidate race, were out, as were prominent conservative Republicans like Sasse and Romney, who could at least have played the role of spoiler.

Striking Out with the Top-Tier Targets

As Kristol looks back, he says that the conventional wisdom of the time—to which he is admittedly "a little sensitive"—was too dismissive and failed to see how close they came to landing a big name. Some thought, " 'Oh, Kristol's going around on some pathetic, Don Quixote kind of thing, tilting at windmills.' [But] we had three serious people, so far as I could tell, seriously considering it. Now I'm not saying they were 50/50, but they weren't at like 1-in-20. I know these people well enough, or know people like that well enough, to tell. And they were, you know, 20 percent chance, 30 percent maybe."[19]

The search party was hampered by a number of factors. First, the potential candidates were more open to the idea than were those surrounding them. "That's the way it went with every one of the high-level political people we talked to," according to Searby. "They have handlers and people around them. And so while we had conversations directly with the principals in some cases, there was a lot of other pressure on them, other voices in their head that said don't do it."[20]

That reluctance had its roots in two other key factors working against the Never Trumpers. One was, to put it bluntly, the kooki-ness factor. Normal, respectable statesmen just don't embark on crazed, last-minute, half-baked enterprises like third-party runs. Before even attempting to convince potential candidates that, on the merits, an independent run was plausible, they first had to be convinced that they wouldn't be volunteering to be a laughingstock. The other, re-lated reason for skepticism was that it was obvious to all that Hillary Clinton was going to win. As Kristol says, "People thought, that's not good, not great, depending on where you were politically, ideologi-cally. But it wasn't the end of the world. She's like an establishment Democrat. We've had those before. But better than Obama, from our point of view, on foreign policy." This sentiment was especially influen-tial among the top tier of potential independent candidates, according to Kristol. Clinton was "acceptable to most of these older, establish-ment Republicans, who, after all, knew her, and in the case of Mattis had worked with her. In the case of someone like Mitt, he probably thought deep down: 'Look, I mean, she's not gonna [be that bad]. We survived eight years of Obama, we'll survive four years of Hillary,' kind of thing. If [Bernie] Sanders had been the nominee, it would have been a different story." The failure to take Trump's chances seriously had the effect of making an independent run look like not just a suicide mission but one that held the potential, even the likelihood, of disgrace. The candidate would go down in history as a traitor to his party—the man who defected from the GOP and elected Hillary Clinton—rather than the white knight savior envisioned by the Never Trumpers. Moreover, as Kristol puts it, a legitimate line of concern for potential candidates (and those soliciting them) was: "You're not going to change the out-come, you're just going to get everyone furious." Quite apart from, say, Romney's personal standing, there was concern that the entire en-terprise would just "antagonize voters who turned out to be more un-happy than we thought, more hostile to the Republican establishment, and to the overall country's establishment than we thought. And more unhappy in a way that wasn't good for the country, frankly. You don't want to make them look like the establishment, as a last gasp, got together to deprive them of a chance to win. I think that was a genuine problem."[21]

A similar mentality had played out in the primary when it was assumed that Trump would fail to get the nomination. Many Republicans desperately wanted to avoid the perception that the fix was in among the party elite, lest Trump's supporters sit out the general election. Once he became the nominee, there was a sequel: If Republican elites had their fingerprints on Trump's defeat, it would hamper their fight for the party's future in the season of recriminations following the election. As Stuart Stevens recalls from his conversations with GOP leaders:

[The response I got] wasn't crazy. It was just wrong. And it was, "Look, if we the establishment put our thumbs on the scale here, we'll get blamed for Trump losing, and it won't be because he's a racist, because he has terrible ideas, because of this alt-right stuff, because he hates women. It'll be because of us. We've gotta just let him lose. Let all this wash out. And then we can rebuild. But we can't be the reason he doesn't win." And I would say, "Yeah, I guess, but what if he wins?" It's like, "He's not gonna win." . . . That inability to imagine Trump winning gave people a pass.[22]

Indeed, the failure of imagination was not only a defining feature of the search for a third-party candidate, but of the entire 2016 election cycle.

French Toast

After Mattis, Sasse, and Romney took a pass, there was a near-miss with David French, a *National Review* writer, lawyer, decorated Iraq veteran, and devout Christian from rural Tennessee. Though a well-known public intellectual in highbrow conservative circles, French was far from a household name and represented a significant lowering of the bar in terms of national stature relative to the top-tier targets.

By this point, the informal circle had expanded beyond Kristol, Searby, Wilson, and Kingston to include top GOP campaign consultants and longtime adversaries Stuart Stevens and Mike Murphy, as well as a handful of other operatives including Katie Gage, Juleanna Glover, and Liz Mair. Erick Erickson, the conservative talk radio host and *RedState* editor, was also actively involved as the ringleader of a separate group of evangelicals and social conservatives. Additionally, there was the interest from key funders, most notably Paul Singer, the Ricketts family, and John Kingston, although it wasn't clear that a candidate of French's stature would enjoy the same level of support that was offered to Sasse at the meeting in Singer's apartment.

The nascent French for President strategy aimed at something considerably short of outright victory, although there were divisions within the team as to what the real objective was. For one group, the plan wasn't to hit 270 electoral votes, but to pick off enough states in the upper Midwest and Mountain West to deadlock the Electoral College, leaving it to the House of Representatives. And in that case, it was thought that French or some other Republican could emerge as president. Another group was simply so appalled by Trump that they wanted to do anything they could to deny him the presidency. If that meant throwing the election to Clinton, so be it. This internal tension was never resolved, although French quickly realized that he didn't want to be the Ralph Nader of 2016; he only wanted to run if there was a chance at an Electoral College deadlock that could prevent both Trump and Clinton from going to the White House.

One final consideration that gave the scheme an air of plausibility was the highly unusual fact that the most important elected Republican had yet to endorse the party's nominee in waiting. In fact, Speaker of the House Paul Ryan had repeatedly and publicly voiced criticisms of Trump, who offered a marked contrast to the Speaker on both policy grounds and personal comportment. Indeed, the contrast was sharp enough that there was a genuine question about whether Ryan would offer Trump his support. If he continued to refuse to endorse Trump— or even better yet signaled his approval of an independent candidacy from a conservative like French—there was real hope for a Republican insurrection that could boost French, provoke a convention fight over the party's nominee, or both. In short, French and his campaign-team-in-waiting thought that there was still a way to derail this seemingly inevitable train, and Ryan was important for both symbolic and procedural reasons.[23]

But there wouldn't be much time to mull things over. The core group had decamped to Kingston's farm in Woodstock, Vermont, for Memorial Day weekend to encourage French to take the plunge and to plan his campaign. The media was on high alert because Kristol had taken to Twitter with a cryptic pronouncement: "Just a heads up over this holiday weekend: There will be an independent candidate—an impressive one, with a strong team and a real chance."[24] It was enough to get Trump's attention. He fired off a tweet of his own two hours later: "If dummy Bill Kristol actually does get a spoiler to run as an Independent, say good bye to the Supreme Court!"[25] Mark Halperin and John Heilemann ran a story identifying French as Kristol's target and revealed that campaign strategy sessions were underway.[26] That's when, from French's perspective, "Everything just goes nuts." On Twitter, the hashtags #FrenchRevolution and #FrenchToast were in common usage. Accustomed to hearing chatter about well-known and respected figures like Rice, Mattis, Romney, and Sasse, many major media outlets dealt with French's candidacy with a mixture of incredulity and mockery.[27] Typical of the more brutal reactions was one from Tina Nguyen that appeared in *Vanity Fair*:

> The elevation of a virtually unknown writer to the status of potential Trump-challenger is the surest sign yet that the #NeverTrump movement has moved beyond principled opposition, blown past frantic desperation, and landed squarely in the realm of the fantastical. For Kristol to champion such a hopeless candidate may simply be his attempt to remain principled to the end, even if that principle is fundamentally disconnected from reality. French has no shot, but at least Kristol can take pride in saying he tried.[28]

Others, including Romney, publicly praised French, but even in less hostile quarters the question of the day was: Who is David French?[29]

Coincidentally or not, Ryan formally endorsed Trump less than 48 hours after Halperin and Heilemann's piece ran. From the perspective of many Never Trumpers, the Speaker's endorsement marks the first chapter in the epic tragedy of Paul Ryan that would continue to play out over the next two and a half years. For the first but certainly not the last time, Paul Ryan—the golden boy of establishment Republicans and elite conservatives—proved to be a deep disappointment to many of his greatest admirers by capitulating to Trump in humiliating and hypocritical fashion and thereby undermining everything he had previously stood for. Because Ryan had been seen as a man of principle, unlike pure partisan apparatchiks like the GOP's Senate leader Mitch McConnell, his endorsement of Trump was a stark reality check for the search party and the wider Never Trump orbit. There was rampant speculation that the Speaker's announcement had been hastily put together in an attempt to shut down the search party's effort to field an independent candidate once Halperin and Heilemann revealed how serious those plans were. Searby notes that Ryan's endorsement did carry real implications for his group's work: "It certainly had a major impact on the overall environment, namely, that some folks who we'd been talking to, especially potential funders, saw that as a signal that the establishment was resigned to the fact of a Trump candidacy and giving up any pretense otherwise."[30]

Soon thereafter, French walked into the kitchen of Kingston's colonial farmhouse where the others were gathered and said, with tears in his eyes, "Guys, no."[31] And with that, the last even remotely viable potential candidate had taken himself out of the running. Looking back, French has no regrets about his decision. During the Vermont retreat, he realized that as soon as his name was announced as the independent candidate, it would be seen as the failure of the Never Trump movement. For some, that was immaterial, but not for French.

A lot of people held out hope for a third-party candidate and had this hope for the general on the white horse and had this hope that it would be a very prominent unifying figure. . . . The people that I let down—and there were people that I let down when I said no— [thought,] "I don't care that it's hopeless. I want to be on record as having done everything that I could to stop this." And my view was, okay, well that's fine for you to say because you're not the guy who would be running! . . . I began to see, well, we don't really have the path we thought we had, we don't really have the money, but, by golly, the "Charge of the Light Brigade" was a glorious moment in world history. But one of the aspects of that poem is someone had blundered, and I realized that if I had decided to do it, the someone who blundered would have been me.[32]

Over the next couple of months, the search party persisted with a two-front mission: secure a candidate, and secure ballot access. Searby even resigned his position as CEO at his consulting firm to continue the fight. Over the course of the search, targets ranged from traditional politicians to various stripes of celebrities. Briefly in the mix, at least in terms of being considered by the search party, were conventional politicians like Arizona Senator John McCain, South Carolina Senator Lindsey Graham, former Secretary of State Colin Powell, former Oklahoma Senator Tom Coburn, former New York Mayor Michael Bloomberg, and Illinois Congressman Adam Kinzinger, among others.[33] As the rejections started to pile up, inquiries were extended to a more eclectic batch of potential candidates. Wilson discussed it with a number of prominent business figures. Searby briefly pursued pro wrestler and movie star Dwayne Johnson. Television personality Mike Rowe took 48 hours to consider the possibility. The idea was also floated to figures including Oprah Winfrey, Starbucks CEO Howard Schultz, Dallas Mavericks owner Mark Cuban, General Stanley McCrystal, and Hoover Institution economist Tim Kane.[34] None took the plunge. It was rough sledding on the ballot access front, too. Because some states allowed organizations to gain ballot access without identifying a specific candidate, the search party had formed an organization called Better for America in an attempt to lock down a spot on the ballot in as many states as possible and then name a candidate whenever they found one. Better for America did manage to land a spot on the Arkansas and New Mexico ballots, but that was it. As it turned out, it was tough to run a campaign without a candidate.[35]

Meanwhile, the Trump campaign managed, with the help of Paul Manafort, to easily see off a floor challenge to his nomination at the

Republican National Convention, which fizzled after suffering from infighting and infiltration by Trump supporters. Finn, who had been among those trying to orchestrate a brokered convention, recalls that "it seemed like a lost cause from the start [and] felt like attending a funeral."[36] Better for America was in funeral mode, too. By the end of the summer, Searby and the rest of the search party had resigned themselves to the reality that all their work to recruit a Never Trump independent candidate had failed. Searby had also paid a high price. He was now unemployed, having walked away from a stable and lucrative career as a Republican consultant.

"The Last-Ditch Emergency Operation"

That's when Evan McMullin, the ex-CIA agent and House staffer, called Searby to say that he was willing to run for president. Soon thereafter, Finn signed on for vice president, and their campaign was underway. It definitely wasn't the ticket the Never Trump operatives had initially hoped for, yet they were happy that someone had finally stepped up. "We viewed it as a last-ditch emergency operation," says McMullin. "It was clearly suboptimal to launch a presidential campaign with a candidate who no one had ever heard of, with no money in the tank, and no fundraising ability."[37]

At the outset, the McMullin campaign attempted to reach a nation-wide audience but quickly realized that their limited resources only allowed for what Wilson called "a live off the land guerrilla army" approach.[38] The Mountain West became the primary focus because that region offered the best opportunity to win a few states. As a Utahan and Mormon, McMullin had the potential for something like a favorite son appeal in the region. Additionally, the Mountain West was attractive ground because Trump and Clinton had both performed poorly there in the primaries. "The best electoral possibility we had was if the race was very close," McMullin explains. The hope was to "block them both and then go to the House and compete in the House. I think we would have done very well in the House, by the way. I think we would have had a good chance of actually winning, but the chances of getting there were like almost zero, so we understood that."[39] Electoral calculations aside, McMullin and Searby insist that theirs was a principled stand for a set of ideas and ideals they saw as being under threat. McMullin, in particular, emphasizes the importance of these principles in his thinking:

> I reject the suggestion that fighting for principles is some sort of naïve Boy Scout activity. Because it's the right thing to do, number one. The second thing is, there had to be such an effort for there to be credibility for the fight that came later on. . . . I say this until I'm red in the face, people just don't understand the importance of it. Maybe you will. It was to stand on principle, to defend ideas that we were afraid would evaporate, certainly on the right, and maybe from the country altogether over time. The idea that all men and women are created equal. This notion of liberty and self-rule, and a government that's accountable to the people. All of these things, everything that goes into that, a free press, separation of powers, Article One, independent judiciary. All of these things, we thought somebody needed to defend those on the right.[40]

Those supporting McMullin's candidacy chose to do so for various reasons. Some thought it was important to keep the Republican candle burning. Still others calculated that McMullin's candidacy was the best way to deny Trump the presidency because they thought that there were some anti-Trump Republican voters who would eventually end up voting for him if Clinton was the only alternative. McMullin, therefore, would draw some votes away from Trump that he would otherwise get.

An obvious alternative, of course, was to support the Democratic candidate, Hillary Clinton. Some prominent Republicans did in fact endorse her, especially those in foreign policy and national security circles. There were also small "Republicans for Hillary" and "Republican Women for Hillary" efforts. Yet many simply couldn't bring themselves to support her. After decades of Clinton being a villainous figure for Republicans, that was simply a bridge too far—even, apparently, when faced with a figure like Trump, whom they argued was an existential threat to the republic.

McMullin's name only appeared on ballots in eleven states. Much of that was due to the campaign's late start. But Wilson maintains that there were also orchestrated efforts by Trump allies to keep McMullin's name off ballots:

In some states we also encountered organized political resistance from the executive branch. Like in Florida, [Governor] Rick Scott's people weighed in quite heavily with the Department of State to keep Evan off the ballot. . . . There was a phone call from the Trump people to the Scott people on the political side. And then Scott people on the government side called the Secretary of State and said, "Don't let them on the ballot. Find a way to disqualify them from the ballot." And they did.[41]

On election day, McMullin and Finn received 728,830 popular votes, coming in fifth behind the two major-party candidates as well as Libertarian Gary Johnson and Green Party standard-bearer Jill Stein. McMullin did, however, make a strong third-place showing in his native Utah with 21% of the vote, just 6% behind Clinton. His only other third-place showing came in heavily Mormon Idaho with 6.8%.

Whatever the final results on November 8, 2016, for McMullin and the hardcore Never Trumpers who stood with him, there was also a long-term strategic calculation at work. They perceived Trump's emergence and the lemming-like response to it from most Republicans as the beginning of a long-term war within the Republican Party. McMullin's candidacy was critical, but it was only the first move in a longer sequence. It was going to pull together a group of Republicans and conservatives who couldn't abide Trump, give them an honorable alternative in the election, and fuse them into a network that would endure beyond the election. "That's what we were doing," McMullin says. "We knew the chances of winning were slim, of course, but we saw it as the beginning of the fight, not something that was self-contained within the election." They had assumed Clinton would win, at which point they'd be engaged in "a fight for the heart and soul of the Republican Party" in which they would draw on the foundation they had laid in the campaign. When Trump unexpectedly won, it only meant "the fight that we had prepared for all of a sudden became much more profoundly important, and much more difficult."[42]

Alone in the Foxhole

"There's a little bit of a ragtag army to it," Mike Murphy says of the Never Trump contingent in the Republican consulting class. "Of the so-called consulting class, 95% of them are hanging in with Trump. There's no consultant revolt."[43] However, some did break away from the herd, often at great personal and professional cost.

Erick Erickson is often cited as one who paid a high price for his opposition to Trump. Even before 2016, the radio host, *RedState* editor, and blogger at *The Resurgent* had dabbled in Republican operative circles as an elected Republican on the Macon, Georgia, city council and as host of *RedState*'s annual gathering of conservatives. Erickson had disinvited Trump from a 2015 *RedState* event following his attack on the Fox News host Megyn Kelly. Several months later, Erickson proclaimed himself Never Trump in a widely circulated *Resurgent* post and later was one of the individuals involved in the search for a third-party candidate.[44] Within the world of Never Trumpers—most of whom are based in Washington or other liberal enclaves and routinely interact with liberals in liberal institutions—Erickson stood out. He had thrived in right-wing talk radio and was based in the bright red Deep South. Underscoring the point, Erickson recounts that *Commentary* editor John Podhoretz "told me one time, 'If I did a list of a hundred people who I knew would go, day one, with Trump, you would be number one on the list.'" Speaking with us in the spring of 2018, Erickson recalls his experience, which coincided with his wife's battle with cancer and his own serious health issues:

> The moment I wrote that [*Resurgent* post], I was done with Fox. . . . I can't fill in for Rush Limbaugh anymore. And we had three people show up on our doorstep. My kids were harassed by someone in the grocery store. They would come home from school in tears on a regular basis about who said I was going to get shot, or whose parents hated me. They've never quite gotten over that one. My wife was in a Bible study where someone said she wanted to slap me. Another woman told her she wanted to punch me. We had to give up going to church for several months because I couldn't go from our Sunday

school class to the sanctuary without getting assaulted by someone angry with me. I didn't expect all of that. And Christy, my wife, and I, we go through these conversations regularly, and we would do it all over again. We still think it was the right thing to do. We would just go in with eyes wide open now, as to what was going to happen. I have never shied away from telling people what I think. It's what I get paid to do. It never dawned on me the professional consequences. . . . I'd filled in [for Rush Limbaugh] after the Megyn Kelly incident, and program directors across the country were inundated with complaints from people that I was filling in for Rush. And this has nothing to do with him. It's local program directors and what they have to deal with. There was clearly, I think, at some point, a level of organized harassment. If I went on Fox, they were going to get inundated with complaints. If I was on a radio program, they were going to get inundated. . . . It was very clearly people trying to keep me off air. I didn't expect that level of coordination to try to shut me up.[45]

Less than a year after his interview with us, Erickson announced to considerable publicity that he had changed his mind and would cast his 2020 ballot for Trump. While Erickson maintains many of his prior criticisms, he explained that he was troubled by the Democrats' move to the left, particularly on social issues.[46] In repenting, however unenthusiastically, Erickson broke decisively from others who vocally opposed Trump all the way to the end in 2016. Of those, the majority continue to hold fast.

What distinguished those in the operative class who stuck to their guns in 2016 and continued opposing Trump even after it became clear that he would be the Republican nominee? Career status was one important separating mechanism. Many A-list consultants had already had successful and lucrative careers, affording them a degree of freedom that many others did not enjoy. As Stevens says, "I'm in a different position. I'm lucky. I made a lot of money working in politics; maybe I shouldn't have. And I'm 65 years old. I write books. I write television shows. I'm not running for office. I'm in a position that some people aren't."[47] Similarly, Murphy explains, "There's just a handful of us who are cranky or independent enough, or late in our careers and fed up enough. . . . Senior people like myself or Stuart [Stevens]—to a lesser extent [Steve] Schmidt—who are in a position where they can do whatever they want because they have enough stature in the party. They've had a successful career. They've made money, [so] commerce doesn't enter into it much."[48] It's easier to ignore the financial incentive to get with the program if you no longer need to worry about making money or climbing the status ladder. Sally Bradshaw, the Bush loyalist and Autopsy co-chair, made a full, clean break. She quit the GOP and registered as an independent immediately after the Republican National Convention, opened an independent bookstore in Tallahassee, and left professional politics for good. As she explains:

> Too many people that I had respected over the years were concerned about their place at the table, and not about doing what seemed to me to be the right thing to do. It just looks so self-serving, it looks so short-sighted, it was just wrong. . . . I knew it was time for me to do something else. It made me sick that people, many of whom I respected and knew well, were immediately becoming Trump apologists. And I just couldn't do it. I'm not a good poker player. People always know my opinion on things, and it's just not in my nature. The *Access Hollywood* tape, making fun of a disabled reporter. I have a daughter who . . . was 16 at the time, and I don't know how you can tell a child to respect other people, love your neighbor, treat people the way you want to be treated, and then say, "Oh, honey, we need to vote for Donald Trump." How do you do that?[49]

Younger operatives were also among the Never Trumpers, of course. Yet many of them had also enjoyed considerable professional success that may have allowed a greater degree of flexibility than your average Republican operative. Many of these individuals have been able to leverage that success into new opportunities as media personalities. But side gigs as pundits are limited. Not everyone was in a financial position to walk away and start a new life. "If I were a young guy coming up," Murphy says, "I think I'd have the moral courage to do it, but economically it would be real trouble for me. Because a lot of the B-, C-, and D-level people make their living from the good graces of the Republican Party."[50] The RNC works closely with political operatives, advising candidates whom to use and steering them away from others.

Few political operatives were comfortable with the professional risk of being on the wrong side of a Trump-led RNC.

On the flip side, for a handful of less established and younger consultants, cutting against the professional grain and opposing Trump has allowed them to stand out. As Murphy notes, there were "a few opportunistically thinking for their own brand who chose to publicly be against Trump." And while Murphy says "most people who are anti-Trump are anti-Trump for the right reason," it's also the case that some have managed to turn their opposition into a professional plus: "You've got lesser-known, lesser-ranked people like [Rick] Wilson and a few others—Tim Miller—who, I think, believe that honestly, but also it's almost a good career thing for them to get noticed from the anonymous herd. I mean, nobody really knew who Rick Wilson was. He'd never really done much in politics until he got on television."[51] There has definitely been a market for outspoken Republican critics of the president in liberal media outlets like MSNBC. *Real Time with Bill Maher*, for instance, has had an all-but-officially designated seat on its panel reserved for Never Trumpers. But those who have found success as disgruntled Republican talking heads push back on the suggestion that it's been a financial windfall. Wilson, for instance, says he can't work, at least not openly, in Republican campaigns anymore:. "I'm not in the political business like I was," he says. "I still do some campaigns, I just don't do them with my name on them. The minute my name comes up, no matter if it's a US senator or a dog catcher, they will get a call from the Trump organization [and] they're told basically, 'If you do this, we will destroy you.' Which is fine. Their ability to use that power is kind of what politics is about. But I have given up financially, as I like to say, a lot of zeros." As for the suggestion that he's cashed in on his Never Trumpism?

I had a [anti-Trump] *New York Times* number #1 bestseller. Okay? Huge, huge selling book. It did great. [But] I would've made more off the average congressional campaign, which I used to do a lot. And so, you know, this idea that Never Trump was this profitable market segment . . . . Look, I'm not complaining, I do fine. I have a lot of interesting new ventures that I'm in. But the fact that people think Never Trump is some sort of financial profit center? Yeah, good luck.[52]

But for most operatives, the new ventures that Wilson speaks of were not realistic alternatives. The path of least resistance was to fall in line behind Trump. Those who stuck to their Never Trumpism recognize the constraints their fellow Republican operatives faced, although their sympathy is limited. Stevens equates the decision facing GOP professionals to that faced by southern whites as Jim Crow was coming undone. The Magnolia State native remains surprised and demoralized that so many picked a variant of what Christopher Buckley calls the yuppie Nuremberg defense, that "everybody's got a mortgage to pay":

> If you're working on the Hill and you gotta work for these people, and you're raising a family, okay, fine. But what about the others? Everybody's gotta make their own choice. I mean, it's so like 1965 in the South. . . . It's very much, to me, like segregation. When I grew up in Mississippi, I knew a lot of nice white folks who believed that blacks should be treated politely, and nicely, and courteously, and kindly. But they were segregationists. And I feel the same way about Trump. I have sort of an extreme view on this. If you look at George Wallace, George Wallace did a lot of good things: free textbooks, he raised taxes to pay for roads. But nobody's remembered as the "free textbook George Wallace guy." You're the George Wallace guy. And I think it's the same with Trump. Trump involves bargaining with yourself. Everybody is transactional with Trump, and Trump is transactional with everybody. It's, "Okay, I'll do this with Trump, and I'll get tax cuts." It's all this sort of bargaining. And I don't think anybody steps back and says, "What does it say about me?" In 50 years, no one's gonna remember that there was a tax cut. They're gonna remember Donald Trump and people who supported Donald Trump."[53]

Those who were deeply invested in the project of diversifying the party were far more likely to stay in the Never Trump camp. Kristen Soltis Anderson says that for the Never Trumpers in the political class, their opposition was grounded in a mix of the political calculation that Trump was "the meteor that is going to nuke" the Republican Party and the personal feeling that "this is not the party I joined; this is not the party I signed up for." She emphasizes that "when you work professionally in politics, you choose a team because that team most closely reflects your views. And this was a moving of the whole team in a direction away from where I think a lot of the professional political class lives personally."[54]

For some Never Trumpers in the operative class, their personal commitment to a diversified Republican Party both fueled their anti-Trump stance while also offering a potential opportunity to reap the professional rewards of being on the victorious side of a major intraparty debate. And at the time, the downside risk of opposing Trump appeared relatively small. Even if Trump did secure the Republican nomination, Never Trumpers would only suffer a short-term hit for the 2016 election cycle because Trump would lose in November. That meant that in the bloody aftermath, the people who had been ringing the alarm bells would be in a position of strength. But even so, as Ruffini recalls, "there were only a small handful that took the kind of public stand that we did even though everyone was kind of . . . with us privately." Ruffini's explanation for why so few others spoke out: "Contracts. If he gets the nomination, you don't want to be frozen out of contracts in the general election for anything. Even if you don't work for the presidential nominee, it potentially jeopardizes your position when it comes to the Senate or the House or the committees." And looking further ahead, even if Trump lost the election, he and his associates would still have considerable sway over the party machine, with the ability to punish those who had turned on the nominee. Ruffini and his fellow Never Trumpers realized that vocalizing the sentiments that others held quietly rendered them outliers and that their actions had the potential to carry serious ramifications. However, he says they were willing to take that risk because of both their principles and the potential upside of winning a risky bet. "We were invested in the idea that the Republican Party shouldn't be just for old white guys. Philosophically, regardless of the political merit of that position, that's what we think. And so we're willing to take a stand for it. We make a bet, maybe it's the wrong bet, but you make a bet. And if you are successful, then hopefully you get recognized for that."[55] It ended up being a losing bet, at least in the short term. But had things turned out differently, Ruffini and other outspoken Trump opponents likely would have been well positioned to reap the rewards, not only in terms of having a stronger hand in guiding the party's future course but also as professional Republican operatives.

While commitment to the Autopsy's vision of the GOP's future does a lot of work in sorting the consultant masses from those who held firm as Never Trumpers, there were some outliers. Notably, three key figures behind the Autopsy jumped ship and enthusiastically entered Trump's inner circle. Reince Priebus, the RNC Chair who commissioned the Autopsy, became White House Chief of Staff; RNC staffer Sean Spicer was tapped as Trump's first Press Secretary; and Autopsy co-chair and George W. Bush's first Press Secretary Ari Fleischer became one of Trump's most visible defenders. Looking back at his work on the Autopsy and where his former RNC colleagues are now, Tim Miller recalls:

> Frankly, one of the funny things is that the person who was most adamant that we needed to address the messaging and [immigration reform] was Ari Fleischer. Because there was some feeling, even among those of us that agreed with the messaging part, that from a strategic standpoint, is it worth the backlash? You know you're going to get backlash from the *Breitbart* crowd, and you know there's going to be heavy criticism of the RNC. [And] the next nominee is going to drive the message anyway. So maybe the RNC should focus just more on the practical elements of party building. But Ari was adamant that this effort needed to include them! And it turns out that Ari threw all those principles out first with regards to Trump. I don't know. I can't get inside Ari's head.[56]

Spicer's conversion was less surprising to Miller: "It's pretty obvious that Spicer, who was there at the time, is the type of person that would have gone along with any Republican nominee, and he sees himself as a party person for better or worse."[57]

Aside from the handful of Autopsy-supporters-turned-Trump-cheerleaders, the political operatives who hung in as Never Trumpers remain adamant that despite Trump managing to eke out a win in 2016, the party's future remains bleak. As Stevens puts it:

> The Autopsy was right. . . . Nothing has changed in the demographic curve of America. . . . There's not *fewer* Hispanics because of Trump. There's not *fewer* Asians. There's not *fewer* African Americans. There's not *more* high school-[only] white voters. It's all still headed the wrong way. . . . It's like going to a party, having several drinks, driving home safely, and concluding that alcohol helps you drive better. It's the wrong conclusion.[58]

Likewise, Anderson says, "I do not walk away from my theory that Republicans are still in really big trouble." Prior to the 2016 cycle, she didn't think it would be possible for a Republican to win by driving up the party's margins among white voters. As it turned out, however, "we did have one more election left in us, as a country," in which that strategy could work. Yet it is instructive to note that the president's unimpressive victory required the perfect storm: the luck of running against a historically unpopular and unlikeable opponent who, despite winning the popular vote relatively easily, nonetheless fell short in the Electoral College thanks to perfectly distributed, razor-thin margins in a few struggling states. "Had the election gone the other way," she says, "it would be extremely fashionable to hold the position that I hold." The Autopsy's arguments are right, "they're just right along different time horizons."[59] In politics, however, being early is the same as being wrong. While they may be proven correct in the long term, the Never Trumpers' big bet failed to cash in, leaving them on the outside of a party they barely recognize.

Finally, and relatedly, the Jeb Bush network is another big part of the story for the political consultant class. Those with ties to Bush were far more likely to go Never Trump than those outside his circle. This can be attributed to a few factors. The first is that Bush himself was closely associated with the idea of diversifying the Republican Party, a factor that made him particularly appealing to some operatives. Others may have been converted to the cause as a result of working for Bush. The second factor that had to be at work for many Bush alums was that Trump seemed to relish singling out Jeb and his family for particularly ruthless attacks. Finally, in the sprawling world of political operatives, many of the alums from Jeb world had developed social ties from their time together on the campaign.

For those in the Republican Party's professional class who opposed Donald Trump, his successful bid for the GOP nomination and his victory in the general election served as both a repudiation of their professional expertise and a rejection of their hopes for the party's future. Trump demonstrated that their theory of the electoral case—the urgent need to diversify the party by reaching out beyond white voters—was, at least for one last time in 2016, unnecessary.

Their final miscalculation was that, like everyone else, the Republican operatives who stayed Never Trump were confident that Hillary Clinton would win. They recognized that in holding strong as Never Trumpers, they were taking themselves out on the 2016 cycle. But the upside was that they'd come out of 2016 as unimpeachable members of the clean team, untainted by the embarrassment of Trump. This meant that in short order, they'd come back off the bench reinvigorated and having been proven right about the need to take the party in a different direction.

Adding insult to injury, the consultants who held the line on Never Trumpism also came to feel a deep sense of personal trauma made more acute because, despite near universal opposition to Trump at the beginning of the campaign, they were eventually abandoned by most of their fellow operatives. Even in the cynical and jaded world of campaign pros, they wonder how so many of their colleagues could turn their backs on what they'd thought was a shared fight on behalf of conservative principles. Stevens expresses his bafflement and disgust:

> They have no courage. Either that or you say, "Okay, I really didn't believe this stuff. I really didn't believe the Jack Kemp, George Bush stuff. Okay, it was fine, I'd go along with it, but I didn't believe it." Because how do you believe that and then support Donald Trump? . . . There's a bunch of people who worked for Bush who

are fine with Trump. Ari Fleischer is an example. I can't square the circle. I mean, look, to do that you have to say all this stuff that we said—"honor and dignity in the White House," all this stuff—it was just a marketing slogan. To buy into Trump, you have to believe that the essence of what the Republican Party stood for—personal responsibility, embracing of legal immigration, character counts, strong on Russia—you have to believe that all of that was just a marketing slogan and it didn't mean anything—any more than "We say, 'Chevrolet's the heartbeat of America.'" You're not making a statement that there's *really* a heart in that Chevy, it's just a slogan. "So okay, we use that for a while, and then when people get tired of that, we'll say something else. We'll say 'America First'; we'll say all this white grievance [talking points]; we'll just say that [because] it doesn't mean anything, it's just marketing." See, you have to believe that [it's just marketing]. And you know what I'm incredibly ashamed about is, I mean, I actually did believe [in the party's principles]. Not that I had some ideological purity or anything, but I believed it. And Trump is a rejection of all of that. . . . He's made every critic of the Republican Party right—that said the Republican Party really didn't care about people, that it wasn't a party that was inclusive. Just go down the list—"didn't respect women." He's made all that true. And he made all the wrong people right.[60]

Stevens's perspective points to an important feature of Republican and conservative identity that is shared by many Never Trumpers, both in operative circles and beyond. A significant part of their identity involves a rejection of the accusation that the Republican Party is racist and bigoted. These individuals had invested a large amount of energy trying to detoxify the party's brand, to highlight the GOP's universal principles, and to bring the party's inclusive message to a wider audience. But the enthusiastic response that Trump's cruelty, racism, and misogyny generated in a large part of the party base lent support to charges that those inclinations were in fact baked into the party's DNA—the very things that many Never Trumpers had minimized or insisted were outdated or flat-out wrong.

Agents Without Principals

Having failed to stop their party from nominating Donald Trump, or the country from electing him, the network of Never Trump operatives has been reduced to keeping the flame of resistance alive, in the hope that the party will one day come to its senses. Kristol launched a number of initiatives explicitly designed to carry on the Never Trump crusade. Several of these enterprises operate under the banner of Defending Democracy Together (DDT), a 501(c)(4) advocacy organization "dedicated to defending America's democratic norms, values, and institutions and fighting for consistent conservative principles like rule of law, free trade, and expanding legal immigration . . . [while] fighting abuses of power that threaten to undermine the integrity of U.S. elections, federal agencies, and the Republican Party as a whole." In addition to Kristol, DDT lists a team of "directors" including many Never Trump stalwarts like columnists Mona Charen and Linda Chavez, former New Jersey Governor Christine Todd Whitman, and operative Sarah Longwell. Somewhat controversially, much of the group's funding has come from left-of-center sources including Democracy Fund Voice, an initiative solely sponsored by tech entrepreneur Pierre Omidyar, and the Hewlett Foundation.[61] DDT is home to Republicans for the Rule of Law, an offshoot that develops and runs occasional advertisements, many of which focused on insisting that the Mueller investigation be allowed to complete its work. Another offshoot, *The Bulwark*, has arguably been the most visible and successful DDT initiative. The website began as a news aggregator but later expanded to produce its own daily written content by *Weekly Standard* refugees such as Charlie Sykes, Jonathan Last, and Jim Swift, as well as podcasts hosted by Sykes and Charen.

Another set of initiatives has been focused on bridging partisan and ideological divides. Joel Searby boosted independent third-party candidates in the 2018 election cycle as part of Unite America, an organization seeking to reform elections and identify and support centrist candidates. Evan McMullin and Mindy Finn now lead Stand Up Republic which "works to ensure that defending democratic ideals, norms and institutions does not become a partisan cause [and to] ensure that the fundamental ideals of liberty, equality and truth remain central to American consciousness."[62] Among other things, Stand Up Republic pushed for impeachment investigations and defended the Mueller investigation. Finally, The New Center is another Kristol project in which he teamed up with Democrat Bill Galston of the Brookings Institution to carve out a space "for the millions of Americans who are tired of the sensational fare served up by the left and right; and who are searching for a credible counter to the growing bias on both sides." To date, the organization has released a handful of policy papers and maintains a website featuring aggregated news articles.[63]

Much of this activity began shortly after the 2016 election and was premised on creating an organizational foundation to challenge Trump in 2020. Among those preparing for 2020, the rough consensus that emerged in the months following the president's inauguration was that the Never Trumpers have to be ready for at least three different scenarios: support a primary challenger, support a third-party candidate, or support the Democratic nominee if that individual has a good chance of defeating Trump. But reflecting the consultant class's geographic dispersal, some saw these organizational efforts more as a reflection of Washington culture than of anything worthwhile. Murphy and Kristol, for instance, are close friends but saw things differently when it came to the efficacy of organizing years ahead of time for 2020. Murphy had been invited to join such efforts but initially kept his distance. That kind of thing, he told us in mid-2018, "is just great fodder for the DC bullshit chamber, but I'm from the world of real political warfare," and until Trump is much weaker, there's little if anything to be gained by organizational efforts. The Washington-based Never Trump operatives are, according to Murphy:

[an] incredibly well-intentioned group of people who I appreciate and admire their moral clarity. [But they] remind me very much of the American proxy forces in the Syrian conflict. ISIS has their stone-cold killers who are out beheading kids, Assad has his stone-cold killers who are out gassing villages, and we've got a hundred sociology professors and librarians out in the field marching around broomsticks trying to figure out how to be a soldier. . . . Hanging out in some Georgetown living room talking about third-party candidates and making paper signs and fighting over a logo is just

busywork for people who aren't involved in practical politics. When I can get ten Republican state chairmen in a secret room, and a couple of $10 million-a-year donors, and people whose first name is Senator or Governor, and they want to have an honest discussion about taking out Trump, I'll be the first guy at the meeting.[64]

The experience of Never Trump operatives in the 2016 cycle remains especially demoralizing. Unlike their counterparts in other nodes of the extended party, the relatively few Never Trump operatives—prominent though they may be—have had fewer places to turn for consolation after being, in their eyes, betrayed by the vast majority of their fellow operatives. As Murphy says: "It's a lonely thing. There are damn few of us doing it right now. And I understand why, but it reeks of Vichy France. So, I can't say I'm not disappointed in my comrades. I thought I was in the fight for agreed-upon principles for 30 years, and they seem to have all been written in pencil, which really disturbs me."[65]

The story of how the Republican Party's operative class responded to Trump—first with near-universal contempt and later with near-universal capitulation—reveals a core truth about their professional network. While they are always close to the light, they aren't the keepers of the flame. Without elected officials to take the lead in resisting Trump, these quintessentially client-serving professionals are like the ronin of ancient Japan—samurai without masters.

PART III

Public Intellectuals

6

Patrolling the Frontier

JUST DAYS BEFORE THE 2016 Iowa caucus, the most venerable and prestigious conservative publication, *National Review*, unleashed what it thought was the intellectual and political heavy artillery on Donald Trump. It devoted the cover and a good chunk of the magazine to a special feature, "Against Trump," that was designed to stop him dead in his tracks by reading him out of the conservative movement.[1] When Ted Cruz managed to narrowly defeat Trump in Iowa just a few weeks later, *National Review* editor Rich Lowry triumphantly tweeted out a simple message above an image of the "Against Trump" cover: "You're Welcome."[2] Lowry's self-congratulation was, to put it mildly, premature. Two weeks later Trump crushed his challengers in the New Hampshire primary, leading to widespread panic among many elite conservatives, and the birth of the #nevertrump hashtag that would give the anti-Trump movement its name. Yet Republican primary voters weren't paying attention. Despite overwhelming opposition to Trump among the conservative intellectual elite, Republican voters had their own ideas of what the party should be about.

That is not the outcome one might have expected at the start of the 2016 electoral cycle, given the outsized role that public intellectuals have played in the GOP over the last half-century. Whatever outsiders may believe, the modern Republican Party has often told its own story as the merger of a conservative intellectual project with a range of grassroots social movements. The idea of "fusionism"—the linkage of social conservatism with economic libertarianism—was thought by the party's intellectuals to be the glue that held together the GOP's various constituencies and activists. Conservative intellectuals were not just eggheads, moralists, and scolds, for they provided a critical coalition maintenance function for a party whose constituent parts could easily find themselves at odds. The party's own leaders paid great respect to conservative intellectual celebrities like William F. Buckley, magazines like *National Review*, and think tanks like the American Enterprise Institute and the Heritage Foundation. And they at least pretended to be familiar with the works of Friedrich Hayek and Russell Kirk.[3]

It is that belief in the Republicans as a conservative party—one defined by its connection to a set of ideas and the intellectuals who generated them—that made the rise of Donald Trump so traumatic for conservative public intellectuals. Among the things that were especially striking about Trump was his dismissal and general ignorance of the history of conservative thought. Conservative intellectuals had just recently experienced the rise of the Tea Party, which many of them optimistically understood to have been, at its core, a recovery of conservative principles in the aftermath of the mushy, soft-headed Bush era of domestic policy compromise. The Tea Party had reinforced their belief that ordinary conservatives out there in the country supported limited government, individualism, and free markets. But now conservative voters seemed to be willing to throw all that overboard in the name of Trump's ethnic and economic nationalism.

This chapter looks at the role played by public intellectuals in the conservative movement, including the historical role of its flagship magazine, *National Review*, as a policeman of ideological purity. It examines the material conditions that permitted it to perform this function in the past, and why that role has come under considerable pressure as the business model of intellectual gatekeeping has eroded. Finally, we examine the efforts by some of those gatekeepers, the Reformocons, to update the appeal of conservatism in a way that anticipated some of Trump's message, and how that not only strengthened their resolve to resist him but also made them ambivalent about the larger Never Trump enterprise.

To understand why so many public intellectuals responded with such virulence to Trump, we need to understand their institutional position and relationship to other party actors. Public intellectuals operate in a more individualistic organizational context than national security and legal conservatives. Lawyers (as will be seen in Chapter 8) and foreign policy professionals have well-defined structures for collective action, common experiences in government, and professional norms of practice that help give them shared interests and the capacity to respond collectively. That is why Part I, on national security conservatives, focused on actions taken collectively, like group letters. But public intellectuals, while often working in institutions like magazines and think tanks, have individual brands, and it is precisely their distinctive judgment and independence that are key parts of their self-understanding and socially recognized role. Therefore, the story of public intellectuals is much more one of actions or positions taken as individuals. While *National Review*'s "Against Trump" issue was a rare instance of collective action, our focus here is primarily biographical rather than professional and organizational in character. This chapter zeroes in on the institutional and material factors in conservative public intellectuals' role and how it influenced their response to Trump, while Chapter 7 focuses on their ideas and personal backgrounds.

The Lifeworld of Conservative Public Intellectuals

The central role of ideological conservatism in the Republican Party has given these idea merchants a range of quasi-partisan functions. Going back to the 1950s, they have taken on the role of defining legitimate conservatism, operating as a kind of secular clerisy, dividing the ritually impure from the clean. Because the brand of "conservative" was so important for Republican elected officials, they granted a certain degree of deference to this border-maintenance work of public intellectuals. This allowed them to draw the line between legitimate conservative ideas and those that stand outside of liberal democratic norms, making them temperamentally more skeptical of populism than are other parts of the Republican Party network.[4] Conservative public intellectuals also link together these general ideas and the work of governance by providing an ideological seal of approval for public policies. They help ideologically motivated policymakers understand, for example, whether the appropriate conservative position on mass incarceration is to support increasing or decreasing imprisonment, or whether it is conservative to support free trade or protectionism—decisions that cannot be read directly off general ideological positions.[5] Finally, public intellectuals can help with the work of party coalition maintenance by providing general ideas that reconcile differences in outlook among groups in the party, and by developing policy proposals that help settle potential conflicts at the level of actual legislative decision making.

Even as they perform important functions for the party, conservative public intellectuals operate in a different social milieu than other Republicans. While the modern GOP has been more ideological than most parties, intellectual consistency and fidelity are core to the professional identity and political motivation of public intellectuals in a way it is not for party regulars. While the intellectual class has connections to party coalition members, elected officials, and grassroots partisans, those relationships are premised on the perception of shared ideas— ideas that public intellectuals play a principal role in constructing. For a remarkably long time, those relationships and conservative ideas did not seem to stand in any considerable or durable tension. But there was always the potential that these commitments would grind against one another—and in 2016 (and beyond) they were pushed to the breaking point.

Conservative public intellectuals also value their audience beyond the movement in a way that ordinary Republicans do not. In addition to their roles of explaining the movement's ideas to itself and waging the battle of ideas against its enemies, they also have had the role of explaining conservatism and defending its dignity to those beyond the tribe. While conservatives take preaching beyond the converted very seriously, party actors focused on internal organization and mobilization generally do not. This difference is especially acute because many conservative public intellectuals are clustered in Washington, D.C., and virtually all work in or interact regularly with non-conservative institutions like universities and the elite media. This physical and social proximity can make them highly oppositional to liberalism, but they also draw their sustenance and friendship networks from within generally liberal institutions and wish to preserve, while also comprehensively reforming, them. To do their work for the movement and party, perhaps paradoxically, conservative public intellectuals need to be recognized by the very actors they are criticizing to avoid being cast as "wingnuts." This distance from the grassroots base of the party gives conservative public intellectuals a somewhat more "entrepreneurial" conception of the Republican Party, a focus not just on serving existing supporters but using ideas to attract new groups. It should not be a surprise that ideas like "empowerment," "compassionate conservatism," "Sam's Club Republicanism," and "Reform Conservatism" all emerged out of public intellectuals but were viewed with at least some skepticism by other party actors.

The political identity of conservative public intellectuals is primarily ideological rather than partisan. For them, Republican partisanship is derivative of their conservatism and rests on the capture of the party by the conservative movement. They think of themselves as guardians of a set of ideas and a bulwark against the drift of their party away from them. By contrast with some of the more prominent conservative media figures on talk radio and Fox News, the conservative public intellectuals associated with Never Trump did not have an exclusively oppositional conception of conservative identity, what political scientists have called "negative partisanship."[6] For all of their often deeply rooted dislike for modern liberalism, they were typically recruited into the public intellectual vocation by their attachment to ideas, books, and specific authors, rather than a defense of a specific group—something they dismiss as unprincipled tribalism.[7] This made them especially hostile to a presidential candidate who seemed to be unaware or even dismissive of ideological conservatism and who embraced a form of cultural class warfare that worked at cross purposes with their understanding of the conservative tradition.

Guardians of Purity

Conservative public intellectuals play a dual role in the American party system. They are partisans, tasked with developing new ideas and policy proposals as well as engaging in intellectual combat on behalf of the party. At the same time, they have deep ideological commitments and believe their job in politics is to preserve the orthodoxy that justifies a close movement–party relationship. It is in this latter role that many Never Trumpers found their ideological and partisan commitments in conflict during the 2016 cycle and beyond. Where their role in sorting the raw from the cooked had been widely accepted before, suddenly they were faced with a nominee who was seemingly unaware of the previous conservative orthodoxy and dismissive of the role of conservative public intellectuals in the party. Faced with a challenge both to their ideas and to their institutional position in the party, many of them responded in ways that would have been inconceivable just one year before.

To understand why so many conservative intellectuals reacted to Trump the way they did, we need to appreciate their understanding of their role in the conservative movement and the Republican Party. And to make sense of that, the place to start is with *National Review*, the magazine that has traditionally understood itself to both contain the various legitimate components of the conservative movement and to define the line between legitimate and illegitimate.

The history of *National Review*—the story the magazine tells itself, in fact—is one of recurrent purges. These began in 1961, when *National Review* famously attacked the forces of the John Birch Society (JBS), which is now seen as wildly nutty but which at the time was a significant force in the Republican Party. Tellingly, in debating how *NR* should relate to JBS (with which it shared many readers and donors), *NR* editor Neil McCaffrey observed that, "We can't afford to jeopardize the grudging status we've earned in the Liberal community, nor renounce our role of tablet-keeper, but the Liberals aren't going to bail us out of debtor's prison."[8] *NR* survived its break with JBS intact, while JBS was hurled into the abyss of far-right craziness, which reinforced *NR*'s role as a "tablet-keeper" and established that it had the power to draw lines for the conservative movement.

This role recurred most significantly in the 1990s, and in almost every case in connection to the relationship between conservatism, race, and immigration. William F. Buckley, *NR*'s editor, had notoriously steered the magazine toward opposition to civil rights in the 1960s, going beyond just constitutional objections to *Brown v. Board of Education* to active support for white supremacy in the South. By the 1970s, Buckley had more or less repudiated the defense of segregation and the related ideas of anti-Semitism (a special concern given the conservative intellectual movement's incorporation of the neoconservatives). But not all conservatives within the magazine had moved with the times as much as Buckley had, who, while extremely conservative, also had a concern for maintaining *NR*'s status in the liberal community as part of the legitimate opposition. In 1993, the magazine fired its long-time writer Joseph Sobran on charges of anti-Semitism and leveled a more nuanced accusation against Patrick Buchanan, a veteran of three Republican administrations.[9] Peter Brimelow, who had been a prominent conservative writer, was fired in 1997 for crossing the line into racial essentialism. Ann Coulter was similarly shown the door in 2001 for writing that, in the aftermath of 9/11, Muslim countries should be invaded and their populations converted to Christianity. John Derbyshire was fired in 2012 after he published a racist article in *Taki's Magazine*, following a number of pieces that tested the outer limits of *NR*'s ideological tent.

Conservatives at places like *National Review* saw in the rise of Donald Trump, therefore, a kind of return of the repressed. The half-century-long effort to hold back the racist, nativist, anti-Semitic, and conspiratorial parts of the right was being, once again, tested. *Washington Post* columnist George Will forthrightly observed of Trump in the summer of 2015 that, "He is an affront to anyone devoted to the project William F. Buckley began six decades ago with the founding in 1955 of *National Review*—making conservatism intellectually respectable and politically palatable."[10] The concern for respectability was, in fact, one of the most important dividing lines between those who opposed Trump and those who were willing to line up behind him. Conservatives like Will and most of those at *National Review* thought that the respectability of conservatism was an accomplishment that had taken decades to produce, and which had yielded enormous returns. The reputation that conservatism had built for being philosophically grounded and culturally sophisticated was also, as we shall see later, of enormous significance for public intellectuals as a class—especially those who worked in and around mainstream and liberal institutions—in a way that it was not for other groups of conservatives who more eagerly embraced Trump.

For many of those who opposed Trump, the concern his candidacy raised was not even primarily about who would be president, but rather the character of the conservative movement itself. As *National Review* editor Jonah Goldberg argued in the fall of 2015:

I am tempted to believe that Donald Trump's biggest fans are not to be relied upon in the conservative cause. I have hope they will come to their senses. But it's possible they won't. And if the conservative movement and the Republican Party allow themselves to be corrupted by this flim-flammery, then so be it. My job will be harder, my career will suffer, and I'll be ideologically homeless (though hardly alone). That's not so scary. Conservatism began in the wilderness and maybe, like the Hebrews, it would return from it stronger and ready to rule. But I'm not leaving without a fight. If my side loses that fight, all I ask is you stop calling the Trumpian cargo cult "conservative" and maybe stop the movement long enough for me to get off.[11]

Opposition to Donald Trump was, for many conservatives, simply a continuation of the effort to read the alt-right—and before that, the paleo-conservatives, and before that, the John Birch Society—out of the conservative movement. The intellectual and media forces that were gathering around Trump were, for them, nothing new at all, and their heightened presence in the party activated historically grounded understandings of the jurisdiction of conservative intellectuals. Goldberg recalls that:

The term [alt-right], all of a sudden, was part of this larger sort of rebranding project of this older, swampier, shittier group of paleocons and racists, some of whom are very, very smart. . . . The alt-right crowd sort of rebranded this old sort of racial essentialist, identitarian right, whatever you want to call it . . . as part of the alt-right. Some of them were quite honest about it. They saw Trump as simply an incredibly useful battering ram for destroying the citadels that had locked them out. They always historically really hated *National Review*, because *National Review* [has] always sort of seen ourselves as the Texas Rangers patrolling the frontier. We're the ones who say, "This is the border and those are the Badlands." *National Review*, sometimes too slowly for sure, has purged those kinds of people, even from our own masthead.

Goldberg saw in Trump a mortal threat to the conservative movement that he had been born and raised into. "If you actually read what the alt-right said, they said . . . we want to destroy the conservative coalition and replace it. We're an alternative right.' The idea that if these guys were all in behind Trump, that I could be part of a movement that had them as fellow members, it was an existential impossibility."[12]

One does not have to look far into the writings of Trump critics to detect a kind of class dimension to their critique, a sense that he and the forces behind him were downscale, tacky, and boorish. George Will argued in 2017 that in the wake of Trump, "conservatism is soiled by scowling primitives whose irritable gestures lack mental ingredients." Similarly, *New York Times* columnist David Brooks makes a distinction between highbrow, literary conservatives and "the people with the arms sticking out of their foreheads." Of the latter, he says, "They were sort of the freaks who were like just around in any movement, and you sort of had to deal with them, but they were off on the fringes, and . . . respectable Republicans and conservatives looked down on them as sort of wackos and yahoos."[13] Trump represented, for those who had cut their teeth on the Ivy League conservatism of Buckley and Will, or the aristocratic philosophy of Leo Strauss, an inversion of the proper status hierarchy of the conservative movement. The firewall allowing conservative elites to keep back the "wackos and yahoos" was eroding, and with it the ability of the right's intellectual class to maintain its historic role in the Republican Party.

The Business Model of Conservatism

The practice of gatekeeping is ideological work, but it depends upon specific material conditions to be effective. Conservatism is a set of ideas, but for thousands of people it is also the way they pay their bills. As James Q. Wilson argued in *Political Organizations*,[14] the behavior of even highly ideologically motivated actors is shaped in fundamental ways by how they acquire resources and mobilize employees and supporters. Wilson had in mind nonprofit organizations, but critically for our purposes the landscape of conservatism is now populated to a significant degree by actual profit-making businesses, for whom conservatism is a product with considerable market value. Within this organizational world, conservatives are divided by modes of political action that interact in complicated ways with how they acquire resources, and by different relationships to liberalism and mainstream institutions. Notably, the opponents of Trump were not randomly distributed across the different ways that conservatives make a career of conservatism, and many took the rise of Trump as a signal that their business model was losing out to another—and in their minds, worse—alternative.

Roughly speaking, one strain of conservatism prizes intellectualism, refinement, and "respectability." This strain of conservative public intellectuals seeks to operate within or at least alongside generally liberal institutions, seeks to persuade liberals that conservatism is a decent, civilized set of ideas, and seeks to compete with it in part by claiming that conservative ideas are better able to achieve liberal ends (including advancing women, minorities, and the poor) than are liberal ideas.[15] This style of conservatism is consciously bookish, identified more with particular texts and ideas rather than a tribal identity.[16] It presents itself as holding liberal institutions to their own standards and beating liberals at their own game. Conservatives in this world take the distinction between different brands of conservatism exceptionally seriously, and argue with themselves about the relative merits of different philosophical schools—libertarianism, social conservatism, Burkeanism—as much as they devote themselves to a critique of liberalism. For these conservatives, respectability is valued in itself and because it is necessary in order for their ideas to be taken seriously outside of the world of conservatism.

Organizationally, conservatives who adopt this presentation of self are much more likely to be found in universities or think tanks and to have their bylines appear, at least part of the time, in mainstream outlets generally run by liberals, such as the *New York Times* or *The Atlantic*. Many of these conservatives draw resources and exposure from mainstream outlets that embrace norms of fair play, or that simply have a desire to reach a larger audience by making space for conservative voices. In other cases, they operate within right-of-center nonprofit institutions supported by conservative donors who themselves care about respectability. Finally, many of these conservatives are in professions like the law or academia that make them insider-outsiders—people who disagree with some of their profession's key ideas, but accept the need for elite professions and the imperative to operate within them. Never Trump draws very heavily on this kind of conservatism.

An alternative style of conservatism, with a very different business model, was much more characteristic of those on the right who supported Trump or more quickly made their peace with him. That style is focused on conservatism as a group—an oppressed identity in a society dominated by liberals—rather than a systematic philosophy. This style of conservatism is not interested in respectability, which it perceives to be the internalization of the norms of liberalism. It is self-consciously pugilistic and sees the other camp of conservatives as too effete to fight and too naïve to recognize the nature of the conflict it is in. It does not want to find a place for conservatism in culturally elite institutions so much as to dramatically weaken their power. Where elite conservatism thinks its legitimacy depends on the ability of the right to speak to a broad swath of the American public, this strain of conservatism sees its function primarily as protecting the interests of grassroots conservative Americans.

By the time of the run-up to the 2016 campaign, the primacy of the more intellectual and bookish faction of conservative opinion makers was coming under considerable strain. David Brooks observes that, "There's a Clayton Christensen book, *The Innovator's Dilemma*, and it basically says the market changes because somebody comes in at the bottom of the market, nobody takes them seriously because they're just bottom feeders, and by the time they take them seriously it's too big, they've already taken over—so Southwest Airlines is the example. [Trump] took over the bottom, we didn't take him seriously, and then he was the whole thing."[17] *National Review* and much of the rest of the mainstream conservative intellectual movement were focused on holding onto the top of the market, assuming that the mass marketers below them would defer to their definition of conservatism. The alt-right centered around *Breitbart*, however, succeeded in chasing conservatism's mass base downscale. With the rise of Trump, the structure of deference in which elite conservatives had a powerful role in shaping the right broke down. That provided an opening for the kind of populist nationalism that elite intellectual conservatives had, with considerable success, previously tried to keep in a subordinate place.

The business model of the purveyors of this populist strain of conservatism differs dramatically from that of the elite conservatives found in more culturally refined environs like the Aspen Ideas Festival.

In particular, the populist conservatives depend, in a way that elite conservatives do not, for their daily bread on interacting with and getting paid by a mass base of those on the right. *New York Times* columnist Bret Stephens argues that over time, the writers in conservatism have lost power whereas the electronic media personalities have gained it:

> Conservatism went from being a fundamentally literary movement, to being a TV movement. When I was coming of age in the '80s, the most important conservatives were George Will, William F. Buckley, Irving Kristol, Norman Podhoretz; and all these guys were writers. . . . And so if you wanted to be a figure in the conservative world, you had to be a writer, period. . . . There was a quality of intellectual selection there, because you have to be pretty smart to write well and to write persuasively. In 1996, with the advent of Fox News, you had a new breed of conservative superstars, none of whom was a writer. They had ghost writers. They sold lots of books, but they were not literary figures, they were TV people. . . . Suddenly, without us really realizing it, they assumed . . . the commanding heights of the conservative movement. So the idea that conservatism had to stand for a set of ideas, that here was the articulation of the ideas, why other ideas were heretical, or dangerous—none of that cut a lot of ice with them. . . . That meant that in an almost imperceptible but very decisive way, the writing class of the conservative movement became less and less important.[18]

Fellow *New York Times* columnist Ross Douthat argues that Stephens's distinction explains a good bit of the line between those conservative opinion makers who went with Trump versus those who resisted. "There's a very basic print versus radio and TV distinction. . . . People who write for a living are more likely to stay anti-Trump, and people who talk for a living are more likely to swing. . . . There's just more pressure on you in the world of talk radio or cable news to conform to where your audience is, than in places like the *National Review* and *The Weekly Standard* and so on, in part because they've never been profitable per se to begin with."[19]

Being a public intellectual may be a calling, but it's also a job. Conservative writers tend to exist in a fundamentally different material universe than their counterparts in TV, radio, and social media. They are insulated from market pressures, the preferences of the actual conservative base, and the political exchanges that occur within political coalitions. *National Affairs* editor and American Enterprise Institute (AEI) resident scholar Yuval Levin argues that public intellectuals' sense of their vocation, as well as their desire to be taken seriously within their world, pushes against the shallow transactionalism that was more natural to other conservatives. "You have to be able to justify to yourself the position you're taking, and so the turn [to support Trump] was just a lot harder. . . . Not only do you not want to think you're being transactional, you don't want to be transactional."[20] *Washington Post* columnist Jennifer Rubin also points to the sense among public intellectuals like herself that transactionalism was inconsistent with their role. "Politics is the implementation of values in the public square. People who look at politics that way, who say that politics is always value-based and it's how we express our political social priorities, those sorts of people were never going to accept Trump, because he was so obviously defective. I guess it surprised me how many transactional conservatives there were as opposed to value-based."[21]

Jonah Goldberg distinguishes public intellectuals' conception of their job, which is the promotion of conservative ideas, from that of radio hosts who think it is defending their side. "There are a lot of people, particularly in talk radio, who think that's their job. It's like they are a Philadelphia sports radio host, so they have to root for the Eagles."[22] In contrast to more literary conservatives, conservative talk radio hosts are exposed to actual conservative voters for hours, day after day, and organizations like the Heritage Foundation are tied directly into the conservative base through their direct mail operation. A rare Never Trumper to emerge from electronic media, Charlie Sykes had been a popular conservative talk show host in Wisconsin, as well as the author of the widely read 1988 attack on the left-wing tilt of the academy, *Profscam: Professors and the Demise of Higher Education*.[23] Sykes recalls that, "I was one of five or six critics of Trump on conservative talk radio in Wisconsin. We were all anti-Trump. I'm gone now. But all the rest that are still on the air are adamantly pro-Trump now. We can apply whatever standards we have to all of that, but the business model for anti-Trump conservatives [in talk radio] in effect evaporated in 2017." The material relationship of those in electronic media to the larger conservative public is, in Sykes's view, fundamentally different from others in the anti-Trump world.

We got ratings four times a year. I know our television partners got daily overnight ratings broken down by 15-minute increments. . . . I remember sitting there and you get the calls, you get the emails, social media, the blowback . . . all media is intensely immediately interactive now, so that's part of it. . . . The Wisconsin people were very anti-Trump, but I felt the shift. There was no question about it, by August [2016] I was telling people, "Look, I know I'm losing the audience. People that have listened to me for 20 years and trusted me, they're not going along."[24]

The material world this type of conservative swims in is inherently populist. Those who make their living in it are disproportionately those comfortable with being in a kind of mind-meld with the movement's mass base. By contrast, Rich Lowry argues, those like himself who run institutions such as *National Review* think their job is to lead the conservative base rather than assimilate themselves to it. "The snapshot way to put it is, [*Breitbart*] runs a website for their comment section, that's the sensibility they're going for. We run a website that wants to correct our comment section or show them where they're wrong."[25]

In sum, many elite conservatives draw their sustenance from organizations generally controlled by the center-left, such as newspapers, magazines, and universities. As a consequence, the legitimacy of conservatism outside of the right is of paramount concern to them in a way it simply is not to those who preach to the converted. Even conservative public intellectuals who work for conservative magazines, think tanks, and public interest organizations find themselves in contact with a relatively small and self-selected group of wealthy conservative donors. That provides a material foundation for their work that serves as a buffer from the conservative mass public and also as the basis for a separate culture of elite conservatism—a culture in which Never Trump flourished. In 2016 that culture of elite conservatism was shown to have been more isolated than anyone had thought, as its organs struggled—it turns out unsuccessfully—to purge what intellectuals on the right thought to be a cancer in their movement.

"Against Trump"

Public intellectuals mainly engaged with Trump as individuals, but *National Review* made an institutional decision in early 2016—at the same time that national security experts were working on their group letters and party professionals were launching their #nevertrump attacks—to try to block his nomination, and, just as important, to resist the ascendance of his populist nationalism as the ideology of the right. In the years to come, *NR* struggled for an identity that reflected its revulsion at Trump the man, distaste for Hillary Clinton, a belief that the conservative movement needed to reform its message, and, after his election, an openness to the possibility that Trump could run a reasonably normal Republican administration. At the same time, *NR* found much to critique in the burgeoning Never Trump movement, and even their most Trump-critical members kept their distance from it.

NR had certainly published a number of critical pieces on Trump throughout 2015, in particular by Jonah Goldberg and Kevin Williamson. But in retrospect, *NR* editor Rich Lowry thinks that the magazine erred by grouping Trump in with other eccentric candidates who had their moments in the sun. "I think we considered Trump a menace pretty early on, but underestimated the gravity of it because we thought it would fade. It was a strong version of a summer phenomenon that we've seen in Republican politics before." *NR* senior writer David French recalls that while many of the people around the magazine disliked Trump, it took a long time to recognize him as a genuine threat. "It takes a while to realize, okay. . . this whole theory that he's going to sink himself is just fundamentally wrong and fundamentally flawed. But when you've had no prior guidance and experience with a politician saying the things he said and surviving, it's just going to take a while for that to sink in, that that's the new reality you're dealing with." When it became clear that Trump was not, in fact, fading, it raised the question of how the magazine should respond. Lowry recalls that, "By the fall, as the weeks tick by, it's clear this is a real thing and the party's going to get swamped and you have to make a stand. There was no dissension within *National Review* about making a stand against Trump. Some people [said] we're against Trump, why do we need to make a big deal of it, but besides that little tactical concern, everyone was on board trying to stand up."[26]

The January 22, 2016, cover of *National Review* bluntly declared, in mock gold, "Against Trump." The lead editorial in the special issue asserted that Trump was personally repulsive but, more importantly, could not be trusted to effectively lead the Republican Party in a conservative direction. "Trump's political opinions have wobbled all over the lot. The real-estate mogul and reality-TV star has supported abortion, gun control, single-payer health care à la Canada, and punitive taxes on the wealthy. (He and Bernie Sanders have shared more than funky outer-borough accents.) Since declaring his candidacy, he has taken a more conservative line, yet there are great gaping holes in it." Tellingly, the *NR* editors expressed a concern for what Trump's rise would mean for the conservative movement that the magazine had so carefully helped shape. "If Trump were to become the president, the Republican nominee, or even a failed candidate with strong conservative support, what would that say about conservatives? The movement that ground down the Soviet Union and took the shine, at least temporarily, off socialism would have fallen in behind a huckster. The movement concerned with such 'permanent things' as constitutional government, marriage, and the right to life would have become a claque for a Twitter feed." Trump was, to *National Review*, a kind of corruption, and its institutional role was to protect the conservative movement from impurities that threatened to infect it. They closed the editorial by observing that, "Donald Trump is a menace to American conservatism who would take the work of generations and trample it underfoot in behalf of a populism as heedless and crude as the Donald himself."[27] More than a concern for the Republican Party, therefore, *NR* was motivated by its historical mission to conserve what it understood to be the essence of conservatism.

Along with the lead editorial, the symposium featured 22 attacks on Trump penned by a wide range of conservative luminaries. These included writers and intellectuals such as Mona Charen, Ben Domenech, William Kristol, Yuval Levin, R.R. Reno, Thomas Sowell, and Cal Thomas. Other contributors included radio talk show hosts Glenn Beck and Erick Erickson; Reagan administration alumnus Ed Meese; Russell Moore, the president of the Ethics and Religious Liberty Commission of the Southern Baptist Convention; and former Bush administration Attorney General and Jeb Bush advisor Michael Mukasey. Many of the contributors emphasized Trump's lack of history with the conservative movement. L. Brent Bozell, a conservative writer and founder of the Media Research Center, stressed this point in especially vivid terms, noting that:

A real conservative walks with us. Ronald Reagan read *National Review* and *Human Events* for intellectual sustenance; spoke annually to the Conservative Political Action Conference, Young Americans for Freedom, and other organizations to rally the troops; supported Barry Goldwater when the GOP mainstream turned its back on him; raised money for countless conservative groups; wrote hundreds of op-eds; and delivered even more speeches, everywhere championing our cause. Until he decided to run for the GOP nomination a few months ago, Trump had done none of these things, perhaps because he was too distracted publicly raising money for liberals such as the Clintons; championing Planned Parenthood, tax increases, and single-payer health coverage; and demonstrating his allegiance to the Democratic Party.

Other contributors argued that not only had Trump not "walked with conservatives" but that his rise would do significant damage to the reputation of the movement itself. Where conservatives had previously cultivated Buckleyite highbrow-ism, *Commentary* editor John Podhoretz compared Trump to the strain of New York culture represented by Andrew Dice Clay and Howard Stern, and worried that Trump as president would drag the "common culture" down to their level. Radio talk show host Michael Medved also worried that Trump would lead conservatives into the gutter, arguing that, "Worst of all, Trump's brawling, blustery, mean-spirited public persona serves to associate conservatives with all the negative stereotypes that liberals have for decades attached to their opponents on the right. . . . Trump is the living, breathing, bellowing personification of all the nasty characteristics Democrats routinely ascribe to Republicans."[28] Conservative intellectuals had taken it as their job to take the movement upscale by leading their followers to a responsible version of their creed. Trump would reverse that, putting what was lowest in conservatism at the movement's head.

Just as *NR* had in its DNA the experience of declaring certain ideas and individuals out of bounds, it had a similar experience with eliminating presidential candidates out of step with *NR*'s style of conservatism. While the magazine has regularly endorsed candidates in the primary, Lowry argues that, "As a practical matter, I wish it were otherwise, but the way things work in presidential politics I found over the years [we are] more effective in the negative and on the attack than trying to create something."[29] A 1991 special issue of *National Review*, which featured a 40,000-word essay by Buckley on anti-Semitism, was among other things aimed at turning back Pat Buchanan's insurgent campaign in the Republican primary. *NR* went on to attack John McCain in 2000 and Newt Gingrich in 2012, and in both cases their target lost.[30] So while those connected to *National Review* realized that their intervention was not the sole cause of the failures of Buchanan, McCain, and Gingrich, this experience did create the impression that the magazine had real influence among primary voters. As Lowry argues, "I use the word 'help' advisedly. . . . Is [*National Review* just] another teaspoon in the potion or whatever it is that destroys the guy? Or is it the 75 percent factor that destroys him? I think it's probably on the lower end, but it's something, or no one would care. The candidates wouldn't care, no one would report about it, no one would think about it, no one would write about it. So it has some effect."[31]

Unlike others in the conservative movement, however, *National Review* was "against Trump" without being "Never Trump"—a distinction that made more sense internally than it always did to the outside world. The "Against Trump" editorial stated that, "he is not deserving of conservative support in the caucuses and primaries." *National Review* Senior Editor Ramesh Ponnuru recalls that:

> It is not the case that we said editorially don't vote for Trump in November. I didn't vote for Trump in November, and I said people shouldn't vote for Trump. Corporately, we did not do that. We had tons of discussion. We had more discussions about what we would do for the general election endorsement than we had about whether we'd do an Against Trump issue or what our stance in the primaries was going to be. In the end, we decided there are lots of presidential elections that we haven't endorsed anybody, nobody here is making us feel like we have to endorse them, so let's not do it.[32]

It is understandable, however, that the tone of *National Review*'s editors would lead those who did not study the issue with Talmudic care to believe that they were saying something more than that they simply did not support Trump in the primaries. Lowry even followed up the special issue with an article in *Politico* accusing those who failed to oppose Trump with being "quislings" and charging that they had become "the mogul's deluded enablers" and part of the "surrender caucus."[33] This would turn out to be a greater point of contention later on than the editors could have anticipated at the time. *NR* had quite diplomatically avoided stating what conservatives should do if faced with deciding between Trump and Hillary Clinton, nor had it established a position about how conservatives should relate to a Trump administration (a prospect that was, at the time, still treated as unimaginable). Had one of the other Republicans in the race overtaken Trump, these would have been distinctions without a difference. But by the fall of 2016, and in some ways accelerating after the inauguration, this hedging, imperceptible as it may have been at the time, would mark *NR* off from many of the other conservative intellectuals who had critiqued Trump.

Trump as Reformocon?

Some of the most strident Never Trumpers thought that, as important as his personal character was, Trump's ideological heresy was even worse. Making Republicans the party of low taxes, limited government, a reliance on civil society, and a morality-based, internationalist foreign policy was, they thought, the great accomplishment of conservative intellectuals. While Trump was lowering the moral tone of the party, he was also dragging it away from these ideas—seemingly embraced in relatively pure form by Speaker Paul Ryan—that they believed were essential to the nation's economic and social flourishing. Trump had to be defeated in order to prevent his populist heresy from spreading and so the party could return to its eternal verities. He also had to be dispatched because he was undermining Republican efforts to present the party's optimistic vision to broader, more diverse constituencies. This was, in effect (and as Chapter 4 discusses), the vision articulated in the RNC's Autopsy that was dominant among conservative funders like the Koch brothers, and that informed the strategy of the Jeb Bush campaign, which in early 2015 looked like a juggernaut. Even after

Trump's election, supporters of this vision held firm, believing that Trump was poisoning the Republican well, making it impossible for the party to ever reach young and minority voters who would be critical in a changing electorate.

As far back as 2008, however, another diagnosis of the Republican Party's predicament began to bubble up among conservative writers and thinkers. The Reform Conservatives or "Reformocons," as they came to be known, argued that the core challenge of the Republican Party was the conflict between the Republican establishment—particularly its donor class—and its increasingly working-class voter base. Republicans could win as a party of the working class, they argued, but only if they were willing to use government in muscular and creative ways that were foreclosed by the party's excessive attachment to libertarian economics. The conservatives who embraced this vision, but who were appalled by Trump, inevitably had a more complicated and internally conflicted view than those associated with the Autopsy. Rather than seeing him as a heretic, Reformocons saw Trump as a kind of comeuppance for the Republican establishment, the demagogic consequence of a party unwilling to face reality. They worried that Trump was close enough to their diagnosis that he would discredit it by associating it with racism, resentment, and his own venality. But they also worried that other Never Trumpers' obsession with Trump would serve to conceal the party's own errors—the very errors that had called him into being.

These Reformocons combined a class-based electoral theory with an account of the legislative shortcomings of the Republican Party that was designed to show the party how to both win and govern.[34] The first salvo in the Reformocon movement was a series of widely discussed essays in 2005 and 2006 by Ross Douthat, then at the *Atlantic Monthly*, and Reihan Salam, the former executive editor of *National Review* and now the president of the Manhattan Institute. The first essay, "The Party of Sam's Club," laid out many of the pillars that would come to define Reform Conservatism over the next decade. It argued that President George W. Bush's agenda—oriented around curtailing entitlement spending, expanding free trade, and liberalizing immigration—was the wish list of the party's elite donor class, not its actual voters. The real GOP, Douthat and Salam asserted, was "an increasingly working-class party, dependent for its power on supermajorities of the white working-class vote, and a party whose constituents are surprisingly comfortable with bad-but-popular liberal ideas like raising the minimum wage, expanding clumsy environmental regulations, or hiking taxes on the wealthy to fund a health care entitlement." Put simply, as Douthat and Salam quipped, during the Bush era—and without the party establishment realizing it—the GOP had transformed from the party of the country club into the party of Sam's Club.[35]

Reform Conservatives' response to the shifting class dynamics of American politics was to reorient Republicans' policy platform around a positive agenda for government that could produce distinctive proposals for conservative governance. They argued that deregulation, free trade, and mass immigration had produced some very important economic gains for the United States, but that the burden of change was increasingly falling on the party's own voters. Failing to deal with the real economic anxieties of these voters could cause them to throw a spike in the machinery of American capitalism. Reformocons argued that the central problem produced by decades of economic liberalization was not, as the left suggested, income inequality per se, but middle-class wage stagnation, declining social mobility, and the eroding economics of family life.

The challenges facing the working and middle classes, Reformocons argued, were not only economic in nature; they were also cultural. The crumbling of institutions that provide meaning and belonging in American society—especially the weakening of marriage, religion, community, and workforce participation—fed on and exacerbated the economic struggles of the American white working class. Reformocons maintained that the party had to move beyond a policy of economic growth driven by tax cuts and deregulation to embrace new economic and social policies that would make life easier for families, increase opportunities for upward mobility, and expand employment opportunities.[36] This would require dramatic changes in the American welfare state. While they agreed with more libertarian conservatives on the need to control middle-class entitlements, they did so not out of fidelity to traditional economic conservatism but because they thought that fiscal space had to be opened up for *new* kinds of programs, like expanded child tax credits and employment subsidies.

By 2013, the Douthat–Salam party-of-two had expanded into a much larger, if largely informal, network ranging from Bush 43 alums such as David Frum, Michael Gerson, and Peter Wehner to libertarian writers like Megan McArdle and Peter Suderman, to cheerleaders in the commentariat like David Brooks.[37] The inner circle of Reformoconism was composed of Douthat, Salam, April and Ramesh Ponnuru, and Yuval Levin, another Bush 43 veteran who had gone on to be the founding editor of *National Affairs*, the wonky policy journal and house organ of Reform Conservatism.

The Reformocons combined a set of new policy ideas, focused on work and family, with an electoral theory in direct conflict with that of the Republican National Committee's Autopsy. Levin recalls that, "the core idea that we worked with . . . was that the center of the country is broadly socially conservative and broadly economically liberal, and that the Autopsy had it backwards and thought that the place to find those voters was by being economically libertarian and socially liberal. [In terms of] theories of the electorate, we were at a very different place."[38] That does not mean that more libertarian, upper-income voters would have to be run out of the party, but that making Republicans politically competitive required putting them in their proper place. Ponnuru explains that, "We thought that an agenda that spoke to the economic interests of working-class voters could keep those voters without alienating the upper-middle-class voters, and possibly while also making some inroads among non-white voters. That was the political calculation." Reformocons thought the way to increase Republicans' ethnic minority share of the electorate was by embracing economic positions that spoke to their working-class interests, while holding onto the social conservatism that they already had in common—not by mimicking Democrats' position on immigration and related issues. Ponnuru recalls:

> The basic theory behind the Autopsy was if we get rid of these distractions from our awesome economic agenda, we will move from triumph to triumph. So we get these pesky social issues and this immigration problem taken care of, then everybody will see how great our economic agenda is. I think there's really just not a word in that Autopsy about what I felt was the biggest problem the Republican Party had, which was the fact that its economic agenda was seen

by voters to cater exclusively to the interests of rich people and big business.[39]

David Frum, a former fellow at AEI and speechwriter for George W. Bush and now a staff writer for *The Atlantic*, recalls being similarly unimpressed with the Autopsy's three-part plan: "What the Autopsy basically advised was: preserve everything that was off-putting in [Romney's 2012 campaign]; change the one thing that had actually attracted some new voters but that the donors had never liked anyway, which was the immigration plan; and then write, basically, a Help Wanted ad for Jeb Bush."[40] At root, Reformocons argued that the GOP was hobbled by its lack of concern for the economic interests of the working and middle classes and the widespread perception that it only served the wealthy, not because it was insufficiently attentive to the distinct interests of minorities.

The Reformocon intellectuals thus went into the 2016 Republican primaries with quite distinct attitudes from some of their allies on the right, attitudes that would shape their response to Trump both during the primaries and afterward. First and foremost, they were aware that they were competing for mind-space with the powerful "Koch primary," a series of events in which candidates were introduced to large conservative donors convened by the Koch network and given strong incentives to embrace its agenda of deregulation, tax cuts, reduced government spending, and comprehensive immigration reform. In 2015, Jeb Bush, Marco Rubio, Scott Walker, and Ted Cruz, among others, all auditioned for the Koch network.[41] While the Reformocons did not disagree with all of what the more libertarian Kochs were pushing, they recognized that the Koch primary was squeezing out the space in the party's policy agenda.

There was one candidate in the race who was immune to the financial siren song of the Koch primary, who had recognized that the sell-by date of Reaganism had been reached, and that the party needed to offer an agenda more directly targeted at the party's working-class voters. Unfortunately, that candidate was Donald Trump. When the prospect of Trump being elected seemed remote, some conservative reformers thought his presence in the race could be positive for the party because it would force issues onto the agenda that could not otherwise break through the Koch primary. Frum recalls that:

> I've been obsessed with the rising threat of drugs since 2007. I thought this could do some good, so when people said Never Trump because we need to adhere to strict conservative orthodoxy and he fails those tests, I thought that's the one thing about him that might be useful. I can't claim Never Trump because I had been—my joke is—"Trump curious" at the beginning. . . . I have a strong belief that conservatism needs to reform. It needs not to reform as a matter of tactics. It needs to reform as a matter of philosophy, and on that Donald Trump is the graphic novel version of my philosophy. Which is to say, many of the things he talks about are things I have argued for well before he walked on the set. But I think he actually discredits the viewpoint by neither having a coherent philosophy nor does he help with his racialism and his combativeness.[42]

Most Reformocons were disturbed by Trump's unstable personality and racism from the beginning, but unlike the figures around the Autopsy, Trump's rise didn't send them into a spiral of despair. That's because his success was in many regards the opposite of the total repudiation—both in terms of political strategy and in their understanding of the party's principles—felt by the Never Trump operatives clinging to the Autopsy. For Reform Conservatives, Trump's victory, while regrettable, was a vindication, albeit a bittersweet one. Days before Trump's Super Tuesday rout, Salam revisited core Reformocon convictions, writing that, more than anything, Trump's dominance in the GOP primaries "has demonstrated that white working-class voters have minds of their own. They will not simply line up behind the candidates selected for them by hedgefunders and industrialists. . . . Ever since the Nixon era, Republicans have relied on the white working class to achieve political victories. Now it has revolted against the GOP elite." For the Reformocons, it was inevitable that these voters would eventually demand that their concerns be taken seriously. The party's failure to do so prior to Trump's rise had been a disgrace on its own terms, but it had also set the stage for an irresponsible charlatan to exploit the legitimate anger among the base. "Why wouldn't they be furious?" Salam asked. "The Republican failure to defend the interests of working-class voters, and to speak to their hopes and fears, has made Trump's authoritarianism dangerously alluring."[43] In a similar vein, three months before the general election, Douthat wrote that Trump was "reform conservatism's evil twin." Though personally repulsive, Trump had managed to activate the same neglected slice of America that the Reformocons had long championed, but with an emphasis on cultural resentment and outright racism rather than material policy changes. Douthat recalls that:

> Our view circa 2014 was probably similar to the Hay Initiative people [in the Republican foreign policy establishment]. We were like: "Alright, we're figuring out some blueprints here, we're steering the party away from where Romney was, we're steering it away from pure austerity of the Tea Party [to focus on] pro-family tax policy and more work-focused anti-poverty programs and whatever else we have." And I think one of the things that Trump proved on that front is that people and wonky policy proposals are all well and good, but when it comes to winning elections, nothing beats going around the country and just saying: "I'm bringing back your jobs!" Right? You know, Rubio's over there talking about vocational training at the debates, and Trump's saying, "They shipped your jobs to China and Mexico, and I'm gonna bring them back!"[44]

Reform conservatives combined profound alienation from what they saw as the donor-driven public policy of the GOP with a deep moral repulsion over the way Trump was appealing to the very voters they had spent years trying to get the party to pay attention to. In retrospect, we can see that the distinctive feature of the Reformocons was that they thought that conservatism needed to change not just for electoral or public policy reasons, but to forestall precisely the kind of demagoguery that Trump would come to represent. A decade before Trump's election, some Reformocons had already sensed that dark forces were building—especially among Republican voters—that urgently needed to be forestalled. Douthat and Salam argued that conditions were "ripe for populist backlash" and "revolt" among the working class. Failure to take Sam's Club Republicans' economic insecurity seriously could "make economic populism ever more politically potent" or "betoken the rise of a more Latin American politics, rife with populism and xenophobia."[45]

Similarly, Frum recalls that—at least with the benefit of hindsight—one of the reasons he had been so insistent on addressing the needs of middle- and working-class whites was precisely because he knew that there was a potential for that energy to be directed in dangerous directions, as it had in other countries.

> I got a call in the last weeks of the 2016 campaign. Because of my interest in the immigration issue, I knew a lot of people who either started or ended up in the Trump orbit. One of them said to me: "Look, Donald Trump is talking about things that you've been calling on Republicans to talk about for a long time, about immigration, about middle-class incomes, about drugs. You should be supporting it." This sort of crystallized something that I hadn't really thought about that clearly until this phone call. I said, "Yeah, but the reason I've been talking about those things now going back to 2007 is that I sensed that something like Donald Trump was coming, and I wanted to stop him. These concerns are not reasons to empower him. The nightmare has shown up, and I'm not going to be reconciled to it because the nightmare is using the issues that I warned were bringing the nightmare into existence."[46]

As Frum suggests, immigration was one issue that held a particularly important place in the minds of many Reformocons, in part for electoral or economic reasons but mostly because they worried that if working-class voters' desire for moderate restrictionism was not met by mainstream conservatives, it would be exploited by the less scrupulous. As Douthat argues, "Being skeptical of immigration is a fairly normal phenomenon . . . that obviously has racialized elements, but if you treat it as this sort of purely racist or racialist position, you'll ensure that its champions are themselves racialist and racist, and you'll create this sort of toxic environment, and that's happened in Europe and I think it happened with Trump."[47]

Conservative parties, as Daniel Ziblatt has argued, have the delicate job of both incorporating and then taming the ethnic and nationalistic attachments of their supporters.[48] While few Reformocons threw their lot in fully with Trump, many saw his success through the prism of the Republicans' failure to adapt their ideological principles to the sentiments of their actual voters. Organized conservatism, with all of its litmus tests, had called Trump into being, and some Reformocons saw in Never Trump a kind of counter-revolution against the changes in the Republican coalition that Trump had wrought. They thought there was something worth conserving in Trumpism and were turned off by what they saw as the snobbish attitudes of other Never Trumpers, whom they thought treated the party's working-class base as tacky, or even pathological. The Reformocons thus became the most ambivalent of Never Trumpers—wholly unreconciled to a man they considered to be a dangerous demagogue, but unable to shake the sense that their fellow conservative critics of the president were largely to blame for his rise to power.

Gatekeepers No More

The election of 2016 revealed that the relationship between conservative public intellectuals and the Republican Party had been deeply shaken, perhaps irreversibly. Conservative intellectuals had cut their teeth on the story of William F. Buckley repeatedly reading racists out of the conservative movement, and had created a myth of the movement in which ideas and intellectuals played a central role. The election of Donald Trump made some conservatives suspect that this myth had always been overstated. Ramesh Ponnuru, for instance, wonders whether the "conservative intellectual class bought into this outsized view of our own importance, at least our own importance in terms of immediate political sway." Goldberg believes that conservatives did, in fact, once have the ability to play an important directive role in the conservative movement, but changes in communications technology have permanently damaged their ability to do so going forward.

> The balkanization of the media, the rise of Fox News, and the rise of the Internet, where you have all of these competing players, means that the bottleneck got so much wider that *National Review* couldn't block it anymore. We still play a really important role in sort of validating people, validating candidates and all the rest, but

the leveling of the media landscape made it just structurally impossible for *National Review* to play that kind of role anymore. The rise
of *Breitbart*, the rise of *Daily Caller*, the rise of all of these competing
things, the rise of talk radio, there are other validators out there.[49]

Rich Lowry agrees that the material foundation for performing
an ideological vetting function has collapsed. "It's hard to maintain
guardrails. . . . Mike Cernovich [the Trumpist Twitter personality]—I
didn't even know who he was probably six months ago. But if you want
to purge him, what are we going to do? We're not Twitter, we can't shut
down his Twitter feed. He's going to tweet about Pizzagate, whatever it
is, no matter what we say."[50]

Communications technology, it turns out, has not been neutral between segments of conservative opinion makers. David Brooks observes
that conservatism, ever since the 1980s, had been divided between a
more bookish version and a more performative and tribal model, but
the distinction had not seemed fundamental. "One of the things I've
gone back to is the *Dartmouth Review*, and so Laura Ingraham and
Dinesh [D'Souza]. When they first came out, they graduated the same
year I did, and they seemed like we're sort of on the same team. But
even in those days, they were much more confrontational, much more
anti-left, much more shock the bourgeoisie, and that turns out to have
been a significant difference."[51] Intellectual conservatives like Brooks
and William Kristol had a structural advantage in competing for primacy in the movement when there was a premium on being able to
communicate within mainstream media, which wanted "respectable"
conservative voices. But they were systematically disadvantaged in the
world of the "outrage industry," which depends on an ideologically seg-
mented audience working within a much more competitive market.[52]
The relentless focus on the idea that liberalism was both hypocritical and
threatening was the core of the kind of conservatism that Trump drew
on, and is one that sells to a mass economic and political market. While
respectable conservatives themselves criticized the mainstream media,
they also depended on it as a way to maintain primacy over figures
like Ingraham and D'Souza. Indeed, the mainstream media has been
an important channel through which Never Trumpers have continued
to maintain their relevance. But it is also decreasingly an effective way

to reach actual conservative citizens. This has left Never Trump public intellectuals, increasingly, without an audience on the right.

Never Trump conservatives had cut themselves off from the economic and political apparatus of the Republican Party, despite deep connections forged over decades. This meant the loss of income, of friends, and of a sense of belonging to a movement that they believed had done great service to the country. Especially for those who persisted with their opposition to the president after his election, this experience was one of profound self-alienation. Why they felt intellectually compelled to resist the president, and with him their former allies on the right, is the subject to which we now turn.

7

Ideas Have Consequences

A SIGNIFICANT FACTION OF conservative public intellectuals responded to Donald Trump with a level of alarm that distinguished them from many of their conservative compatriots in other parts of the Republican extended party network. While the institutional and economic factors discussed in Chapter 6 go some way toward explaining that extraordinary response, they only go so far. Indeed, some conservative intellectuals drifted away from Never Trumpism as the president proved surprisingly orthodox where taxation, regulation, and the courts were concerned. What some public intellectuals describe as a "remnant" maintained their stance of determined opposition despite these policy achievements, seeing in Trump something more disturbing, and more corrosive, than their former allies did—something that no policy victory or judicial appointee could assuage.

The intellectual world of conservatism in the era of Trump resembles the classic Japanese movie *Rashomon*, in which different characters view the same events in drastically different ways based on their own experiences and motivations. The continuing critics of Trump see him as a source of deep corruption, a man who represents an existential threat to liberal democracy and the inherited principles of the conservative movement. That is not, to put the matter gently, what most Republicans see when they view the president. To understand why the Never Trump intellectuals perceive the president—and increasingly the movement and party that have followed him—through such a dark lens, we need to take their professional identity as intellectuals seriously.

These are people for whom words are their stock and trade. They do not view the utterances of the president as simple annoyances that are easily ignored next to a record of conservative governance. They believe words are the raw material of culture and that, in a phrase they use often, politics is downstream from culture. They believe the president's words—as well as his actions—have driven a cultural decline that far outweighs short-term policy victories.

For some, the cultural decline they associate with the rise of Trump has led them to reconsider conservatism itself, either because they came to see dark elements on the right that they had previously ignored, or because they concluded that the party they thought was committed to conserving the nation's liberal traditions had become irredeemably illiberal. These thinkers tried to keep the flame of Never Trumpism alive, even as they found themselves drifting further and further from the party. For conservatives associated with the Reformocon movement, Trump presented a profound and inescapable conflict. They were repulsed by Trump the man and his form of governance, but they recognized that his rise was abetted by the conservative movement's own failures and inability to change with the times. But most Never Trumpers have come to feel estranged from the party and the movement that had been at the center of their identity. Trump initiated a rupture that could not be fully repaired.

How Bad Is It?

One of the fundamental divisions that mark off Never Trump public intellectuals from those who embraced or at least tolerated Trump is their sense of the political moment in 2016. Many in the conservative movement had come to believe that the election represented a hinge point in history, a critical juncture in which foundational and irreversible matters would be settled. For conservatives of a particularly exercised imagination, it seemed plausible that what was on the ballot in 2016 was whether they would be rendered a subject population if Democrats won the presidency. This made even conservatives for whom Trump was dead last on their list of primary candidates willing to embrace him, out of a particularly acute version of negative partisanship. Never Trump conservatives, for one reason or another, rejected the belief that Democrats could not be trusted with control of the White House, as much as they had reasons to shudder at the prospect.

The ur-text of the idea that 2016 marked a kind of last stand for conservatives was Michael Anton's "Flight 93 Election," published in the *Claremont Review of Books*. The critical feature of Anton's argument analogizing the election to the heroic passengers who stormed the cockpit and brought down the hijacked plane on 9/11 was a claim of irreversibility. A failure to win in 2016, Anton argued, would lead to an entrenchment of Democratic power that would render Republicans politically unable to turn the wheel of history back in their direction.

> A Hillary presidency will be pedal-to-the-metal on the entire Progressive-left agenda, plus items few of us have yet imagined in our darkest moments. Nor is even that the worst. It will be coupled with a level of vindictive persecution against resistance and dissent hitherto seen in the supposedly liberal West only in the most "advanced" Scandinavian countries and the most leftist corners of Germany and England. We see this already in the censorship practiced by the Davoisie's social media enablers; in the shameless propaganda tidal wave of the mainstream media; and in the personal destruction campaigns—operated through the former and aided by the latter— of the Social Justice Warriors. We see it in Obama's flagrant use of the IRS to torment political opponents, the gaslighting denial by the media, and the collective shrug by everyone else.[1]

Anton's argument reflected Steven Levitsky and Daniel Ziblatt's model of democratic decay in almost all its particulars, especially the argument that the other party can't be trusted with power because they will use it to eliminate the possibility of future political competition. It was not surprising, therefore, that Anton ended the essay by stating that, "The election of 2016 is a test—in my view, the final test—of whether there is any *virtù* left in what used to be the core of the American nation." The sense that America faced a "final test" raised the stakes such that it could make sense to "spin the cylinder and take your chances" with Trump.

The rejection of the Flight 93 view of history is one of the most common features that ties together Never Trump public intellectuals, regardless of how intense their opposition is to the president. They rejected the idea that a Democratic victory would represent a break from which the country—and the Republican Party—could never recover. Bret Stephens, writing in the *New York Times*, zeroed in on the illiberal roots of the Flight 93 analogy's theory of history: "It is the mark of every millenarian fanatic to assume that the world stands on the verge of a precipice, and that only radical or violent action can save it. That's the premise of Anton's essay. It's also the kind of thinking that has inspired extremists from time immemorial, including the people who grabbed the planes on 9/11."[2] The Flight 93 analogy, Trump critics argued, was an effort to convince conservatives that what, in reality, was a normal democratic election was instead an emergency so dire that it represented a historical disjuncture in which the normal rules no longer applied. Never Trumpers thought this was irresponsible and was in fact a deflection from the reality that, if anything, it was Trump who was the threat to democratic norms. Jamie Kirchick, a hawkish journalist who previously focused most of his fire on the left, argued in the early days of the administration that, "if any candidacy posed an existential threat to the American republic, it wasn't the unexciting, predictable, left-of-center continuity represented by Hillary Clinton, but the reckless, impetuous, populist disruption promised by Donald Trump. The Flight 93 moment, in other words, is now."[3]

Many Never Trumpers simply could not comprehend Anton's belief that, given Trump's manifest unfitness for office, the potential election of Hillary Clinton required a suspension of the normal rules of politics. The conservative humorist P.J. O'Rourke, for instance, endorsed Clinton by arguing that her election was "the second-worst thing that can happen to this country, but she's way behind in second place. She's wrong about absolutely everything, but she's wrong within normal parameters."[4] Clinton had seen off a primary challenge from a man who proudly claimed he would bring socialism to America, something that really would have been a break in the trajectory of history. But for Never Trumpers, Hillary was not an Allende-figure whose radicalism required summoning their own Pinochet. Instead, a number of Never Trumpers offered an alternative account of history, in which the cyclical dynamics of democracy still held. David Brooks, for instance, recalls:

> Some people thought a Hillary Clinton win would just be devastating for the country. A lot of us thought it would be bad having an opponent win, but it wouldn't be devastating. I mean, during Barack

Obama's president years, we seemed to survive Hillary Clinton. We all had interactions with her, she wasn't Satan personified. So why did some people have an apocalyptic mindset others didn't? I'm not quite sure what the answer is. I understand from the evangelical point of view why you might have an apocalyptic mindset, but I think that was a little overwrought too. That's a key . . . determinant of where you came out, of how you conceived a Democratic victory.[5]

Orin Kerr, the conservative law professor and blogger for the libertarian Volokh Conspiracy, expressed a similar incredulity at the idea that the 2016 election was different from all the elections that preceded it.

I think it's just inevitable that the Republicans are going to win some elections and the Democrats are going to win some elections and each side gets its turn and they screw it up. Then the other side gets its turn and they screw up. . . . So even if you get a window of time with the Democrats controlling the presidency and controlling, hypothetically, the Senate, and having judges that I think are not interpreting the Constitution in the way that I would like, that's the swings of America politics.[6]

The former Hoover Institution fellow and current George Mason Law School Professor Adam White recalls of the 2016 election that, "I didn't think it was an extinction-level event. I thought actually . . . that one of the worst parts of the presidential campaign was the Flight 93 election article. . . . I felt it was horrific, and I just thought its author was a total demagogue and that it really misperceived the stakes of the presidential election. But others held that belief."[7] Most Never Trump intellectuals felt that the prospect of a Clinton presidency simply represented the normal rotation of parties. Accordingly, what Levitsky and Ziblatt call the fundamental democratic rule of forbearance still held, and there was no need, or justification, for suspending the normal rules of politics.

More interesting were conservatives who shared much of the worldview that caused their allies to embrace the Flight 93 narrative, but nonetheless chose to reject it out of something like a democratic faith. They believed that a Hillary Clinton presidency would put things they cared about deeply in serious jeopardy, but thought—for some just barely—that Trump would represent a kind of damage that would be even more serious and lasting. Princeton Politics Professor Robert George, a key social conservative and vociferous anti-Trumper, for instance, observes that people he respected thought, "This is it. It's over if Hillary Clinton's elected. Religious liberty is smashed. Abortion is made permanent. There's no going back on same-sex marriage." The conservative law Professor Jeremy Rabkin recalls:

> Having lunch with a . . . quite successful, accomplished lawyer in town, we were all talking about Trump . . . and he said, "Look, I know all the bad things but this is the last chance. If Hillary is elected, the Supreme Court will be destroyed, and I won't be able to practice law anymore, because we won't have law." . . . At least a current in that world [was] we must at all costs have a Republican because the alternative is the federal courts will be destroyed by eight years of Hillary Clinton on top of eight years of Obama.[8]

Faced with this extreme tension, George expressed his position in the election as one of choosing under conditions of radical uncertainty and picking between what was, for him, nearly equally awful choices. In the end, he concluded that:

> We're against her, but it could be even worse. We don't know. It could be. It's unpredictable. . . . If Trump is elected and taints our causes to the point where there is no going back to them, we taint ourselves. We discredit ourselves by associating ourselves with a man of such bad character, to the point where we will have no future. People like me believed we could survive Hillary if we absolutely had to. It's not a good prospect. We could survive her and live to fight again with our integrity and our strength intact. We didn't believe it was Flight 93, but we worried that if we got a Trump administration and we embraced him, he could discredit us and taint our causes. That's still, by the way, a worry of mine. You throw in your lot with Cyrus, you get the bad as well as the good.[9]

The brand of conservative represented by George worried that, by "throwing in your lot with Cyrus," conservatives were abandoning any possibility of a return to normal, decent conservative politics. Better to accept defeat with their principles intact, and then fight the Democrats with all their might, than to win with Trump and accept the stain he would put on them forever.

Never Trumpers saw in Flight 93-ism a disturbing inclination that had been welling up on the right for some time, a willingness to give up on the liberal values undergirding conservatism and accept that American politics was simply tribal warfare and, along with that, a willingness to abandon all scruples about how power could legitimately be wielded. Jonah Goldberg heard in the Flight 93 narrative a justification for turning toward illiberalism. The mentality of those who embraced it, he explained, was:

> We put one hand behind our backs while the other side embraces identity politics fully, and then we get called racists for wanting colorblind standards. We just need to embrace identity politics too, because that is the nature of the political struggle now. This defeatism, in the more normal sense, the sense of the liberals have already won, that's why these guys all went in for Alinsky. This is how they already won, so we've got to be like them now. We've got to adopt their patterns. We've got to adopt their tactics. We've got to adopt their logic. . . . They now want to have identity politics for white people.[10]

Other Never Trumpers shared much of the alarm about Trump's behavior, but because they were more critical of the state of the country before 2016, they had a harder time viewing him as a sickening aberration against which it was possible to return to a basically healthy status quo ante. Ross Douthat explains that this attitude "contributes to my lack of 'Trump is threatening the Republic' mentality. I think Trump is threatening the republic, but the republic isn't much of a republic anymore to begin with . . . I think it's bad that Trump is a corrupt asshole, I think he's degrading our country in all kinds of ways, but I think he's an accelerant on a process that was already in motion. And since I don't see him installing a dictatorship, I think it's a better use of our time to sort of think about where he came from than to act like it's a five-alarm fire every day."[11] The repeated claim by Trump critics that his behavior is not "normal" cuts little ice if, like Douthat, one was unsatisfied with normality. Charles Murray, a political scientist at the American

Enterprise Institute and the author of, among other books, *The Bell Curve*, also places his criticism of Trump within the context of national decline. He believes that "essentially, the American project is dead already. We are still a great nation, we still have a lot of positive characteristics in our people, all that sort of thing. But people like me who have been trying to push for a return to more limited government and more traditional understandings of America, we've just been wasting our time. . . . The country is in the grip of a kind of decline that Donald Trump's not going to arrest."[12] While Murray was sharply critical of Trump during the election, and has been during his administration, his criticism, like that of Douthat, is tempered by the sense that Trump reflects a much deeper rot. Flight 93 had, in essence, already crashed.

Taking Demagogues Seriously: Corruption and Culture

Never Trumpers sensed something deeply insidious in Trump's candidacy, a suspicion they believe has been vindicated by his performance in office. What they saw in Trump was corruption, not just in the ordinary, material sense of the term, but also a corruption of the nation's republican character. Trump seemed to have all the essential qualities of classic demagoguery, an appeal that works by debasing those to whom the demagogue appeals. They expressed this idea in often quite simple moral terms, as a kind of temptation that they were obligated to resist— and one which they were disturbed that many of their former comrades had embraced. Trump was not, in this understanding, idiosyncratic or new, but represented a recurrent danger as old as ancient democracy.

In sharp contrast to progressives, conservative intellectuals tend to emphasize the permanent character of human nature, and thus the recurrent features of political behavior. Influenced by the thought of Leo Strauss, among others, they have stressed that democracy is always in danger of falling under the sway of demagogues and decomposing into mob rule.[13] It is the job of constitutional government, along with civil society and education, to, in Straussian political theorist Thomas Pangle's term, "ennoble" democracy by elevating popular rule into genuine constitutional government—rule by reason and deliberation.[14] Representative democracy, in this understanding, has the capacity to embody some of the virtues of aristocratic government, while avoiding its risk of decomposing into oligarchy.

An ennobled democracy is far from natural or automatic. For Straussians in particular, demagoguery must be countered by giving democratic societies what University of Virginia political scientist James Ceaser refers to as a "constitutional tone," one "enforced, if not always by the political leaders themselves, then by enlightened parts of the public." According to Ceaser, this is necessary to counter what *The Federalist* called the "'artful misrepresentations of interested men' who encourage the people to indulge 'the tyranny of their own passions.'"[15] Straussians in particular were critical of what they take to be the tendency of Progressives and their successors on the left to dismantle institutional constraints on demagoguery by, for example, reducing the role of the institutional parties in the presidential selection process, encouraging direct appeals to the public, and attacking constitutional formalities that maintain the "constitutional tone" of government.[16]

More generally, conservative intellectuals have been inclined to at least look somewhat skeptically upon the populist spirit because of its tendency to encourage the public to succumb to their passions rather than their long-term interests. The role of the "enlightened parts of the public," which in the modern age is a way of describing public intellectuals, should be to elevate these public passions and to resist the populist spirit that is characterized by a "leader" (which Straussians distinguish from "statesmen," who embody constitutional norms) appealing directly to and inflaming these passions, and attacking the institutions that stand between the leader and the people.

It is this background that explains some of the unwillingness of many Never Trumpers to be assuaged by the arguments that their fellow conservatives have made in support of Trump. Numerous critics have argued that Never Trumpers' repulsion from Trump mistakes personal for political virtue, failing to recognize that political good can be done by bad men, especially if channeled through the right institutional structures. The most prominent such conservative is Charles Kesler, the founder of the Claremont Institute[17] and leader of "West Coast Straussianism," a dissenting sect from which a large percentage of conservative intellectual defenders of Trump are drawn. Kesler argued that "[Trump's] religious friends find it instructive that in the Bible God repeatedly found ways to use even very flawed human beings for

His purposes—from King David, who procured her husband's death so he could enjoy adultery with Bathsheba, to Saint Peter, who fearfully lied about his association with Jesus."[18] These defenders of Trump find the excessively delicate moral compass of the Never Trumpers to be a denial of the compromises that are inherent in the political vocation— which explains their exasperation with Never Trumpers' guise of moral superiority.

Never Trumpers, by contrast, argue that no amount of tax cutting, regulatory reform, or judicial appointments can compensate for what they see as a kind of insidious corruption that threatens to accelerate the decline of constitutional government into mob rule. They describe the job of intellectuals as the preservation of this more elevated, constitutional tone in public discourse, and it is why they have been alarmed, rather than simply perturbed, by Trump's rhetoric and late-night tweeting. Bret Stephens observes:

> I grew up in Mexico City, and I've always sort of been aware of Latin American politics, probably to a greater extent than most other conservatives, because I read the Spanish-speaking press. Demagoguery is a category in political experience that Americans kind of weren't prepared for, because it's largely been a kind of fringe phenomenon in the American experience, with a handful of exceptions. . . . The fuel was seeded by Fox News and Mark Levin and so on, and there's a great deal of truth to that, but I don't think you can discount the sheer power that Trump alone had in debasing the conservative mind and corrupting it. He's not just symptom, he's also cause. I was thinking about it this morning—pornography is debasing, right? Well, it wouldn't be debasing if our minds weren't already in some ways prone to being turned on by pornography, right? But in its turn, it acts as a kind of catalyst, or accelerant, or whatever, and that too has to be taken into account with Trump. He was the porn of the right. Trump was like a striptease act; the dirtier he got, the more it turned out we liked it.[19]

While those who have made their peace with Trump point to his short-term impacts on policy, Never Trumpers weigh more heavily his longer-term impact on the national character. They see in their fellow conservatives' willingness to apologize for, or even just minimize, Trump's impact, a surrender to the demagogic temptation, a willingness to use an evil man for what they take to be good ends, only to find that they have let loose forces they cannot control. In appealing to the low, demagogues attempt to obliterate even the existence or desirability of the high. Demagoguery, understood this way, is inherently debasing—the demagogue insists as a condition of his rule that his followers embrace their debasement. Never Trumpers believed that it was their role to insist that there had to be some standards below which the party should simply never go. Yuval Levin recalls:

> A lot of my friends who liked Trump didn't think there was anything beneath the dignity of the presidential race. They just thought that's the lowest there is, and Trump belongs there. I found myself differing with people about whether . . . there just had to be a certain level that someone had to reach before you could imagine them being president. . . . I just could not imagine Trump being in the president's seat at any moment in that whole race. It had to do, for me, I think early on, with just a total absence of dignity and seriousness. . . . The presidency does take a certain human type, and Trump is just not there.[20]

Never Trumpers regularly describe their unwillingness to go along with Trump in surprisingly visceral, instinctual terms. David Frum argues that: "The essence of Trump is that he's disgusting, and there are people that have a strong disgust reflex. The line of separation is between those who are able to swallow this toad and those who, for one reason or another, have not been able to swallow the toad."[21] While other conservatives have responded to Trump in terms of instrumental calculation, and criticized Never Trumpers for moral preening, the Never Trumpers themselves describe Trump as ritually impure. Because of that sense of Trump as unclean, and hence corrupting, they think that it is impossible to successfully engage with Trump in an instrumental way. For Frum, "One of the things that is remarkable about Trump is the way you get drawn deeper. Because there is no part of him that isn't rotten, you will be drawn into an entanglement that will end up changing you."[22]

In particular, they see in Trump's appeal a willingness to weaponize the tribal dimension of party polarization for his own ends, thereby extending a disturbing trend already present in conservative media culture. Frum argues that, "The Romans built the Coliseum, and it stood and was busy for the next like 400 years, putting bums on seats twice a week to watch men hack each other to death. There is a market for cruelty. Some people find it exciting. People with grievances and resentments find it exciting."[23] The essence of Trump's instinctual appeal, therefore, is his willingness to activate a kind of revenge fantasy on the part of conservatives, to engage in cruelty to those who have looked down on them. Trump's lack of manners or character is, therefore, a feature rather than a bug of his appeal. What Fox News does on a daily basis is the template for what Trump the avid TV-consumer has made a key element of his presidency. As Frum puts it:

> What they do is they bring on a tethered goat and then have their paladin beat the hell out of it. Then they feel better about being outmaneuvered by their son-in-law who went to college. There's a lot of Fox that's about saying every day, "I'm not dumb, I'm smart, and I want respect." Watching Tucker Carlson find the one professor in North America with something good to say about the North Korean regime and then confront her with photographic evidence, that makes up for all the times that you had to put up with your son-in-law pointing out that actually Obama did cut taxes.[24]

Trump is, for Never Trumpers, the natural endpoint of the conservative media culture that had transformed political polarization into partisan tribal warfare, preparing the way for the public to be comfortable with real, material cruelty in addition to symbolic media cruelty.

Never Trumpers express a kind of incomprehension that others could not and cannot see in Trump's character what was, for them, manifestly obvious. Charles Murray, for instance, reflects the attitude of many Never Trump conservatives, who found the president's behavior to be transparently that of a deeply disturbed personality, one characterized by "three things—grifter, malignant narcissist, and the [onset] of increasing dementia. . . . I consider that to be . . . an objective appraisal—with caveats, because we don't know everything of the man. And I don't think that we should have a malignant, narcissist grifter with dementia in the presidency."[25] For Murray and other Never Trumpers, the fact of Trump's pathological character was self-evident, and the lack of alarm by their friends on the right incomprehensible. "For conservatives, character is a big deal. The central requirement for a limited government is, as the founders put it, government of the self. . . . You can't have a successful limited government unless you have a population that itself is virtuous. And so, that means character in the leaders is important—not just so they can perform a job effectively, it's extremely important as an emblem of what the country's all about."[26] Just as leaders in a liberal democracy can ennoble the sentiments of ordinary citizens, they can also corrupt them.

Never Trumpers believed this insight was a core part of what conservatism was, and experienced a kind of whiplash in finding that their allies no longer did. Bret Stephens recalls cutting his teeth on this insight, only to find his fellow conservatives abandoning it:

> A fundamental conservative insight is that politics isn't simply a matter of getting the policy you want. There is that. There is, of course, a transactional element. But politics is also about culture and values. After all, what the hell was [Trump supporter Bill Bennett's] *The Book of Virtues* about? Or [Bennett's] *The Death of Outrage*? Or *Slouching Towards Gomorrah*, as Robert Bork put it? In the United States, because we don't have an aristocracy and because we don't have a monarch, the functions of head of state and head of government are combined, and they are combined uniquely in the person of the president. So he's not simply a political figure. These [pro-Trump] conservatives had been telling me how important culture is, right? And that culture is in a sense set from the top, which is why you care about what's being taught in the academy. Because if your best professors are all professing a bunch of garbage, this will infect the souls of the young, and it will tell them terrible things, and so forth and so on. Do I have to sit there and read Alan Bloom to these motherfuckers? Excuse my language. But why were they praising Alan Bloom?[27]

Never Trumpers held to a vision of culture in which the personal morality of the citizenry is deeply intertwined with the political morality of the regime, embodied in part by its leaders. This was a vision that some conservatives, especially traditionally religious Christians, took less seriously than those associated with Never Trump, because they thought the state had become a parasite on morality—and hence the best they could hope from it was protection rather than elevation, even if from a very bad man.

"Our People Can Smell This Thing Coming"

There is no question that Jews are overrepresented among the most persistent conservative critics of the president, what we might call the bitter-enders of Never Trump. While there certainly were a large number of non-Jewish Never Trumpers, there is a quite distinct sense in the response of Jewish conservatives to the president that he was surfacing dark currents in American society that had been—mostly—repressed. The response of Jewish conservatives to Trump can seem, to those outside of the postwar culture of Jewish America, more than a little hysterical. It makes a great deal of sense, however, when seen from the inside.

A number of the Jewish conservatives we spoke to emphasized that their response to Trump was rooted in their feeling that the norms of liberal democracy that Jews count on for their protection in America are easily unwound. Columnist Mona Charen, for instance, argues that, "It's just part of your psyche that everything is fragile. Everything could be temporary. You have to keep some wealth in jewelry because it's small and easy to transport. You know, land, not so much. Two thousand years of wandering will do that. Not to mention persecution. My parents had that view. My parents lived through the Holocaust. Not there, they were near, but I think were always ready to flee if it came to it. Things can go very badly very fast."[28] Bret Stephens also expresses the resonances that Trump had for some Jewish conservatives, ones that might have seemed hyperbolic outside of that specific cultural and religious frame of reference. "There's no blinking at the fact that an overwhelming number of prominent Never Trumpers were Jewish, and I think it's because if you're Jewish, there's just an odor to Trump's politics that reminds you of something else, something your grandmother told you about." Those memories of the Holocaust, as Peter Novick has argued, were an important, deeply embedded part of the culture of postwar American Jewish life, even for a community growing increasingly secular.[29] Charen relates that culture directly to her response to Trump:

> I may be a little hypersensitive to threats to our liberal democratic order. . . . I spent my teenage years—not the best way to spend your teenage years—[when] most American kids are hanging out and smoking dope and doing whatever it is they do, I was reading all about the Holocaust. . . . I just couldn't stop reading about it. And watching the movies . . . I felt like I had some sort of an obligation to grieve, and to fully take on myself the pain of what my people had suffered. But I also felt that if I could really understand it, then I could prevent that from ever happening again. So, perhaps that early . . . weird preoccupation of mine [explains why] I'm so aware of the fragility of our civilization. It's really hard to build a civilization, it's really easy to destroy one.[30]

For some, their relationship to the Holocaust and what they took to be its lessons was quite personal. Law Professor Orin Kerr also made the connection between his opposition to Trump and his family's own experience of the Holocaust. "My father was a . . . concentration camp survivor, and as a kid I had a sense of the world is fragile and institutions are fragile. And when Trump was celebrating dictators and talking about how great the Chinese Communists were for killing the protestors in Tiananmen Square . . . and so clueless about the Constitution . . . . That triggered I think, in me, a sense of American institutions are fragile. You don't want to ever get anywhere close to toying with these ideas."[31] For Kerr, given his own family's experience, opposing Trump was, in part, seen as a kind of moral obligation. "When I think through my own reaction, I think, 'How could I react otherwise in light of my family background and in light of that?' Not that Trump is a [Nazi]. He is not. But the methods of propaganda that Trump uses and the rhetorical strategies he uses, they're frightening in a way that I think . . . pulls on a different cultural understanding of the threat. It's because I'm Jewish and because my father is a concentration camp survivor, et cetera, that does sort of take it outside of the normal 'how bad can it get, whatever, it's just politics, it's just a game' kind of attitude."[32]

Eliot Cohen echoes the sentiment that the Jewish experience creates a frame in which it is harder to dismiss rhetoric as cheap talk. "There is a Jewish sensibility that when somebody says terrible things, you pay attention. That's a direct outgrowth of the Holocaust. When people say they're going to do awful things, or that they're willing to do awful things, or that they're kind of playing with violence, or encouraging violence, you don't say, 'Oh, those are just words.'"[33] That insight informed the neoconservative approach to foreign policy (which emphasizes the character of the regime and its leaders more heavily than traditional conservative realpolitik) held by many Jewish Never Trumpers, and it shaped what they saw in the figure of Trump.

The specifically Jewish conservative experience helps explain why Trump's mode of leadership, which other conservatives found annoying but not fundamentally threatening, was seen as specifically menacing to Jewish Never Trumpers. Trump's rhetoric loomed especially large. Stephens argues that, "Many of us are Jews, and I do think it's because the Jewish experience is saying that certain rhetoric just isn't funny, these aren't just words, this kind of language has echoes that ought to concern us."[34] Gabe Schoenfeld, a former senior editor at *Commentary*, advisor to Mitt Romney, and now a senior fellow at the Niskanen Center, similarly argues that:

> There's certain things that happened in the Trump world . . . the vio-
> lence at the rallies, the character of the rallies, the fact that they were
> kind of mass rallies with some fascist qualities, response to chants to
> lock her up, the presence of open anti-Semites in his ranks, and his
> refusal to distance himself from them. I'm not charging him with
> anti-Semitism at all, but I think there was a kind of toleration of it,
> around him and in circles around him. And I think some Jews were
> particularly sensitive to these things, and they found it to be all the
> more unacceptable and also I think fueled some of our energy, or at
> least my energy in opposing him.[35]

Those echoes of the Holocaust come out of what we might call the catastrophic imagination, the ability to easily access the possibility of history taking a sudden, communally threatening turn. This is some-thing that Jews, suggestively, have in common with Mormons, who were the other religious group that was overrepresented among the most alarmed Trump critics such as Evan McMullin and Mitt Romney. Mormons, too, live in a culture in which the near-destruction of their community at the hands of the majority, specifically the "Extermination Order" issued by the governor of Missouri in 1838, is part of their communal memory.

In sharp contrast to the acute state of alarm that possessed those who saw Trump through this historical frame, *National Review* under Rich Lowry has projected a pose of non-excitability since Trump became president, arguing that his administration is a mix of good and bad, rather than a historical break requiring emergency measures.

> I'm fairly certain it's not a threat to liberal democracy. It's a threat to the nation's political culture and he is participating in and driving its degradation, which is a bad thing and should be called out. But I don't see him having violated any law, the Constitution, in any respect. Most of what people take to be threats of that nature, is him popping off on Twitter. He attacks a judge; the norm is presidents don't attack judges. People say, "Oh, my gosh, this is a violation of separation of powers." No it isn't. He's free to say what he wants. [It's] not prudent for him to say it. It doesn't respect various proprieties for him to say it, but it's not a threat to our constitutional system. . . . Obama clearly violated constitutional lines, or at the very least, pushed the envelopes as much as he could to a much greater degree than anything we've seen from Trump. He was just polite about it.[36]

Jewish Never Trumpers are not as confident as Lowry that the liberal democratic regime that has been so important to their community's thriving in the United States is not threatened by Trump. Cohen points out that this is partially explained by their distinct historical sensibility, which led Jewish Never Trumpers to pick up resonances that their co-partisans simply did not. "Jews tended to be much more sensitive to even the faintest overtones of the sort of white supremacist . . . things that were there. So that even when he's saying nice things about Israel, he's got an Orthodox Jew as a son-in-law, you just knew this man's playing with fire. I remember . . . somebody who's not in politics but very eminent senior person who's Jewish, grabbing me by the arm and saying, 'Eliot, our people can smell this thing coming.'"[37] But additionally, Jewish Never Trumpers brought a theory of leadership to their assessment of the president that marked them off from other conservatives. Cohen specifically points to the differences between Christian and Jewish conservatives around how they think about the morality of political leaders.

> I had some very interesting conversations with people who were devout Christians who could bring themselves to support Trump even though they knew what a morally compromised individual he is. And one of them said, "Well, you know, render unto God the things that are God's and unto Caesar the things that are Caesar's." And I understand that sensibility, but that's not the Jewish sensibility. . . . At least my version of the Jewish sensibility, which is really rooted in our attitudes towards monarchy and towards rule, is that you don't separate out personal behavior in quite the same way that I think that Christians sometimes find it easier to do.[38]

Whereas Christians might envision bad men being used for good purposes, Cohen thinks that Jews are more likely to see disordered personal character as a sign of what sort of things a political leader might be willing to do if equipped with the power of office.

Not all Jewish Never Trumpers shared the sense that Trump was a proto-fascist, or that liberal democracy is quite as vulnerable as some feared. Jonah Goldberg observes that, "I have Jewish friends who play this [game], 'Who will hide us when the Nazis come among the Christians?' I don't like that because I think it assumes wrong things about America." But even Goldberg now looks at his fellow conservatives in a way he did not before: "This whole experience is like a dye marker. I know, that if the really bad shit did happen, who wouldn't hide me in their rumpus room." Goldberg recalls seeing how the rise of the alt-right was bringing anti-Semitism to the surface. "You see how evil and shitty these human beings are and the kind of stuff they do. . . . I remember we were talking on Twitter one night . . . someone was talking about drug addiction, and I said, 'Look, I kind of take this stuff seriously. My brother was a drug addict. He's dead.' Immediately, the Pepe the Frog alt-right crowd start making jokes, asking whether he was turned into a lampshade."[39] From this point of view, the rise of Trump is viewed as continuous with the alt-right's anti-Semitism in a way that it is not for other conservatives. Yuval Levin also had a sense that what was most concerning about Trump was not so much any anti-Semitism of his own, but that his campaign had given those who did hate Jews permission to come out of the closet.

> By the end of it, being Jewish was part of this. Trump unleashed some anti-Semitism . . . some of it in my direction when I wrote against him. That probably meant that it would've been hard if not impossible for me at some point to just say, "Well, I've changed my mind about him, actually. It's fine." . . . I experienced anti-Semitism directed to me in a way that I had not before in my life in 2016. It wasn't much, I don't want to give the wrong impression, but it certainly raised questions in my mind about what the hell this was unleashing. That's part of why . . . I wasn't going to join this train.[40]

A number of Jewish conservatives experienced quite frightening levels of anti-Semitic abuse online, not unlike the racism that the Christian conservative David French, who as we saw in Chapter 5 came close to running against Trump, experienced aimed at his adopted daughter.[41] Goldberg speculates that, "Being subjected to the kind of shit that those guys did made you lock in and sort of think, 'I can't have anything to do with these people.' David French, how many times do you need to see a picture of your daughter photoshopped into a gas chamber, before you're like, 'These people are my enemy?' "[42] Never Trumpers weighed the actions of the president's supporters more heavily in the balance than did other conservatives, and were concerned that he had released forces—even if not actively intending to do so—that were if anything more menacing than the president himself.

It is precisely because of their historically informed sense of vulnerability that some Jewish Never Trumpers took Trump's threats to the rule of law so seriously, even as other conservatives focused more on his (for them, positive) impact on the composition of the judiciary. Jennifer Rubin, for instance, recalls that "his attacks on judges and the courts struck such a visceral feeling, that he was so obviously looking to knock away the small-l liberal institutional protections that

Jews and other minorities have always relied upon in democratic societies. If you get rid of the courts, if you get rid of the free press, if you begin to demonize business and trade and foreigners, who's first in line?" For Rubin, that explains why the prospect of Trump's impact on the rule of law was interpreted so differently by some Jews than by other conservatives, who were more focused on judicial selection. "The Catholics and also the evangelicals look at the court purely in terms of religion and right-to-life. I think a lot of Jewish and other right-leaning conservatives look at it as a stalwart of constitutionalism, that there's a reason we don't have mob rule in our society. There's a reason why we have protection of individual liberties."[43] Many Jewish Never Trumpers were especially committed to a creedal, constitutional conception of the country, since it was one in which they had a very clear place, whereas an ethno-national conservative would inevitably leave them out in the cold. Goldberg argues that, "In that world, where it's just nationalism or socialism or tribalism, then your Jewish identity kind of locks you out."[44]

Finally, a number of Jewish Never Trumpers emphasized that because of prior experience, they could envision the possibility of abandoning their party loyalties. Gabe Schoenfeld, for instance, observes that Jewish neoconservatives had in their own memory the experience of leaving a party they felt had abandoned its principles, and so the idea of doing it again was not so unimaginable as it might have been for other conservatives. "These particular Jews . . . are the intellectual successors of the neocon movement that came out of the Democratic Party, left the Democratic Party as I did. I was working for Pat Moynihan in the late 70s, and then I became a Reagan Democrat. Then I became a Reagan Republican. So I left the Democratic Party, and all of us did that, or had parents who did that, or had mentors who did that."[45] Among the sons of the original neoconservatives were two of the most outspoken Trump critics, William Kristol and John Podhoretz. Rubin also supports the idea that the history of neoconservatives provided a template for Jewish Never Trumpers.

I think, if you look at the early Never Trumpers, many of these were the people who left the Democratic Party in the 1970s. This was the neoconservative movement, the people who left the Democratic Party over social order issues, over foreign policy issues, to some degree over affirmative action issues, and that both in their willingness to leave a party and move where they intellectually felt more at home, and in the issues that they chose to leave the Democratic Party over, they were more willing to see Trump, more able to see Trump, for what he was.[46]

For Charen, her Jewishness prepared her to be willing to stray from the herd, a position that terrified many people in the conservative movement. "I said to somebody, when they said, 'You're all alone, you Never Trumpers. You've got a constituency of none.' I said, 'Look, I'm used to being a despised minority in every way. As a Jewish conservative, as a conservative Republican who was Jewish, I'm used to my own people finding me a weirdo and peculiar, so that's just normal.'"[47] While it was certainly painful, some combination of their preexisting sense of apartness in American culture, their awareness of Jewish neoconservatives separating themselves from the Democrats, and their heightened, historically rooted sense of the stakes involved in the Trump presidency made Jewish Never Trumpers willing to go further in their opposition to the president than other conservatives.

Their Party No More?

Most of the public intellectuals who became critics of Trump could never have imagined becoming separated from the rest of the conservative movement. Most of them had been—in some cases, literally—raised in the movement, and their tie to it was bound up with deep personal relationships and memories of battles fought together. They had not gone into the 2016 race with any expectation that it would wrench those relationships apart. Yet hey saw, one after another, their friends and allies make peace with Trump, and as a result, at least some Never Trumpers were forced to ask questions that they had never entertained about conservatism itself. Some embraced a sense of themselves as a remnant, holding fast to the eternal verities until such a time as the Trump fever broke. The experience of the Trump era caused others to wonder whether conservatism was what they once believed; to look at the movement's past in new, darker ways; to see things that they had not permitted themselves to see before. For some, that experience was a kind of intellectual awakening, as they could no longer defer to the opinions of others in the movement to inform their judgment. For almost all, there was a sense of sadness as their participation in a decades-long collective effort cracked apart.

For some Never Trumpers, the break with their fellow conservatives is one that they view as irreparable. Bret Stephens compares seeing so many other conservatives throw in their lot with the president to discovering a horrible secret about a relative. "I think there must be people who finally figure out that Grandpa is a monster and they have that shock of discovering that a benevolent figure they respected, and even loved, has a dark side. I had something of that feeling watching the Republican Party give itself so wholly to Trump."[48] Similarly, Jennifer Rubin relates her experience to finding out that everything she had based her political beliefs upon was a lie.

> Never Trump has been world-changing, intellectually dislocating, for many of us on the right, who have spent decades arguing, "No, conservatives aren't racist. They're just opposed to race quotas. Republicans aren't in favor of rich people, they just have an economic theory of trickle-down economics, which happens to benefit rich people but really it's all about economic growth and the wonders of a democracy." It's as if you wake up in a Cold War spy thriller and realize you've been married to a spy for decades. You really have the veil lifted on many things and it has been extremely disorienting, disturbing.[49]

These conservatives had assumed that their side was the conservator of what was virtuous in the American experience, that their allies were those who could be trusted. In the light of something as traumatic as they experienced with the rise of Trump, they looked around and wondered anew at whether other things they took for granted were wrong.

The role of race in the Republican Party looms particularly large in the list of things that Never Trumpers view themselves as having filtered out in the past, but were suddenly able to see in the light of the Trump phenomenon. Charen recalls a shift in her thinking:

> It's the harsh glare that this experience, that this moment has shed on . . . some of our population. For my entire career, I've been very interested in racial issues, racial solutions, how to help black people . . . but I was very hostile to the "racism explains everything" argument. I had written many a column about how it isn't racism, it's other things. It wasn't entirely just with Trump, it had started before then, it started with the Trayvon Martin thing, where I saw white people immediately assuming that this black kid in a hoodie must have been a criminal, must have committed a crime, and I remember bristling at that. Anyway, in the light of the response to Trump, and the open racism of a lot of his supporters . . . it's made me . . . realize that racism wasn't as fringey a phenomenon as I had thought it was. I thought it was just in the fever swamps, but I don't think that anymore.[50]

Conservative public intellectuals had seen their role, in part, as vindicating American society—and ordinary conservative citizens in particular—against the left's charge that racism was a deep and constitutive component of the American experience. The forces unleashed by Trump's campaign, however, forced them to wonder if they had dismissed that critique simply because of its source. Stephens, for instance, puts it, "The left wing's critics of the right, the ones who had always said, 'The right is racist, the right operates according to a bigoted playbook.' Maybe they had a point that I didn't see, because I was too into it, or because I simply thought it was kind of a fringe element."[51]

For some Never Trump conservatives, race became the entry point from which to reassess their entire relationship to the conservative movement. Ross Douthat recalls that, "When I would read conservative intellectuals praising Rush Limbaugh in the late 2000s or something, I think there was a blindness to how much . . . racialized appeals and race-baiting was woven into populist conservative entertainment. I think there was a willing blindness about that."[52] George Will also points to Trump's open willingness to appeal to racism as the straw that broke the back of his Republicanism: "I can tell you exactly when it happened. The 2nd of June 2016. Paul Ryan endorsed Trump. The next morning, I came in and changed my registration. . . . This was about ten days after [Ryan] had said the attack on the Mexican judge from Northern Indiana was textbook racism."[53] David Brooks also points to the centrality of race in the intensity of his and others' opposition to Trump: "For a lot of us the race thing is the bridge you can't get over. That's a core wound of American history, and you can't be on the wrong side of that one. I think for people like me, Mike Gerson especially, that bigotry endemic in the project is just a thing you can't get over."[54]

One of the consequences of seeing the conservative project differently is a changed relationship to their colleagues on the right. Charen describes the conservative movement as a kind of intellectual logroll in which people deferred to others in determining their positions beyond a core area of expertise.

> Once you're on a team, and you are engaged with other people who think like you and you all read the same books and you reinforce one another, you come to believe in the good faith of the people that you know and that you've learned from and that you're dealing with. You believe that they are right. . . . If they're in a fight with somebody on the left, I'm going to be inclined to believe that my guy has the better of it and the guy on the left is all wet and his arguments are not valid because my guy is the good guy. He's my guy.[55]

The open racism of Trump and his supporters had, for Charen, broken a kind of spell that made deference to her fellow conservatives sensical, causing a reassessment of a whole range of positions.

> The whole business of the whole racial stuff, I mean, seeing people making excuses for Trump after Charlottesville. At a moment like that, I just say, "You are not on my side anymore. You're just not. . . . It's a break. It's a rupture." Because it's straight up good and evil. Not tough. No gray. Simple. Simple. Simple. You guys flunked. So then, once you've had that disillusionment, it is possible to say, "Maybe if I was wrong about them being good people, then maybe I was wrong about them having the right views on other issues." . . . When you're

in a situation like we're in now, you don't any longer quite give the benefit of the doubt that your side is the good side and that your people are the right-thinking and the morally upstanding people, because you've seen them do things that are so morally compromised that it shakes your whole faith in their intellectual structures.[56]

Most conservatives critical of Trump found his racial appeals morally disqualifying. But they also had more consequentialist concerns about the impact such appeals would have on the ability to get a hearing for their approach to public policy. Conservatives had been arguing, at least as far back as Jack Kemp (who was a key touchstone for many Never Trumpers), that reforms that would increase the power of the market and civil society would be better for racial minorities. Yuval Levin argues that reform conservatives, in particular, thought:

Trump was dangerous because he was discrediting exactly what we were trying to do. . . . [He allowed people to say] this is just racial or it's just resentment. And that's the most dangerous thing there is to the kinds of arguments we were trying to make which I think were not racial or about resentment. It got to a point where that was a big part of why I worried about Trump in '16. But I'm sure that's not where it started. . . . I think the discrediting part of it wasn't just about losing. It was about being associated with what really was just demagoguery and racial appeals and the kinds of things that I think the right just has to be especially careful about, that everyone has to be careful about.[57]

Charen had been Jack Kemp's speechwriter in his 1988 presidential campaign and was thus as invested as anyone in the idea that Republicans should have an appeal beyond their white base, and that their ideas were in fact better for the flourishing of blacks and Hispanics. For her and other Never Trumpers, it is very important to "get these questions about race right, and to not be on the wrong side of that question, which is the biggest question in American politics and has been for my entire lifetime, and arguably for the nation's existence."[58] While other conservatives certainly agreed at an intellectual level with ideas like school vouchers, the kinds of people who remained Never Trumpers stood out in believing that the dignity of the Republican

Party depended on appealing to racial minorities, whether they voted for the party or not. Accepting the direction that Trump was taking the GOP, for them, meant surrendering to the left-wing narrative on race and conservatism that they had spent their careers believing was wrong and trying to debunk.

Race is thus wrapped up in matters of character, morality, and an elevated conception of politics that the most committed Never Trumpers felt far more deeply than those who were more lukewarm in their distaste for Trump. Many of those who opposed Trump in the primary but now believe that, so long as he is president, they are obligated to get the most out of him, find this attitude exceptionally hard to take. They see Never Trumpers as guilty of moral preening and willing to sacrifice the achievement of what they take to be essential goals for the sake of their own purity. Lowry, for instance, thinks that:

> it comes down to character and how much you value it. Some of my colleagues just think that's the most important thing about the presidency. And if that's what you think, then being 110% against makes sense. I think that's important, but it's not the entire story of what we're seeing. Some Never Trumpers just won't say anything positive about anything he does, even if he's advancing policies that two years ago they supported [under] Marco Rubio . . . . So that's where I think some folks are letting their distaste for him distort their judgment and actually change where they are politically.[59]

Ramesh Ponnuru echoes this sentiment, arguing that the comprehensive criticism of the Trump administration has isolated the most committed Never Trumpers by making it seem like they have to choose between Trump and abandoning conservatism itself. "This idea that those of us who are praising him sometimes are making it harder to have an anti-Trump resistance, I think is basically mistaken because if you want conservatives to be anti-Trump or skeptical of Trump or less in love with Trump, I think probably telling them [that] you've got to stop being conservatives to do it is not going to be a productive way of doing that. If the idea is we all have to become Jennifer Rubin—again, nothing wrong with Jennifer rethinking her positions on these issues— but I think that it is not going to get a lot of takers on the right."[60]

The attitude that Lowry and Ponnuru reject, that treats Trump as a kind of acid test that overwhelms all other ideological considerations, is deeply embedded in those who have stuck with a Never Trump identity. As Bret Stephens argues, "I don't think I'm becoming left, I actually think my politics are pretty much exactly where they were three or four years ago, with the exception that I now see Republicans and the entire conservative movement, and so many of its leading lights, in a very different way, because I think Trump has been a great surfacer of character. . . . A certain perversity of character is required to take a liking to this guy or to make excuses for him."[61] For Stephens, seeing so many conservatives go along with Trump has stamped his perception of them in ways that cannot be reversed.

> [Joachim] Gauck was the president of Germany [who] made available all the Stasi files. So you can go and read your file, and you would learn who was spying on you. . . . "Wait, my girlfriend was spying on me. Or my brother-in-law was spying on me. Or I did all those favors to that guy, and he was spying on me." You suddenly see the truth. And then all of a sudden you discover people you think were jerks, turned out, refused to spy on you. It's filled with surprises. I feel that way with Trump. It's like opening a Gauck file and discovering the inner truth about people.[62]

The experience of losing faith in one's ideological allies has, for some Never Trumpers, led to a loss of the instinct of partisanship. Some experience this as a kind of liberation. Rubin, for instance, has experienced the time since Trump's takeover of the Republican Party as one in which she has discovered a level of political commitment more fundamental than ideology and partisanship.

> The experience of Trump has made people of goodwill and people who care about ideas, on the right and left, appreciate one another more than in the past. We've gotten down to some basic fundamentals here about objective truth in the world, about democratic norms. I think it's Tom Nichols who likes to say, "I'll never go back to being as partisan as I used to be." I think there's some truth in that, that in the political wars over specific policy issues, those are

very fierce and very important, but they're not as important as what we're talking about now. We're really talking about the survival of the American ideal of what it means to live in a pluralistic constitutional republic.[63]

Similarly, Charlie Sykes points to how the increasing organizational linkages between Never Trumpers and those to their left have created a respect for those outside his party that he had not experienced before.

> To be able to convene us together and then to have a respectful and intelligent dialogue about these issues with some folks from the center-left, I found incredibly valuable. I think it's created relationships that are going to have a lot of consequences. . . . For example, in about half an hour I'm going to do a podcast here at the Bulwark with Ian Bassin from Protect Democracy. Now, Ian's a leftie, but I think we have a lot of common ground on issues of the status of democratic institutions. I never would have had a discussion with him, or a relationship with him had it not been for these new organizational structures.[64]

The rise of Trump has led to a flowering of groups in the political center like Protect Democracy, Better Angels, David Brooks's Weave, and, more immediately political, the Niskanen Center's Meeting of the Concerned. For Never Trumpers like Sykes, the lesson of the Trump era is that partisanship itself was the core poison of American politics, and finding ways to short-circuit it is the most vital service Never Trumpers could provide.

Most Never Trumpers have not given up on conservatism, with some analogizing their situation to that of a remnant, a term that originated with Alfred Jay Nock (who was an early influence on William F. Buckley) and which has become the name of Jonah Goldberg's podcast. For some, like Sykes, this idea is inspiring: "I was actually talking to David French about this the other day. I asked him, 'Do you feel irrelevant?' And he gave this sort of eloquent little speech about what it's like being in the remnant, and sometimes a small group of people who pull back at moments when they are regarded as irrelevant can actually do incredibly important and consequential work, and that the value can't necessarily be determined by [what's happening] tomorrow."[65]

For others, however, the loss of a sense of partisan spirit has mainly been negative. Charles Murray, for instance, has experienced his separation from conservatism as both personally painful and as reinforcing a sense of depression at the state of the country.

> I feel as if in the latter part of my life I have been deserted by large numbers of people that I thought were my allies, and that I am stuck with a few friends like Jonah and some others, and it's not coming back. I see populism as being the dominant feature of conservative politics from now on. Painting with a very broad brush, I see America as a civilization in decline—not economically, not militarily, but as a system it's [just] another great power, we are . . . losing our exceptionalism, we have lost it, it's gone.[66]

Charen describes this as almost a loss of a kind of vital energy.

> I've discovered that when you are completely demoralized and don't really feel like you have a side any more, that is a very, very hard way to try to make a living as a writer. . . . Because that energy that you've got from being a partisan and being on a side is gone. Even if motivated reasoning is a bad thing in some instances, in other ways it can be good. It can be a spur to making you sharp and able to express yourself. . . . When my former people are now saying, "But, look, the left, they just shouted down somebody on a campus. Let's get excited about this," I'm thinking, "Yeah, they do that, and I'm against that. But it's not really what's bothering me right now. I'm just not there with you anymore. I used to be, but I'm not anymore." My friends sense it, and they don't like the drift and they worry that I'm being taken over by the left. It's not that I'm being taken over by the left, it's that I'm just disgusted with the right. And so it affected my life in a lot of ways and some of my dearest friends, some of the people that we socialized with the most, we haven't seen much of at all. Some not at all in the last couple of years. It's painful.[67]

Sykes analogizes the situation of Never Trumpers, cut off from their previous friends and allies in the conservative movement, to "the astronauts floating off from the capsule in space. We did feel like that for a while."[68] While some of the Never Trumpers have found new homes to shelter them, the sense of disconnection that many of them continue to feel is palpable.

For some Never Trumpers the fight against Trump has inspired them to resist surrendering the Republican Party to populist nationalist arrivistes. David Frum, for example, views partisanship of some sort as inevitable, and thus engagement with parties—in his case the Republicans—as unavoidable.

> Okay, so be an independent, sure. But as I learn from political scientists, it's like the joke about Northern Ireland. Are you a Catholic independent, or are you a Protestant independent? . . . You don't build center parties from the center out, you build center parties from one party in. So it may be that . . . the Democrats, a group over whom I have no influence . . . choose a path away from Bernie Sanders and Elizabeth Warren toward an Eisenhower-style party of the center. If that happens and the Republicans remain committed to Trump, I will find that attractive. But I can't make that happen.[69]

Moreover, for Frum, many of the reasons why he became a Republican in the first place still hold. Whatever else they are, parties are distributive coalitions. So long as Democrats are the coalition of the public sector's material self-interest, the Republicans are the only game in town for those who believe in the primacy of a basically free market economy and a thriving civil society. Frum illustrates the point:

> I was just in California last weekend, spent a lot of time there. California has this huge pension crisis at the state and at the local level. The question is what are you going to do about it? And one answer is you raise taxes to cover the pension, and another is you rewrite the pension deal. And I'm in group two. I'm not a liberal. I think if your pension obligations are unpayable, then you have to revisit those agreements, rather than load all the costs of adjustment on the taxpayer.[70]

Just as important, Frum has come to believe that, as Levitsky and Ziblatt argue, liberal democracy requires that both parties adhere to certain fundamental norms of political competition. While it might be comfortable for Never Trumpers to simply abandon the Republican Party for mobilization in the center, or even throw in their lot with the Democrats, that would produce a self-reinforcing cycle that would make the Republican Party even more dangerous than it has already become. "It does no good at all to have one political party out of two committed to democratic norms, and it is really important to stay inside the Republican Party and to continue to challenge it, because I think the drift to acceptance, especially at the state level, of ever more explicitly anti-democratic means of holding onto power [is] self-accelerating. And as the future that is implied by this tendency becomes more clear, you have to say, 'Look, I think it's really important to compete in these elections rather than manipulate these elections.'"[71] Quite simply, for Frum, "This has been my ideological political home for a long time. It's in trouble. That's where I'm needed."[72]

The idea of the conservative movement as "home" underscores the depth of sentiment involved in political commitments. People like Frum have a sense of that home being illegitimately occupied by a band of squatters—but they are not ready to abandon occupancy to Trump and his followers. At least not yet. Most Never Trumpers believe that the conservative movement needs to adapt to the concerns that Trump has surfaced, while cleansing itself of the populist demagoguery that their former allies have so willingly embraced. Few, however, have a clear vision of how the conservative movement can be stitched back together again and made a force for decent, liberal democratic governance. That may be a challenge that requires an electorally potent political movement that public intellectuals can hitch their ideas and policies to. That is something they can hope for, but which they have only a limited capacity to call into existence.

PART IV

Lawyers and Economists

8

In Scalia's Shadow

IN THE FALL OF 2018, an inside the Beltway fight broke out within the ranks of conservative lawyers—professionals who are more accustomed to training their guns on their adversaries on the left than their own ideological allies. The creation of Checks and Balances, a new group of conservative legal critics of the Trump administration, led the Federalist Society Vice President Leonard Leo to declare, "I find the underlying premise of the group rather offensive. . . . The idea that somehow they need to have this voice because conservatives are somehow afraid to talk about the rule of law during the Trump administration. And my response to that is, no, people aren't afraid, many people just don't agree that there's a constitutional crisis and don't agree with the people who have signed up with this group." The former Acting Attorney General and Federalist Society co-founder Peter Keisler struck back, arguing that, "We do think the words of a president matter. When a president demands that the Justice Department investigate his political opponents and protect himself and his political allies, those words undermine confidence in the fairness of our criminal justice system and convey to the country a corrupt set of values and priorities." Tellingly, however, even George Conway, the acerbic Trump critic and founder of Checks and Balances, who had once been considered for a number of senior administration positions, acknowledged that, "We love the judges. . . . [The administration]deserves a tremendous amount of credit for that. I'll be the first to clap my hands for it."[1]

From the moment he came down the Trump Tower escalator in June 2015 Donald Trump offered a cornucopia of reasons for conservative lawyers to mistrust him. From his racist attack on the federal district judge ruling on the Trump University case and suspicions that he would appoint his own sister to the Supreme Court, to his threats to revise libel law so as to silence his rivals, and his nearly total ignorance of the constitution, Trump was almost no prominent conservative lawyer's first choice.

Once he dispatched all his Republican rivals (including Ted Cruz, who had been a prominent member of the conservative legal movement as solicitor general of Texas), however, conservative lawyers were in a quandary. The death of Antonin Scalia, the most celebrated conservative jurist of his generation and a leader of the conservative legal movement, put the future of the Supreme Court squarely on the ballot. And in a poetic irony, the alternative to Trump was Hillary Clinton, with whom many conservative lawyers had been locked in battle for decades and who represented much of what they hated about liberalism. Even those with considerable reservations were pushed into grudging silence by Trump's announcement of a list of potential Supreme Court nominees chosen by prominent conservatives at the Heritage Foundation and Federalist Society. Trump was seemingly offering to formally subcontract the choice of federal judges to the conservative legal movement, expanding their jurisdiction even as he was openly challenging that of conservative economists and national security experts.

Even so, a relatively small number of conservative lawyers, mainly academics, produced an "Originalists Against Trump" letter, while a small group of former Justice Department officials (mostly not in recent administrations) generated a relatively obscure letter of their own. Once the character of Trump's governance became clear, Checks and Balances emerged to criticize the administration's legal conduct. Overall, however, the participation of conservative lawyers in the administration, and the cooperation of conservative legal organizations with it, has far outstripped that of right-of-center economists or national security professionals. The relatively few conservative lawyers who have publicly criticized Trump and his administration are the outliers. What motivated this small band of conservative legal critics to row against this very powerful tide, even as the victories of the conservative legal movement in the courts seemed to be mounting?

Kissing the Lawyers' Ring

Lawyers have an effective monopoly over nominees to the federal bench, the Department of Justice, and the White House Counsel's office, and they serve in a range of appointed positions across the federal bureaucracy. Beyond just staffing the executive branch and the courts, conservative lawyers play an especially important role in the Republican Party. They provide a powerful constitutional language for Republican Party politics, one that reverberates even beyond the narrow world of the courts.[2] Ideas that have played a central role in Republican governance, like originalism and the critique of the "administrative state," have come from lawyers associated with the Federalist Society. The Society, with its hundreds of law student and lawyer chapters, provides a powerful network for connecting legal professionals to each other, deepening their knowledge of conservative legal ideas and linking them to positions in the executive and judicial branches.[3] Through the Society, conservative lawyers have a capacity for collective action far greater than any other expert community on the right, making them a source of both fear and envy among their counterparts on the left. When not in control of the executive branch, this capacity has helped them coordinate a range of challenges to Democratic governance, including litigation on environmental regulation, the Affordable Care Act, abortion, and religious freedom.

The influence of the conservative legal movement is particularly significant in the area of judicial selection, where they have attained a professional jurisdiction that has eclipsed the once-prominent place of Republican elected officials. The conservative lawyers who did openly criticize Trump all agree that the most important reason their colleagues chose to stay on the sidelines was the prospect of a transformed judiciary. John Yoo, the Berkeley law professor who still gets accused of being a war criminal by those on the left for his willingness to provide legal justifications for the War on Terror in the Bush administration's Justice Department, was firmly critical of Trump in 2016 (and when we interviewed him in 2017), although he reversed course later. He recalls that Trump was willing to make a direct commitment to conservative lawyers and to defer to their organizations, something he did not do for other professional groups. "I kind of saw it as a deal. He knew he needed to get all these conservatives on board. He knew at that crucial point a lot of conservative legal people were not on his side. What more could you have done, and more prominent signal that you were going to be reliable, [than to] not just put out the names, but say the Federalist Society did it. . . . I've never seen that in judicial appointment politics before."[4] Adam White, who was at the Hoover Institution and would soon move to George Mason Law School, had written a number of very biting pieces about Donald Trump in *The Weekly Standard*, among other places. He recalls that it was the announcement of the list of potential justices, in the context of the highly symbolic Scalia seat, that pushed conservative lawyers toward, at least, quiescence in the face of Trump.

> Scalia dies in the middle of the primary season, and then suddenly the stakes for lawyers who care about the Supreme Court and the Constitution is huge. And candidate Trump issues this list of judges. I think that was enough to make conservative lawyers think, "even if I don't like him, even if I profoundly dislike him, this election is uniquely important because of the Supreme Court and I'm not going to get in the way of this." It was such an innovation, it froze conservative lawyers in their tracks. And that gave them something concrete to point to and say, "He's not just saying he'll appoint good judges who don't legislate from the bench, he's actually giving us names."[5]

Yoo recalls that before this, "Trump had this reputation for not keeping his word and changing positions all the time," but as White argues, the list functioned as "a good reassurance, that one part of the administration is going to be normal as we understand it."[6] The removal of this uncertainty as to Trump's reliability allowed a number of Republicans to swallow what were genuine, serious reservations. As Yoo recalls, "I had a number of friends—conservative Federalist Society members of long standing—who are very traditional morally and in terms of personal conduct, and worried about the decline of values . . . who would normally be utterly turned off by a guy like Trump, and [who] said only because of [the] appointment to Justice Scalia's vacancy I'm going to support [him]."[7]

It was precisely because Trump recognized how important his relationship was with conservative lawyers, as compared to other professional groups, that he was willing to bend over backward to publicly defer to them. Yoo argues that this is a classic example of practical game theory. "I'm going to do something expensive as a signal for you to trust me. . . . In all those other areas he's like, 'I'm making the decision, no one's gonna advise me, no one controls me.' But on judges, he did the exact opposite."[8] A number of Trump-critical lawyers make the point that Trump has, in fact, exceeded their expectations where judicial selection is concerned. Marisa Maleck, a former clerk for Justice Clarence Thomas, argues that, "I didn't want to be complicit in this presidency. Despite that, I think he's doing amazing things with the judiciary. I think he's much better than Bush on the judiciary because he's listening to the right people."[9] Will Baude, a professor of law at the University of Chicago and former clerk to Chief Justice John Roberts, also recalls that, "I wasn't sure he was in fact going to pick the judges [on the list]. I've been pleasantly surprised on that front."[10] Trump made a contract with the network of conservative lawyers, one that was narrowly focused on judicial selection, and he has more than kept his side of the bargain.

A Marriage of Convenience

Facilitating a transactional relationship to the Trump administration reflected the very different professional character of lawyers, as opposed in particular to those in national security. As we saw in Chapters 2 and 3, the kinds of people who conduct diplomatic, intelligence, or military jobs in Republican administrations take the character of their boss to be a matter of the utmost seriousness. They come from a professional culture that is far more hierarchical than that of lawyers, whose dominant professional mode is client-serving. Jeremy Rabkin, who for decades taught public law at Cornell University and is now at George Mason Law School, thinks this derives from the differing responsibility that lawyers and national security professionals have for the actions of government.

If you're a foreign policy specialist . . . if you're in an administration with a lot of bad policies or any policies that end up badly, you're really tarred by that. . . . [That] is not actually true for most lawyer jobs in the federal government. . . . Whatever people might say about the . . . Nixon Justice Department, except for the very top people it didn't taint them. I mean, they went on to something else because it's what it is to be a lawyer, that you defend a client that you have. And if your client is the tax division in the Nixon Justice Department, well, then you do that.[11]

Adam White also believes this client-serving ethos explains the willingness of legal conservatives to serve the Trump administration. "Lawyers are uniquely well-suited and uniquely comfortable with working on behalf of people who they dislike or whom they know to be profoundly flawed or even sometimes bad people. . . . Lawyers can stake out positions on behalf of their clients that are separated from the problems of those clients, whether we're talking about criminal defense attorneys or lawyers who represent corporations. There's always, inherent in the work of a lawyer, this gap between him and the client, and also this bond between him and the client."[12]

Just as some conservative lawyers could justify working for a president they disrespected because they could analogize him to a client, some conservative lawyers found it difficult to openly oppose him because of the pressures associated with having actual clients in their firms. Jonathan Adler, a libertarian law professor at Case Western Reserve Law School who was actively involved in the legal challenges to Obamacare, found in organizing legal critics of Trump around Checks and Balances that, "Taking certain sorts of controversial stands is something that can have consequences for firms. . . . It's one thing if some firm has its stable of former people that were in one administration or another, but going beyond that can be perceived as sticking your neck out in a way that certain firms and certain employers don't like their lawyers to do. . . . I know that there are some people who, either because of funders or clients, didn't feel they could publicly associate themselves with the group."[13] Even some law professors found that their role as teachers constrained how comfortable they were in joining an active opposition to the Trump administration. White believes that, "My role as a scholar at Hoover and a professor here at the law school really counsels against [participating in] any kind of political movement. Here at the law school, I teach students and I want to be a credible teacher to students, so that requires a certain amount of detachment from organized political movements. I think I'm a better teacher when, even if I'm writing on these issues, I'm not seen as an arm of a political movement."[14]

Finally, conservative legal critics of Trump thought that relatively few of their colleagues joined them because the alternative was equally grim or even worse. Yoo notes that during the election, the prospect of a President Hillary Clinton was simply indigestible, even for many lawyers who had strong reactions to Trump. "They've been fighting her for decades. . . . [Something] a lot of conservative law people would say that may be less prominent than the average conservative is, 'I don't care who are our nominees, I'm never voting for Hillary.' . . . A lot of these people are veterans of Whitewater, or they've seen Hillary's hand in judicial appointments. . . . Trump could've been anybody, but if it's Hillary as the Democratic candidate, you're still gonna have a lot of conservative law people who [have] prolonged scars from fighting with her in the past."[15] Others emphasized the idea that, independent of her personal qualities, a Hillary Clinton presidency would be hard for legal conservatives to stomach. Peter Keisler, a prominent Trump critic, thinks that what Clinton represented to conservative lawyers, as compared to national security professionals, played a large role.

> To the extent you accept the critique . . . that the administration is outside a rule-of-law consensus . . . you would think that lawyers in particular would flock to that kind of thing, would particularly want to express it. These are ideas they kind of care about and know and focus on. But it was really a striking comparison that the national security community was coming out in force and the legal community was absolutely not. And I've thought since then that that was probably a reflection of the fact that . . . there wasn't the partisan divide on national security policy issues that there is on legal policy issues. And Hillary Clinton was actually, from a foreign policy, national security perspective, considered very centrist and mainstream

by people in that area. That wasn't, obviously, the view on the legal policy side where these divides are much sharper and the gulf between the parties is so much broader. . . . So you're giving up more if you jump ship and oppose your side's guy and give support to the other side.[16]

In addition, opposition to Trump among Republican lawyers was partially a function of how disturbed they were by the prospect of being governed by the kinds of people who would be appointed in a Hillary Clinton administration. Orin Kerr, a law professor at Berkeley, contributor to the libertarian-leaning blog The Volokh Conspiracy, and an advisor to Senator John Cornyn on past Supreme Court nominations, observed that his aggressive opposition to Trump was connected to the fact that in his areas of expertise, such as cybersecurity, the ideological differences separating Republicans and Democrats are not as deep as they are in other areas of the law. That, combined with his relative moderation, has allowed his institutional preferences to dominate:

> It matters . . . that the Obama staffers, in a lot of areas—not only areas that I work in, but in the legal sphere—were for the most part pretty mainstream technocratic types. And an example might be the nomination of Merrick Garland, who is as centrist a person as you could find. We're not talking about crazy radicals on the Democratic side, and so I just couldn't see it as that much of a [difference]. . . . If Jeb Bush was a candidate, I would have voted for Jeb Bush and would have never imagined voting for Hillary. But I wasn't in a position to see the Democratic side as this sort of existential threat or something sort of crazy out there. [It was] sort of the 45-yard line one way versus the other.[17]

Lawyers with other priorities, especially those who were focused on social issues like abortion and religious liberty, thought that a Clinton presidency would be quite far from the 45-yard line, which explains why they were scarcer among the most engaged Never Trumpers.

Not in Our Name

The most important act of collective action by Never Trump lawyers during the campaign was a letter organized by two right-of-center law professors who had clerked for Chief Justice Roberts: Will Baude of the University of Chicago and Stephen Sachs of Duke University. The letter, which had 62 signatories, including many of the most prominent conservative law professors in the country, was published in October 2016. Sachs recalls that he had been mulling the idea of some sort of statement, but was hesitant:

> both for reasons of time and because it didn't seem worth sticking my neck out. As the summer went on, though, it seemed to me that too many people were already staying quiet and were keeping their serious objections too close to the vest. . . . I wrote to Will at the end of September with potential language for a statement, and we spent a little while deciding what to do. For me, at least, the delay was less about hoping that someone else would say it first, and more about getting up the gumption to oppose one's own party's nominee. Eventually we decided to go ahead and began drawing up a list of potential signatories. As it happened, the *Access Hollywood* video was released shortly before the emails went out. While not quite on the same topic, I imagine it made some people's choice to sign a little easier.[18]

The letter was not framed as "Republicans" or "conservatives" against Trump, but "originalists," a school of legal thought closely associated with the late Justice Scalia (as well as the late Judge Robert Bork). While the exact meaning of the concept has been the subject of innumerable academic conferences and law review articles, its most widely accepted claim is that judges should interpret the law according to the original public meaning at the time of its enactment.[19] The purpose of the letter, according to Sachs, was as much about inoculating the honor of originalism from Donald Trump as anything else.

> To me, the letter was a way of saying "not in our name" as originalists. In my circle, the single most prominent argument for Trump was

that he, unlike Clinton, would appoint originalist judges and would respect the Constitution in office. That seemed wrong to me. In addition to every other reason to vote against him, what he said and did on the campaign trail showed no firm commitment to the Constitution, originalism, or the rule of law more generally. Clinton would have surely been bad from an originalist standpoint, but Trump ran an unacceptable risk of being truly disastrous and may yet [be]. We were being asked to pay far too high a price for judges, with no guarantee that we'd even get the judges.[20]

Baude argues that, "The letter came from 'originalists' because that's how we really identify ourselves, me especially. I'm actually not even a Republican, although I often vote for Republicans. And I think we were especially concerned about this argument that if you care about preserving the Constitution then you need to vote for Trump in order to fill the seat with an originalist."[21]

While we do not have data on the number of signatories as opposed to rejections on the Originalists Against Trump letter, it does appear that there were more rejections than was the case with the national security letter. Sachs recalls that those choosing not to sign had varied reasons.

We did have a fair number of rejections, which were very polite, though they rarely expressed their reasons. Of those who did, some disagreed with us about what Trump would likely do in office, some objected to Trump for policy reasons unrelated to the joint statement, some were conservatives who chose not to identify as originalists, etc. In any case, I didn't find the number of signatures surprising. A Republican president might help realize decades of aspirations of the originalist movement, which Clinton would undoubtedly set back. And those who signed were taking a fair deal of professional risk by doing so.[22]

No one stepped up to generate a letter earlier, and so many lawyers declined to sign, largely because these conservative lawyers could never have imagined themselves, before 2016, doing anything other than supporting, advising, and working for a Republican administration.

Marisa Maleck recalls that, "If someone told me I wasn't going to vote for the Republican candidate for president a year ago, I would have laughed in your face. There's just no way in hell."[23]

There is no evidence that the organizers of, or signatories to, the letter expected it to have a significant impact electorally, but like a number of national security conservatives (and unlike most economists we spoke with), they thought it was important to take a stand against Trump. According to Baude, "It seemed important to try something. And I guess I did think it was important just as a matter of almost intellectual integrity to make clear that originalism isn't a purely partisan movement."[24] Regardless of its impact on the world beyond the academy, the letter served the function of providing a kind of firewall between originalism and Trump, which, given the toxicity of Trump in the academy, was especially vital for the many conservative professors who signed it. Originalism had carved out a kind of legitimacy in the modern legal academy to the point where its supporters could get jobs at elite law schools, and their ideas were taken seriously by their liberal counterparts.[25]

Those who chose to sign the letter emphasized that while they thought putting Republicans on the bench was important, they also believed that there were even more important challenges to the American constitutional system raised by the prospect of a Donald Trump presidency. Baude recalls that while conservative lawyers were focused on the Court, especially because of the open Scalia seat, they were "not paying as much attention to all the other ways the president influences the law. And I think that ultimately was what motivated us to speak up, is that there was more than the [Scalia] seat at issue."[26] This was reflected in the letter's claim that, "We do not trust him to respect constitutional limits in the rest of his conduct in office, of which judicial nominations are only one part."[27]

The priority that they placed on the rule of law beyond the courts, what might be called constitutional culture, is a significant factor distinguishing Trump's conservative legal critics from those who, often through gritted teeth, went along with the administration because of its impact on the judiciary. Baude, for instance, focuses on "the idea of having a president who cares about following the law and the separation of powers, the idea that individual rights like free speech and due process are things to be celebrated not to be condemned at rallies. . . . The basic idea that government officials, not [just] judges, are supposed to care about the constitutionality of a law and want to uphold it, or at least follow it most of the time."[28] A similar instinct can be found in a much less prominent letter by previous Republican legal appointees, which emphasized the long-term impact of Trump on the legal culture of the United States. "We have no reason to believe that Donald Trump understands or would act prudently to advance and preserve the hard-won system of legal rules and evenhanded law enforcement that make this country the envy of the world. To the contrary, his every word seems calculated to create an atmosphere of arbitrariness and unpredictability much better suited to an authoritarian regime."[29]

Other Trump critics in the conservative legal movement were motivated as much by a more diffuse sense that Trump represented a dangerous trend in American life and a turn in conservatism away from what they thought it represented. Rabkin worries that Trump was bringing out in American culture elements that he previously thought were mostly alien.

> Since college I've had this awareness of Europe as kind of sick. . . . They like really dark currents there. America, whatever anyone says about politics, it's basically really a good country. It's solid because people are calm. And now you really have this sense [that] you just don't know where this is going. I do not think in any way that Trump is racist, I don't even think his followers are racist. I don't think they're anti-Semitic. I'm not going there at all. But there is a kind of petulance, this kind of rancor, this kind of [attitude of] fuck all of you. . . . And I'm very aware that I'm reacting to comments that are posted online and those are not representative of anything. But there just seems to be this undercurrent of real resentment, real troubling polarization. I mean Trump is a symptom of a country in turmoil.[30]

Adam White also sees Trump through the prism of larger, darker forces in American politics, which Trump both reflects and potentially encourages. "A few months ago, the Federalist Society brought me to Oklahoma and Kansas to speak to some chapters. And while I was driving around, I got to visit the Oklahoma City memorial. It's astonishing how quickly we've forgotten that. That somebody believed there was a deep state and he backed up a truck to the building and blew it up."[31] However, many other conservatives consider Trump's rhetoric to be annoying but not fundamentally important. For example, Leonard Leo has dismissed Never Trump lawyers, arguing that, "I measure a president's sensitivity to the rule of law by his actions, not his off-the-cuff comments, tweets or statements."[32] One of the features that sets the critics of Trump apart among conservative lawyers is their inability to shake off the suspicion that his language was helping to authorize darker sentiments in the body politic, with consequences far beyond his term in office.

A surprising number of those who signed the Originalists Against Trump letter described their motivation as some combination of self-sabotage and self-binding. For instance, Maleck recalls that:

The reason I signed that letter was because when I go to a party and I know I'm going to drink, I'm not driving. I leave the keys at the door or I take the Metro. This is leaving the keys at the door. I knew that if I did not sign this letter, someone was going to approach me from the White House, ask me to go in and do something that I wasn't going to be able to say no to. Which in fact, has happened. People have asked me to work on judicial selection, which would be my absolute dream job. As soon as they found out I [signed] that letter, they were like, "This conversation is over."[33]

Baude recalls that he had a very similar motivation:

It was also I think a matter of just putting my own cards out there. Maybe the opposite of virtue signaling. There are a lot of people who were going to be tapped to be part of the Trump administration, if there was a Trump administration, and I wanted to make clear beforehand where I stood, and if that had the consequence of cutting opportunities for myself, that was a plus not a minus. If there was a future administration that decided they didn't care about the letter, obviously that wouldn't necessarily bind you. But it was binding you from sucking up later. . . . I think everybody needs that. I think law professors especially. I think it's very easy to be corrupted by power or the possibility of power.[34]

Finally, Adam White expressed almost the exact same sentiment. "I had laid down a marker. I knew I would not work in this administration. Sometimes I think that I was vocal in order to remove myself from the possibility of government service."[35] The powerful network of conservative lawyers brings potential appointees to the attention of a Republican administration and creates strong expectations of working in a common cause. Precisely because the pull of working with their movement allies is so strong, these lawyers needed a profound self-binding mechanism to commit themselves to sticking to their guns.

The decision to stand back when so many of their friends and colleagues were making their peace with Trump was, in effect, a choice to preserve a "remnant" of what they considered real conservatism (a choice that might have seemed less daunting when it still seemed unlikely that Trump would win). As Maleck argues:

> I do feel a deep obligation to young women conservatives I have mentored and my other mentees who are male, too, to say, "You don't have to think that way." There are other people who feel like this is distasteful. . . . I felt an obligation to be a person who is on that alternative path. . . . I'm willing to sort of put myself out there in a way where I don't care if I don't get an administration job. . . . Yes absolutely I want to become a judge. . . . To some extent that still is my goal, but I'm not going to pretend to have views that I don't hold to get there.[36]

Maleck chose quite consciously to go against the grain of the rest of the movement that, from working for the Federalist Society before going to law school and all the way through clerking for Justice Thomas, had groomed her and shaped her professional development. The strong network ties created by the conservative legal movement thus created significant pressure, even when unspoken, to not push too hard on opposition to the Trump campaign and subsequent administration.[37] "The downside or the dark side maybe of the mentoring and unity of the conservative movement is a sense that you don't want to go against the president. You don't. We're working on something together here."[38]

The Semi-Organized Resistance

Curiously, despite the fact that conservative lawyers as a whole have had a more durable cooperative relationship with the administration than most other right-of-center professional networks, the greatest effort to create an organizational presence for critics of Trump has been among elite lawyers. Checks and Balances began as the brainchild of George Conway, a prominent corporate litigator, and quickly included a number of high-level appointees from previous Republican administrations. Conway had once been on Paula Jones's legal team, making him an honorary member of the "vast right-wing conspiracy," but he declined to join the administration because he concluded it was "like a shitshow in a dumpster fire."[39] Conway had made a name for himself for his acerbic tweets and op-eds at the expense of the president, which were especially newsworthy because his wife, Kellyanne Conway, has been one of Trump's most prominent defenders. Lori Meyer (a private lawyer and wife of the president of the Federalist Society, Eugene Meyer) recalls talking to Conway in the summer of 2018: "He basically went on a 45-minute diatribe about how he was really alone and the reason he was sending out all these tweets was because he didn't feel like he had other people that he could sympathize with."[40] Conway's sense of isolation and frustration was a common experience. As one conservative lawyer recalls, "I was so frustrated at that point because I'd spent so much time watching CNN and screaming at it. . . . I was like, anything is better than the amount of time I'm spending screaming at the TV."[41]

By the summer of 2018, Conway began calling around to other senior Republican lawyers who had signaled that they were critical of the president's conduct, and early in the fall the first organizational lunch of what became Checks and Balances was convened. It included Peter Keisler, Paul Rosensweig (former Deputy Assistant Secretary of Homeland Security), Carrie Cordero (among other positions, Counsel to the Assistant Attorney General for National Security), Marisa Maleck, Lori Meyer, Orin Kerr, and Jonathan Adler. One participant recalls that the idea was to:

Get some lawyers together and have a formal resistance group, sort of a Republican Party in exile and be set to come in when this administration finally implodes. We're putting our hopes in Ben Sasse and Mike Lee and other sensible Republicans that eventually there'll be a preference cascade, and enough of them will defect that there'll be an impeachment and have the people ready to go to serve as impeachment council and be this untainted vanguard to say, "No, look, there are principled Republicans out there, there are principled conservatives who believe in separation of powers and rule of law."[42]

Jon Adler recalls that a conservative anti-Trump lawyer put up a notice on Facebook in the summer of 2018, "saying if you're a conservative lawyer that would like to be in a position to lend your expertise to efforts . . . [in case] there are impeachment hearings, and there are Republicans that want to take the process seriously. You might need legal support, legal help. If that's something you might be interested in, let me know. The status was up on Facebook for like a day, and I said I would be happy to . . . be involved in that."[43]

In the summer of 2018 the idea that Special Counsel Robert Mueller's report could, in fact, bring down the administration or lead to impeachment was not at all outlandish, so putting together an organization of conservative lawyers publicly opposed to Trump, who could potentially contribute to a congressional investigation and trial, was a significant move in and of itself. This was similar to the motivation of many Never Trumpers during the campaign, who expected Trump to fail spectacularly, after which they could form a "clean team" of principled conservatives who weren't compromised by their relationship with him. But, at least in the short term, this aspiration for the organization never bore fruit.

From the start, there was significant reticence within the group at the prospect of being the legal activist auxiliary of Never Trump. Instead, the organization settled on two functions fairly early on—networking and preserving the idea that legal conservatism was distinct from the actions of the Trump administration. Checks and Balances was created so that Republican lawyers disturbed by the conduct of the administration could identify each other in a world where it was easy to believe that everyone in the conservative legal movement was on board with

Trump, and to make collective action outside the organization's aegis easier to engage in. Peter Keisler, who was one of the founders of the Federalist Society, recalls that it was one of the models that Checks and Balances drew on when they thought of the potential role for the organization. Keisler argues, "The Federalist Society doesn't take positions, but obviously it's a nucleus of people who do a lot of things and come together under its umbrella in part just to find each other. And so you can think of Checks and Balances a little bit like that."[44] Another participant in Checks and Balances also recalls the impact of the Federalist Society analogy. "I approached my network of friends, and George [Conway] approached his network of friends, and ultimately we decided, well, let's just have a smaller group to start with and then use that as a proto-Federalist Society where it doesn't itself take any positions, but people are there to network and come up with ideas on what it is they can do." Most of the members of Checks and Balances held the Society in high regard and continued to be active members, despite the close work of people like Leonard Leo with the Trump administration. Thus, the Society's model was available and appropriate for the participants in the organization, and it also helped to bridge the different sensitivities the members had. For Keisler, the core role of Checks and Balances was to facilitate the work of lawyers critical of the Trump administration, but not to actually conduct that work.

To the extent there were lawyers who were really concerned and troubled by the administration, and in particular by its posture on what I call rule-of-law issues, I certainly felt it would be valuable to have a place, in an organizational sense, where we could get together and share ideas, and to the extent individuals were so moved, work together on individual projects. It wasn't going to be necessary that the organization as an organization take a whole lot of positions on a lot of issues. It was more important that [we] create a space in which people who were interested in these things could collaborate as they saw fit. . . . And if you think about what's happened since then, there's a fair amount of that that's going on. And so, for example, one of our number is leading one of the cases against the president's emergency declaration on the wall. Others of us have done various writing or speaking or amicus briefs or things like that. Most of that, by far, has not been in the name of Checks and Balances, but a fair amount of it has.[45]

The second function that members of Checks and Balances hoped the organization could perform was to prevent the brand of the conservative legal movement—and to some degree the larger conservative movement—from being entirely captured and corrupted by Trump. Orin Kerr recalls that he thought that the role of Checks and Balances was, in part, to conserve conservatism during a period in which its traditional ideological principles were being forgotten. He sought to:

> Have it be known that there are people that are disagreeing with the direction of the Trump administration and have all these concerns . . . give people an opportunity to express their views. . . . Remind conservative lawyers of how conservative lawyers would normally think through these questions. And the conservative values— like the rule of law, like separation of powers, like the importance of judicial review—[values] that conservative lawyers were very outspoken about in the past, bringing them back into the fore. And then let people decide whether they think that ultimately leaves them in a pro-Trump or anti-Trump position . . . . And also let law students who may be conservative, but against Trump, know that that's okay, that a lot of people feel that way.[46]

Likewise, Keisler expressed the purpose of Checks and Balances as reminding conservatives that their principles were distinct from the actions of the Trump administration.

> There are certain ideas and propositions that are so basic that no one ever used to think they needed defending, because they were generally accepted—things like honesty in government and the need not to politicize the criminal–law enforcement function, and things like that. And not only have we gotten to a place where they actually do need public defending, but they've become partisan in the way they're perceived such that it seems like on the Republican side, there's near uniform support for what the president is doing. And, paradoxically, in order to communicate that these need to be

nonpartisan values and they need to transcend some of the policy debates that we're always going to have . . . it becomes important to have a group that's identified, in some sense in a partisan way— "We're Republicans" or "We're conservatives and libertarians" or "We're right-of-center" or whatever you want to call it—that says, "No, we too think that it's important not to use the criminal justice system to punish your enemies and protect your friends. And that's not a Republican–Democratic issue." . . . And so partly the agenda was to make clear that there was this view within at least some segments of that side of the spectrum and that political party so that others who might feel that way, but might feel reluctant to speak out or wonder if they were alone, could feel more emboldened.[47]

Jon Adler similarly says that "the signaling effect of a group of people saying we all agree with this would be more significant than all of us doing our things independently."[48] Because of the prestige and unambiguous conservative credibility that people like Conway and Keisler brought to the group, it was hoped that the organization could help arrest the sense that conservatism and Trumpism had to go together.

Despite these high hopes, however, many involved in Checks and Balances were disappointed by how little it had actually done in its first year of existence. One participant observed:

What's concerning me is that it was [like the *South Park* episode]: Step One, underpants; Step Three, profit. And nobody could explain to me what Step Two was. What is it that this group is going to do that's actually going to make a difference? And when I saw that all the group wanted to do was issue tweets and the occasional press statements, and didn't actually have any sort of viable strategy for changing things, [I became frustrated]. . . . I wanted to be actually doing something, taking on Trump from the right, and the only thing the group really wanted to be doing was to occasionally lob a "me too" statement when the left was taking on Trump. I hate to use the word "virtue signaling" because that's gotten so broad as to mean nothing, but I didn't see that it would make a difference for me to be on there.[49]

Checks and Balances had relatively limited impact because one theory of the organization's purpose—to be a clean team in the case of administration implosion—never became activated. But equally important was the fact that no alternative set of objectives beyond networking and solace ever emerged. As one lawyer involved notes:

> I made a suggestion that maybe we can help whistleblowers, maybe we come out and try to find whoever wrote the "lodestar editorial"[50] and . . . nobody wanted to do anything other than write an op-ed. And I don't know whether it was a collective action problem or just nobody was tasked with the responsibility. So it was a question of a preference cascade, and somebody needed to be the primary mover. And since nobody was the primary mover, nobody became the second person to help and nobody became third person to help. And just the preference cascade never happened.[51]

Connected to this, one lawyer in the group suggests that part of the explanation has to do with the kinds of people that lawyers are and the skills they bring: "Lawyers aren't naturally good organizers. That's why you see in law firms, some people turn out to be really terrific managers, but it's not a skill that everybody has, and similarly with this political organizing thing."[52] A wide range of the participants in Checks and Balances believe that the organization's problems have less to do with the motivations and skills of the participants, and more with the resources they have been able to mobilize for collective action. One lawyer recalls:

> If you want something more, in which you are having big events, having a lot more press attention . . . mobilizing large numbers of people . . . the difficulty is that if you think about the people who are part of this, we all have other jobs and we're all kind of interested in helping and contributing, but . . . to do something like that, you'd probably have needed somebody who was a full-time staffer . . . because it takes a lot of time . . . [to] take a bunch of people who come to a cocktail party, get all the names, get back in touch with them, organize chapters, kind of arrange, do the kind of thing that the Federalist Society, for example, did when it was first starting. . . . So

instead, you have this group of people who are very busy doing a lot of things, care a lot about this, but aren't quite at a stage in their careers where they're going to be doing the kind of intensive work that is required to really build . . . a broad-based membership organization, or [one] that as an organization has a very large public profile. . . . And a bunch of partners at law firms or academics affiliated with important institutions who have teaching and writing responsibilities aren't, at their heart, spending all of their day organizing events and things like that. And so to some extent, I think the organization is what it is, and isn't what it isn't, just in part because of the nature of the people involved in the structure.[53]

In the same vein, John Bellinger argues that it was challenging for Checks and Balances to move beyond its relatively modest public role without resources and full-time staff.

Why has it been sort of underwhelming? . . . Every one of us is extraordinarily busy with full-time legal practices and other things, and it's just been hard for people to put in the amount of hours to organize events, write statements. There's no staff to do this, and so, on a sort of a week-to-week basis, one person has got to take the initiative and say, "Okay, we want to say something about the Mueller Report today. I'm doing a draft. Will people have a look at it?" . . . You need a leader or one or more leaders who will really push, push, push, push, push, and then you've got to have people who will be able to have enough time. I think our group certainly has the passion. . . . But there just have not been enough other people who have been willing to do that.[54]

Although at least one prominent foundation on the center-left was prepared to help support Checks and Balances in building out the organization,[55] a number of participants were not particularly comfortable with that. Jon Adler recalls:

To do more, we need things like funding and staff. We all have pretty active day jobs, and we're in the process of putting that stuff together, and we want to be very cautious because there are folks that want to come after us as some kind of [progressive funder George] Soros front because of the Bill Kristol efforts, Republicans for the Rule of Law, something like that. And these allegations of where funding for some of those things comes from . . . . We're really worried about making sure we get money from places that aren't going to allow anyone to tar us, and we are hoping to do some things in the [future] that will serve the purpose of raising these issues within a conservative framework.[56]

But as of this writing, there have not been any explicitly conservative sources of funding that have been willing to support the organization.

The organization may do more in the future, and there are certainly members who have hopes that it will. Yet it has fallen short of the aspirations of some that it would be a "formal resistance group." Given how cross-pressured many conservative lawyers are, perhaps the greater surprise is—in sharp distinction with the economists we will encounter in the next chapter—that any lawyers' organization has formed at all.

Some Things Are More Important Than Judges

Even the most outspoken leaders of Never Trump have been at pains to say that they enthusiastically approve of Trump's selection of judges, something they describe as an example of behaving like a normal Republican administration. Ed Whelan, the president of the Ethics and Public Policy Center and a harsh critic of Trump during the campaign, observes that, "I've made the judgment to do what I can to help the administration make good judicial appointments. I'm going to try not to do anything that seriously impairs my ability to contribute there."[57] Jon Adler reflects the general attitude of Trump-critical conservative lawyers who view supporting the administration's judicial picks as part of protecting constitutional norms.

I think that they are the sort of people who actually are going to be part of a bulwark against some of the things the administration might try and do. . . . I do genuinely think the vast majority of the appellate nominees have been the sort of people that I've always wanted to see get nominated to federal courts, and one of the reasons why

I've been supportive of that while being against Trump is because I think it's good for the country to have good judges, and it's better to have good judges confirmed than to have seats left open, and I also never supported the obstruction of Democratic nominees, so I've always felt that if any president nominates somebody qualified, the presumption should be that that person should be confirmed.[58]

Many legal conservatives, both during the election and afterward, found themselves in a state of profound internal conflict. They thought Trump's conduct was deeply damaging to constitutional norms, but they believed that Democratic control of the Supreme Court would be quite threatening as well. Even more than economists, their enthusiasm for the administration's judicial selections has rendered Trump-critical lawyers—in sharp contrast to national security conservatives— profoundly cross-pressured.

Most of the participants in Checks and Balances are active members of the Federalist Society, the kinds of people who would have served in a normal Republican administration, some in very high positions. Many of them had not been strangers to hard-edged partisan combat. Adler, for instance, had been one of the most aggressive lawyers challenging the constitutionality of the Affordable Care Act; Conway had helped represent Paula Jones; others served as clerks for the most conservative members of the Supreme Court. Peter Keisler helped found the Federalist Society, and served in senior positions—including Acting Attorney General—throughout the Bush administration, when the Justice Department was at the center of highly partisan conflict. While there are a few like Orin Kerr who think of themselves as relative moderates, most of these conservative lawyers are not particularly ideologically distinct from those who chose not to criticize the administration.

Although Svolik's theory, discussed in Chapter 1, that institutional fidelity is more likely to come from relative moderates, has a great deal of explanatory power in other areas, it reaches its limit in explaining the behavior of lawyers. That may be because the ideology of lawyers is, fundamentally, about institutions rather than about policy outcomes (although those are certainly important for many lawyers as well). Lawyers who opposed Trump regarded him as a kind of test for conservative lawyers, measuring how deeply they were actually committed to the idea of the autonomy of constitutional principle from politics.

While the signatories to the letters opposing Trump in the campaign might have been reassured by the possibility that Trump could not possibly win—so that their actions could be dismissed as cheap talk—those who joined Checks and Balances did so in the face of an administration that was delivering on fundamental conservative goals such as sweeping deregulation and changing the ideological direction of the courts. Many of these conservative lawyers believed that their collective efforts would be called upon—and soon—when the scale of the president's undermining of constitutional norms was revealed by the Mueller investigation. When the Mueller Report failed to lead to impeachment, they focused instead on what they thought was the movement's legal orthodoxy—and even its dignity—in times when it was in danger of being corrupted by the party's own president and his administration. Never Trump lawyers acted out of the constitutional conservatism they associated with the Federalist Society, rather than out of an absence of ideological fervor.

9

The Marginal Value of Economists

AT LEAST AS FAR back as the 1980s, the Republican Party has been joined at the hip to free-market economics and advised at the highest levels by conservative economists. Donald Trump directly challenged the core beliefs of conservative economists during the campaign, almost gleefully dismissing many of those beliefs and openly spurning their advice. In his inaugural address, Trump announced, "We must protect our borders from the ravages of other countries making our products, stealing our companies, and destroying our jobs. Protection will lead to great prosperity and strength."[1] Just as he attacked the belief of national security conservatives in international alliances, Trump challenged the core creed of the economics discipline which held that an expanded scale of markets—for goods, capital, and people—was essential to economic growth and human flourishing.

On an even deeper level, Trump's entire worldview clashed with that of modern economics, which, since its birth with Adam Smith, has promoted a vision of human interaction based on exchange for mutual advantage. Trump, by contrast, advanced a profoundly zero-sum worldview—perhaps rooted in his career in real estate—in which the good of some, be it nations or individuals, always comes at the expense of others. Trump had built a real estate empire on political deal-making and subsidies, and when he needed it he relied on outright government coercion in the form of eminent domain. In Trump's worldview, and in sharp contrast to the libertarian vision of conservative economists, the government is ever-present, so questions of its proper scope are less important than whose side it is on. Rather than envisioning a world in which economic interdependence makes all nations wealthier, Trump advanced a darker vision in which America was constantly exploited by other nations, a trend that he would counter by making "great deals" that put "America first." Trump also rejected the distinctly conservative economic belief in the virtue of fiscal restraint, advancing the idea that—again, just as in real estate—leverage would be as good for the nation as it was for his business.

Republican economists had every reason to fear Trump and what he was doing to the party, and they responded by keeping their distance. Whereas previous Republican candidates for president were able to generate endorsement letters signed by the country's most prominent conservative economists, the best Trump could muster was a letter that, while signed by economists, merely expressed concerns with Hillary Clinton (and lacked the names of the most prominent conservatives).[2] Since he became president, only a handful of high-status economists have gone to work for the administration, and a number of posts traditionally held by economists have been left unfilled. But unlike national security professionals, there has been little to no collective action by economists. What little they have done has been on an individual basis. Despite Trump's direct attack on their ideas and their jurisdiction in the Republican Party, why have economists largely absented themselves from battle with the president?

A Seat at the Table: Economists in the Modern State

The American economics profession has co-evolved with the modern administrative state. Unlike their counterparts in France, whose pinnacle has been the elite civil service, the highest status location of American economics has been in the academy.[3] The relatively weak American civil service is split into a low-status permanent bureaucracy and a larger number of appointed, partisan positions than in any other advanced industrial country.[4] By the 1970s, economists had established an enormous scope of influence in the modern state, as their ideas became dominant in areas like monetary policy, regulation, and antitrust.[5] In both Democratic and Republican administrations, a large number of critical appointed positions came to be filled by economists, and some (like the chair of the Council of Economic Advisers) were effectively reserved for the most prestigious members of the profession. Consequently, each party has developed a cadre of prominent economists who combine status in the economics profession with an aptitude and willingness to advise ambitious presidential contenders.

The influence of economists in the extended party network goes far beyond staffing the sprawling administrative state. Glenn Hubbard, who was the chair of the Council of Economic Advisers (CEA) under George W. Bush and served as an Assistant Secretary of the Treasury under George H.W. Bush, argues that even in campaigns, where we might think their expertise the least valuable, economists had an important role:

> There were always three primaries. The first was a primary for money, where a candidate had to find individuals or groups that could help him or her. The second was a primary for experts, and not just economics. I mean defense, a variety of topics. Because without those people the candidate couldn't sound smart or couldn't prove to the first group—the wealthy people—that he or she is serious. This sounds so quaint describing it today, but major editorial pages would pay more attention to proposals they thought were, A, coherent, and, B, there were people they could talk to. So people would spend hours and hours . . . talking through positions with leading reporters and editorial boards. . . . Even reporters who might not have had the same political views that I had took me dead seriously. . . . That was something that could be offered a candidate.[6]

To perform that legitimating function for a political campaign or administration, economists drew on a hybrid form of status. Their position as spokesperson for a campaign gave them a public platform that their academic credentials, on their own, did not. But their academic credentials provided a perception of seriousness and expert validation that was valued among certain pivotal audiences and that politicians could not generate on their own. This provided economists a serious power resource, but also a degree of professional insulation, since their influence among certain audiences only existed to the degree to which they were understood to be operating within the bounds of their profession. As John Cochrane of Stanford's Hoover Institution argues, "When your reputation is that 'I give scientific fact-based advice,' you want to keep up that scientific fact-based advice and opinion in [government]." While not as strong as the Hippocratic Oath, elite economists in Republican administrations could only stray so far from the one true god of supply and demand if they wanted to return to the economics profession with their status intact. Economists hold up for high esteem luminaries like Harvard University Economics Professor Martin Feldstein, who openly criticized others in the Reagan administration for their unwillingness to raise taxes to reduce the deficit.[7] Their ability to ground their positions in the prestige of a highly respected academic discipline, combined with the jurisdictional clout that economists have carved out for themselves in a number of parts of the executive branch, provide a formidable platform for influence.

That influence is especially high among Republicans, since economics is one of the only policy-relevant academic disciplines in which they have a sizable representation. Surveys of the ideology of academics vary, but most find that between a quarter and a third of economists identify as conservative or Republican, while sociologists and political scientists on the right register in the single digits.[8] As a consequence, Hubbard argues, "I think virtually every regulatory idea, tax idea, financial idea, healthcare, has come from Republican academic [economist] stalwarts."[9] In addition, Hubbard claims, the institutional expectations for what constituted policy seriousness provided a sizeable jurisdiction for the kinds of skills and credibility economists possess. "Remember there was once a day when a politician would have his or her head handed to them if they went out with proposals that didn't add up. And so economists were very important in that process in campaigns. Again, it's not true right now, but there was a time when that definitely was true."[10] So long as there were rituals of legitimation that only economists could perform, Republican politicians needed to include them in senior positions in campaigns and government.

Because Republican presidents and office seekers relied upon mainstream economists for a number of critical functions, they included in their campaigns and their administrations economic experts with political preferences that were, at the least, different in intensity from the rest of the party. The function of economists in politics, as described by Hubbard, was not only to provide a source of policy solutions but also to act as censors of bad ideas. "[Just] the notion that a policy has to add up, that you can't just promise the moon. I remember telling many presidential candidates, you cannot simultaneously increase defense spending, cut taxes, [and] not change entitlements. It's just not coherent. No one will take you seriously. We're doing exactly that, of course, right now. But there was a day when you wouldn't have done that."[11] While there were no Republican administrations in which professional economists had a monopoly over economic policy, there were equally none in which they did not play a central place in advising candidates, or have a prominent place at the table in government.

Economists brought to Republican politics the very broad range of positions they shared with their disciplinary colleagues who counseled Democrats, a feature that they have in common with national security experts and that makes them different from lawyers. Within their professional and academic network, the connective tissue unifying economists runs deep, often much deeper than their partisan identities. As Cochrane argues, between liberal and conservative economists, "our debates are much narrower and the framework is the same. So, if you raise the marginal tax rate, how much will people work less? . . . We have a framework for our community."[12] That "framework" is one in which at least certain basic assumptions about the economy are taken as nearly axiomatic. As Tim Kane of the Hoover Institution puts it: "Think about free trade or the minimum wage. There's a right answer. Just right. Sometimes it's the economist in me that feels like we're physicists. That's [just] how gravity works. You can pretend it doesn't. You can make laws against it. . . . [But] free trade makes us richer. It's better for poor people. It's better for world peace."[13] Professor Greg Mankiw of Harvard, who succeeded Hubbard as Chairman of CEA, also sees the role of economists in government as expressing the relatively simple home truths of the discipline, a task somewhat parallel to their function as teachers.

> I am a big believer in textbook economics being useful for understanding the world . . . so I think it's great when economists are in the middle, whether it's people like myself and Glenn Hubbard . . . or people like Larry Summers, Jason Furman, who are center-left, [and]

go and do policy jobs. Basically what we're doing is, we're applying the tools that we teach in the classroom to the policy issues of the day. . . . One of the few reasons I spent fourteen years teaching introductory economics at Harvard is because I really do believe that what we teach, even as the first-year course, is incredibly important. . . . There are certain elements in Washington that don't have the same respect for sort of mainstream economics and are willing to make outlandish claims. And I think it's useful to push back against that whenever we can.[14]

Michael Strain, the director of economic policy studies at the American Enterprise Institute, similarly was "worried about a retreat from—I wouldn't even call them the basic tenets of conservative economics—I would just call them the basic tenets of economics. . . . That almost sounds like a parochial concern. And I don't intend it to be because . . . the idea that free trade makes people richer and helps societies to advance . . . is something that economists all believe. It's also just a fact of the world. I think it is not a controversial proposition."[15]

Mainstream economists of both parties believed that their role in the policy process was justified by science grounded in a rigorous discipline and that the institutional role carved out by that discipline was a vital brake on the preferences of politicians. This somewhat attenuates the partisanship of economists, who—again, like national security experts—often have a high degree of respect for their counterparts in the other party, as well as a sense of shared struggle against politicians who fail to recognize the basic truths of economic science. Trump brought this perennial tension to a much higher degree of intensity.

A number of Republican economists claim that their opposition to Trump is attributable to the fact that he violated certain basic concerns of conservatives in the economics discipline. Tim Kane believes that, "Our biggest risk as a country—our existential risk—is national debt. Super boring. Everybody says, 'Oh yeah, it's a big risk,' and then they don't do anything about it. He seemed to be in that mold."[16] Unlike previous Republican politicians, Trump did not even offer rhetorical gestures toward budgetary discipline, proudly declaring that, "I'm the king of debt. I'm great with debt. Nobody knows debt better than me. . . . I've made a fortune by using debt, and if things don't work out

I renegotiate the debt. I mean, that's a smart thing, not a stupid thing."[17] And Strain was concerned about the negative effect Trump would have on the party's hard-won, Paul Ryan–ish position on entitlements: "I was worried about a four- or eight-year reprieve from taking entitlement reform seriously, [what it would] do to the US economy."[18]

Conservative economists part ways with their liberal counterparts by embracing a more moralized conception of the economy featuring promotion of a culture of self-reliance and greater worry about dependency. Strain articulates these concerns about how Trump might impact the moral foundations of conservative economics. "I was also worried about what effect he would have on the conservative movement, in terms of its adherence to the importance of personal responsibility as a kind of guiding value. . . . A bedrock principle is a strong belief that personal responsibility is important, that individuals have agency, that people aren't just victims . . . that everything is not just luck and circumstance, that effort actually matters."[19] Like other conservatives, most notably *National Review*'s Kevin Williamson, Strain worried that Trumpism represented a kind of white-victim politics, one that conservatives rejected when the same language had been used by the left for racial minorities.[20] Trump's populism, some conservative economists fretted, spilled over into trade protection and demagoguing immigrants because it inherently sought out an external cause of individual problems. The conservatism they cut their teeth on, by contrast, was one whose cultural foundation was individual responsibility.

Table for One: Economists' Response to Trump

Despite Trump's many violations of Republican professional economic orthodoxy, there was no significant collective action by conservative economists and relatively few public statements of disapproval by them. Hubbard, like almost all conservative economists, chose not to sign the "Economists Against Trump" letter because, "In general, I don't sign petitions where I'm not involved. Even if I like the person, I just don't do it." He wasn't alone. Of the 673 economists who endorsed Mitt Romney in 2012, only one signed this anti-Trump letter.[21] Hubbard continues: "What I did tell people who were putting together letters is that the candidate, now the president, doesn't care. So you're not hurting him by saying we're against Trump. He could care less what you think. In fact, it almost makes him happy."[22] Greg Mankiw had a similar reaction and worried that, if anything, collective action would actually backfire, leading to less influence by conservative professional economists.

> One of my more liberal friends tried to induce me to organize a collective letter of center-right economists opposed to Trump. And I thought about it, and in the end I decided to state my own position on it on my blog. I was very happy to state my position, but I was actually apprehensive about a collective letter on the grounds that if he did get elected, everybody on the letter would automatically be disqualified from a position in the administration. And you didn't want somebody to become president who . . . crossed off every reasonable economist. . . . The fact that a bunch of pointy-headed economists are opposed to somebody doesn't really convince any voters.[23]

Cochrane went even further, expressing a degree of bemusement at intellectuals who made more comprehensive assessments of Trump:

> I studiously avoid any public pronouncement on the moral fitness or character of presidential candidates. I talk about economic policies . . . so Trump or not Trump has never made any difference to me. A lot of people felt the need to go out and say, "Oh, Trump is horrible" and become Never Trumpers. They regretted that when Trump won and they wanted jobs. Trump's been pretty effective about if you tweeted mean things about Trump, you don't get a job. So that was a stupid thing to do. You know, keep your mouth shut. Who cares about your opinions about the moral fitness of candidates? . . . I guess there were fewer "Trump is a disaster" comment letters from economists. Maybe economists just have a little more humility about our scope of expertise.[24]

Whereas a number of national security conservatives openly eschewed consequentialist reasoning in explaining why they thought it was important to make it clear where they stood on Trump, if only for the history books, this sentiment was all but absent from conservative economists.

A number of economists expressed concern about how appropriate it was to directly criticize Trump given their institutional position. Strain was also worried that if AEI was viewed as taking an aggressively anti-Trump position, it would reduce its influence on a Trump administration. "I assumed that . . . a potential President Trump would have people around him who wanted to seek out a range of views to help inform internal discussions and things of that nature. So I wasn't worried about that. But I mean, I was worried about potential negative ramifications if the institution [AEI] has people who are supposed to be doing cool policy analysis but who are publicly opposing a presidential candidate based on issues of moral character. . . . That rubs off on the institution."[25] Faced with a choice between what he considered to be unacceptable alternatives, Douglas Holtz-Eakin, the former Congressional Budget Office Director, chief economic policy advisor to John McCain in 2008, and now head of the American Action Forum, fell back on assessing the merits of individual policies rather than offering an evaluation of Trump himself. He recalls that:

> If you walked into this office the day after the election, I've got about 28 full-time people, and I've got at least five of them crying and probably another ten who were walking around in open disbelief and scared to death. I literally had to sit and talk to people and say, "Look, we're a policy shop. We evaluate policies. It doesn't matter who says them. . . . That's what we've done before and that's what we will continue to do." That's what I did during the campaign. It wasn't really about Trump, it's about Trump policies.[26]

When he cast his presidential ballot, Holtz-Eakin chose to write in his old boss McCain, because "I had no idea what [Trump's] economic policies were. When he did say something it was usually crazy and wrong. So I can't endorse that." And yet, his concern didn't rise to that of the national security professionals. For them, "this was an extinction-level event [but] it was something I thought I could wait out." And in the meantime, Holtz-Eakin also thought his position running an activist think tank meant he was obligated to make the best of the situation, rather than sitting on the sidelines criticizing the president:

> We have a mission. If it was just me hanging out at Syracuse, I'd have probably said some pretty unflattering things. . . . I could have, but I choose not to. I focus on the policy, not the personality, not the character, none of the things that people I think have correctly criticized the President on. . . . [What I] don't think Greg Mankiw is thinking about [is] I'm sitting in this office every day thinking about three sets of conservatives, White House, House, and Senate. . . . Paul Ryan's got task forces that he has set up to do tax reform, health-care reform, regulatory reform, policy-rich initiatives that he has for his members, designed in part for their reelects. That's interesting. I'm paying my attention to that. . . . Those things turned out to be the live action once Trump got elected. The things that he's been successful on were things that were in those initiatives. They were the tax reform, they were the regulatory reforms.[27]

Not all Republican economists chose to avoid offering an assessment of Trump's overall merits. Mankiw took the decidedly minority option of openly stating that he would not be voting for Trump, not just because of his "disqualifying" position on international trade but also because of "issues of temperament. I am not a psychologist, so I cannot figure out what Mr. Trump's personal demons are. But he does not show the admirable disposition that I saw in previous presidents and presidential candidates I have had the honor to work for."[28] Michael Strain joined Mankiw in focusing on Trump's character as well as his economics. In February 2016 he argued in the *Washington Post* that "the American president is not merely a package of public policy proposals. The president is our head of state—our chief public representative, a living symbol of the nation. However he would actually govern, Trump is simply unfit to hold this office."[29] Strain emphasizes that his criticisms of Trump diverged significantly from the overall brand of AEI, in which it was important for the think tank's various audiences to not think of it as "Never Trump or pro Trump. I want the major reaction to be, 'a bunch of serious people who are doing the highest quality work on economics and economic policy, and who are driven by sound reasoning and sound evidence.' . . . And some of the things that I did in 2015 and 2016 were a departure from that." Trump was so exceptional both in his economics and his character that Strain believed he had to push the envelope of his own organizational interest. "I felt like I had a platform and a voice. And that this was a pretty unusual situation, both in the conservative movement and in the country as a whole. And I wanted to use that platform and use that voice."[30]

Some conservative economists were surprised, however, at the relatively muted criticisms that have been lobbed at the administration even when it was making decisions that were directly in the wheelhouse of the profession, in particular the potential Federal Reserve nominations of Heritage Foundation and Cato Institute veteran Stephen Moore and former Godfather's Pizza CEO Herman Cain (neither of whom holds a Ph.D. in economics). Mankiw recalls that, "I first stated on my blog and then I wrote it up in the *Times* [that I was] opposed to Moore, and also the Herman Cain nominations to the Fed. But I was personally surprised that I didn't have more people join me in that. And it did seem to be just general silence on a lot of center-right economists and that surprised me."[31] Strain similarly argues that economists' sins with regard to Trump have been of omission rather than commission.

> What's disappointed me . . . has been the silence. For example, the president nominated Steve Moore to a be a Fed governor. I would've expected the economists with a public voice would have come out and said, "Hey, the Fed's a really important institution. . . . It's pretty clear that the president doesn't like Chairman Powell, and maybe trying to set up one of these governors to be the next chairman. It's bad to have a very partisan person like Steve Moore or like Herman Cain as a Fed governor. But it would be really, really bad if they were being put in place so that they could be moved over into the chairman seat in four years. And I need to come out against this." I would have expected there to have been a large number of people who would have come out and said that. And you just didn't see that. That was confusing to me.[32]

Mankiw has chosen to speak out publicly on issues where he feels he has distinct professional authority, especially in challenging the appointment of conservative economists whom he did not recognize as representing the discipline.

> If you compare what they're doing to children on the southern border, that's obviously much worse than nominating Steven Moore to the Federal Reserve. I just thought I had some credibility as an economist to have an opinion about the Steven Moore thing. Whereas I could write stuff on my blog about how terrible the southern border is, and how terrible it is that there are a bunch of empty slots throughout the government, that Washington is not functioning. But I feel like that doesn't speak to my expertise particularly. So that's why I sort of decided to lay in to the Steven Moore thing. But lots of other things I don't, just because it's not my area.[33]

Conservative economists are both empowered and constrained by their professional identity as scientists and guardians of what they view as a set of fundamental truths. While some have continued to question the morality of the Trump administration's overall policy, however, most express a degree of cynicism that anyone cares about their views.

Economists' Collective Action Problem

What explains the relative absence of significant collective action by conservative economists, both during the election and since, given the numerous ways in which Trump has challenged their professional jurisdiction and fundamental beliefs? Holtz-Eakin emphasizes the culture of conservative economists that limited their willingness to push others toward collective action. "Economists of my ilk place a heavy premium on individual freedom and the choices they make. We don't tell people what to do with their lives. The national security guys tell people what to do with their lives. They would pressure people not to serve [in government under Trump]. They're happy to do that. We are far more libertarian."[34] Tyler Cowen, a professor of economics at George Mason University and director of the Mercatus Center, chalks up the difference between national security conservatives and economists largely to network factors: "All those neocons know each other and hang out. Economists, it's just larger and more numerous."[35] National security conservatives are heavily based in the Washington area and have numerous structures that bring them into personal contact on a regular basis—including with their counterparts in the Democratic Party. Relative to that, economists have weaker formal organizational structures, apart from those that are specifically academic in character. Tim Kane saw the weaker coordinating structures of economists as a reason why they didn't engage in more collective action where Trump was concerned: "There's not a Federalist Society of economists, like, 'Hey, here's our list of nominees.' There are different think tanks, and we're friends with each other, but we don't have that coordinated institutionalism."[36]

A number of conservative economists also stressed the importance of public choice theory, as well as a general disrespect for politics, as factors in the profession's somewhat numbing reaction to Trump. Public choice theory is a large and diverse school of thought and not exclusively right-of-center, but it has an especially large following among conservative economists. While more sophisticated public choice theorists avoid assuming that those in politics are exclusively self-interested, the "folk theory" of public choice generally assumes that those in politics have the same self-regarding motivations as those in any other sphere of life. Politicians are best understood, therefore, as pursuing ends such as reelection or agency budget maximization rather than higher, idealistic goals.

Hoover Institution Senior Fellow Russ Roberts, who runs the widely followed EconTalk podcast, recalls that his initial perceptions of Trump were shaped by this public choice frame. "Sure, [politicians] try to differentiate themselves. But when it comes down to it, the incentives that they face, they're the same whether an R or a D is in front of their name. Of course, Trump promised some diversions from that because he's not a party animal. But I just assumed that a lot of the things that he was advocating would, quote, never happen. . . . I was sure there was no way he would ever be stupid enough to start a trade war. . . . So I just sort of assumed that a lot of his platform was just going to be cheap talk."[37] Similarly, Cowen, for instance, argues that among right-of-center economists there is a prevailing "sense that so many politicians are liars, and previous politicians lied in a higher-status way, and now Trump is lying in a lower-status way. That's objectionable, but with that framing it seems a little less urgently bad than a lot of non-economists would view it."[38] Because they generally had lower expectations of politicians in the first place, economists were less shocked by Trump than other conservatives, even where they agreed, as Holtz-Eakin did, that "He lacks honor. He has no character. He's a horrible human being. . . . [But] I wanted to get tax reform done, and I wanted to get healthcare reform done, and I want to get entitlement reform done. I've been working on regulatory and education reform. I have my bucket list, and I'm not going to give a rat's ass who's there."[39]

A number of conservative economists accepted the reality that, whatever they thought before November 2016, the election represented the end of the viability of any collective professional resistance to Trump. Michael Strain shows the tension and real internal conflict felt by many economist critics of Trump.

> I think there's such a thing as democratic legitimacy. And I think the guy won an election and is the president, and this is his administration. . . . I don't question his legitimacy per se, and I guess if I did . . . that would change the way I think about it. . . . I went way outside my lane, so to speak, during the election. And now, the election's over and now he actually is in power. . . . I can see . . . the point that if you're helping out, then you're just helping this enterprise to be more successful. But policy matters. I think if you're helping out, you're also helping people's lives to be better. And that's important, too. But at the same time . . . the things I was worried about in the election are things I'm still worried about. I'm worried about normalizing all this, and I'm worried about the longer-term effects on the Republican Party and the conservative movement, and, really, American democracy. . . . I think striking the balance in those cases is difficult for people who are trying to have an impact on this.[40]

While economists overall have not been particularly outspoken in comparison to national security conservatives like Eliot Cohen or Tom Nichols, most of the economists we spoke with felt that the profession has been significant largely through its absence in the administration. Holtz-Eakin believes that the relative lack of economists in the Trump administration has had a noticeable impact on its performance.

Among the things that Trump doesn't believe, he doesn't believe he needs to staff the federal government. He thinks all these people are swamp [creatures]. He ran Trump Enterprises with his family and a couple of folks, and this is how he's going to run the government. I would politely disagree. I don't think you can be effective that way. I think he's been less effective than he otherwise could be. They have done relatively little to roll back the labor regulations of the Obama administration. They have done relatively little in terms of western land issues, which are a traditional strength of the Republican Party. . . . Those are all extremely difficult, ground-level, inch-by-inch battles that you run through the agencies. You can't run them out of the White House. You can write all the executive orders you want, but you need foot soldiers to make those things happen. I think that they have too few.[41]

Hubbard similarly thinks that even in some areas where Trump has pushed policies that economists would not generally support, he would have been more effective with their advice.

Trump proves you could be elected without [the advice of professional economists]. Has he proven that you can govern effectively without that? I would say, no. . . . Let's start with the headlines now, with China and globalization. If he had had a different economic team, that team might have said, "You know what? Let's have a fundamental challenge of China." Which would mean getting the European Union, Japan, Canada, and others with us for a fundamental questioning of whether China should even be in the WTO. President Bush was sold a bill of goods. . . . But of course that wasn't the discussion. Or when Trump is mystified that tariffs lead to a strong dollar. Well, that's just textbook. So nobody was there to say "that's just the textbook," and it shows. Even the tax bill, which had some excellent stuff in it, like cutting the corporate tax, also had just a grab bag of ancillary provisions that nobody who designed real tax bills had spent much time with. . . . President Trump actually was smarter than people are giving him credit for. Some issues hitting the populist vein were right before people's eyes, and they didn't see it. And frankly, his challenge of China is absolutely right. Where it hurts him not to have experience and expertise is even when he finds a vein of rich gold, he's not able to mine it.[42]

For all their criticisms, many conservative economists believe it is important to give Trump his due, a recognition that explains why most conservative economists have not been as outspoken as Strain and Mankiw. Hubbard in particular thinks that Trump recognized some important blind spots in the profession.

> Free trade or economic disruption makes people better off on average. That was true, is true. I think what people didn't focus on was that what we say in textbooks, which is that the gainers can compensate the losers . . . that really wasn't happening. And if you think about the way politicians, not just on the right, I would even put President Obama in this group, dealt with people . . . they were speaking mainly to elite experts and wealthy businesspeople, who of course had a different view of the world, perhaps, than people on the ground. So I do think that President Trump deserves a lot of credit for picking that up. . . . Trump saw the dam breaking in a way that many elites on the left and the right just missed.[43]

A number of economists also recognize the significant policy victories that conservatives in the economics profession have won in the Trump administration, and the way that these gains have impacted the prestige of their organizations. Michael Strain was concerned, for instance, that his outspoken criticisms of Trump might reduce the impact of AEI, but"

> I don't think it did. Or if it did, it was marginal. There were parts of it that were, I think, positive. Kevin [Hassett, Trump's first chairman of the Council of Economic Advisers and before that director of research for domestic policy at AEI] was a real champion in the academic policy communities [for] lowering the corporate tax rate. And Kevin was part of the group that got that done. And that enhanced the brand. . . . Kevin did real research and real work on this topic. And that ended up having real impact through his presence as [Council of Economic Advisers] chairman. So that's a good thing. And I'm glad that our [corporate tax] rate is down 14 percentage points, and that

we have expensing for a few years, and whatever else. I think the kind of deregulatory efforts that the administration has engaged in are certainly brand enhancing.[44]

Conservative economists are generally mixed on what the Trump administration means for the future influence of the profession on the policies of the Republican Party. Hubbard, for instance, notes that, "About five or six years ago, Adam Davidson did a big Sunday Magazine *Times* cover story on Larry Summers and me as the future.[45] Like one of these two guys will be advising [the next president]. It's just a complete laugh. Larry is no more influential, I would think, among Democratic candidates than I would be with President Trump. So in that sense it looks pretty bad for economics."[46] Holtz-Eakin, by contrast, is more sanguine, believing that, "I don't think he's rewritten the economic orthodoxy of the conservative movement. . . . There are no principles at all. You can only have an orthodoxy if you at least have some principles. And he has none. There is nothing that distinguishes between the game and the real strategy. They're indistinguishable. He's fine with that. What's underneath [Trump's rhetoric] are people trying to get done things conservatives have always tried to get done."[47] Tim Kane similarly agrees that, "There is no Trumpism. There's only Trump. There's not this core underlying philosophy. I don't think people will look back in 50 years, like you would talk about Reaganism or Goldwaterism. . . . I don't think he's trying to win the 20-year intellectual battle for where America is going."[48] There have been people in Trump's orbit—like Steve Bannon and Peter Navarro—who have aspired to replace traditional Republican economics with something more vigorously nationalist and dirigiste. But conservative economists appear somewhat surprised that the administration has not pursued a more effective challenge to the basically libertarian economic status quo ante in the party—a bullet they may have dodged because of Trump's disinterest or inability to build such an alternative economic philosophy.

Where economists generally see a sea change is in the overall influence of experts generally in the American political system, a shift they think is embodied in Trump but not necessarily just a function of him. Tim Kane sees:

A discrediting of expertise. The populists in both parties don't give a damn about expertise. They just want people that are going to execute against this general principle. . . . You need expertise in a society. . . . I think it is troubling when any president talks about firing someone off the Fed [for] a policy disagreement. That's new, and that's dangerous. I think it's dangerous because Trump won't even act on some of these things, but there will be a future president, and I don't think it has to be Republican, [it could also be] a Democrat, who will say, "Well look, Trump did these things, so everything is justified." That's dangerous when you get a Fed that's both politicized and not independent.[49]

Economists less enamored of the technocratic character of the discipline and its role in politics, however, are less worried that the shift in the status of expertise—economic or otherwise—from the Obama to the Trump administrations represents a kind of decay in the quality of democratic governance. Russ Roberts recalls that most economists thought the potential Moore and Cain nominations to the Fed showed that Trump had "really gone off the reservation. . . . To appoint Herman Cain to that, to a slot that belongs, in quotes, to a serious professional economist, is unimaginable to us. . . . I think that the elevation of economists to priesthood class, or caste even, is a bad turn of events over the last few decades."[50] Cochrane similarly considers himself "a little allergic to the credentialism. You know, the Federal Reserve is now a wholly owned subsidiary of the economics profession. Ph.D. economists have gotten a whole lot of stuff a whole lot of wrong in the past, and the Fed is a public institution which ought to represent different constituents. . . . Moore himself, I don't know. But the instinct that a larger range of views should be present on the Fed than Columbia New Keynesian versus NYU New Keynesian strikes me as a reasonable one."[51]

While only a handful of elite conservative economists endorsed Trump during the campaign, and relatively few have worked in his administration, it is also true that there has been no significant oppositional collective action by them. Even lawyers, who were rewarded by Trump with an expansion of their jurisdiction over the choice of judges, managed to generate two letters of opposition (albeit relatively minor ones) during the election and a nascent anti-Trump organization that began in the second year of the administration. Economists were relatively quiescent in the face of Trump's challenge to their most sacred beliefs due to their relatively weak skills and temperament for collective action and their level of cynicism about politics overall, rather than from a lack of ideological motive. Both lawyers and national security conservatives had a more professionally embedded sense of the elevated nature of the public realm than economists, and thus launched themselves into collective action, largely in response to Trump's degrading of the norms of governance. Conservative economists, by contrast, have mainly sat on the sidelines awaiting the day when the populist fever in the Republican Party breaks and they are called back to service. It may be, however, that Trump was not an aberration, but a sign that the jurisdiction of economists in both parties has been eroded beyond repair.

10

Conclusion

ONE STORY THAT COULD be spun about the Never Trump movement—already prominent in many circles—is that it was a rather pitiful last gasp of a decadent, exhausted, and now vanquished elite. The Republican Party had once thought it essential to build up its own "counter-establishment" of right-leaning professionals to oppose the forces of liberalism.[1] In such disparate areas as national security, law, and economics, and based in think tanks, magazines, and universities, conservatives created a parallel network of experts and intellectuals—what we call the Republican extended party network—who were in conflict with their counterparts on the left, while also operating inside their world. The rise of Donald Trump, however, repulsed the party's class of experts. Not only did he reject many of their key ideas and spurn many of their claims to jurisdiction in governance, he also expressed disinterest or even scorn for the history of conservative thought they held dear, and his approach to governance lacked any role for the expertise they had grown accustomed to providing. Trump demonstrated in his rhetoric and actions all of the calumnies thrown against conservatives that Never Trumpers had devoted their careers to refuting.

All of these forces led to a rebellion by a remarkably large segment of the conservative extended party. That rebellion, in this telling of the tale, quite simply lost. Having been ground into the political dust by Trump, and abandoned by many of their former allies, the various professionals and party operatives who made up Never Trump essentially scattered to the four winds, some of them slinking back to a more or less fully Trumpified Republican Party, a handful switching their allegiances to the Democrats, others simply drifting away, and a few holding out, far from the levers of power, against Trump and Trumpism while clinging to their identities as conservatives.

That scenario, in which the forces of Never Trump once burned brightly but have now gone all but dark, is certainly one possibility. But it is not the only one, nor the most likely.

There can be no doubt that the Republican Party has been substantially transformed by the experience of having Trump at its head. The president's reelection in 2020 would only deepen that transformation. Deep sociological forces—in particular, a Republican Party base that is increasingly white, working class, Christian, less formally educated, and older—will lead the party to go where its voters are. What Trump started, his Republican successors will finish. Just as parties of the right across the Western world have become more populist and nationalist, so will the Republicans. A party that always had a relatively high degree of ambivalence toward intellectuals and experts—even its own—will now become entirely populist. That, of course, bodes poorly for most of the Never Trumpers, who combined a deep distaste for Trump personally with a professional interest in a less populist governing style and a disinclination to see their party go ideologically where he wanted to take it.

However, there may yet be a parallel, contrarian story to tell about the Republican Party. That story begins with the historical observation that American parties are rarely homogenous and are more typically deeply divided. While our institutions push strongly in the direction of two parties, our enormous population, vast geography, and demographic heterogeneity make it hard for those parties—especially in Congress—to be internally coherent. The consequence is that the ideological and coalitional diversity that in other systems is processed through multiple parties is institutionalized in the United States through durable factions within the two dominant political parties.[2]

Despite that, for the last couple decades both parties have been remarkably lacking in factional divisions. The Republicans in particular have not had organized groups with significantly different ideas, institutions, funders, and geographic bases. There has been, of course, the Freedom Caucus in the House of Representatives, but even there it disagreed with the leadership less on first principles than on tactics. Both Mark Meadows and Paul Ryan basically agreed where the ship should sail; the only question is whether it needed to tack to get there.

That kind of internal coherence is unlikely to persist in either party. The Democrats are already seeing the first signs of durable factional divisions emerging in their ranks, with some members openly calling themselves socialist and rallying behind a presidential candidate—Bernie Sanders— who has always resisted membership in the party itself. The left wing of the Democratic Party now has an increasingly large membership organization, the Democratic Socialists of America, that funnels party participation through a factional structure and is prepared to engage in primary challenges to the leadership's preferred candidates. They have their own information networks, focused on social media, and increasingly their own think tanks to provide the faction with ideas such as the Green New Deal, free college, and Medicare for All. They have their own ways to raise money, focused on large groups of small-dollar donors. Some members of the budding left faction of the Democrats appear eager to openly challenge the party's leadership and will likely become even more aggressive as their ranks in the congressional caucus increase.

By contrast, the moderate wing of the party is somewhat less developed, although it has a significant base of large donors, a group of loosely affiliated members of Congress (the New Democrat Coalition), and a few think tanks like Third Way. But both of these burgeoning factions are likely to only grow and deepen in the future, potentially squeezing politicians, activists, donors, campaign professionals, and intellectuals to join one or the other. It remains to be seen which faction will be dominant. The energy is certainly with the Democratic left for now, but it could be countered by growth in the moderate faction driven by refugees from an increasingly populist Republican Party. Whichever faction gains the upper hand, the Democrats in the future will almost certainly be a more deeply divided party than they have been since the implosion of the conservative Southern Democrats.

The Republicans are likely to also become more factionally divided. Going forward, the dominant faction of the GOP is almost certain to be populist and nationalist and have little space for most of the people who stood against Trump. Yet the populists will not have the party all to themselves. They are going to be being forced to share it with what we call a *liberal-conservative* faction, in recognition of their grounding in classical liberal principles of free markets, pluralism, and constitutionalism. The Republican Party in most of the South and Mountain West, along with a good part of the Midwest, will be Trumpist in character. But such a party will be all but uncompetitive in the Southwest, the Pacific Coast, New England, and the Acela Corridor, even as far down as Virginia. Notably, these are also the parts of the country where the left wing of the Democrats will be the strongest—possibly even dominant. That dominance will make it potentially beatable, especially in non-federal races, by a Republican Party that champions racial and ethnic diversity, is in favor of economic competition and entrepreneurship, and embraces market mechanisms to protect the environment, internationalism in foreign policy, and aggressive measures to fight poverty and enhance economic mobility without growing the public payroll or handing over power to public sector unions.

The core voters of this liberal-conservative faction will be the educated middle class, business, and more upwardly mobile parts of ethnic minority groups. This faction will find significant financial support in the technology and finance sectors of the East and West Coasts (support it will share with moderate Democrats), which combine cultural liberalism with a pro-market but reformist and less thoroughly antigovernment ideology on economic matters. This faction will still be recognizably conservative, especially on secular questions of social order like crime and homelessness, opposition to public sector unions, and a general pro-market orientation. The competitiveness of a Republican Party faction like that in the bluer parts of the country can already be seen in the reelection of Republican governors in Maryland and Massachusetts who, in a somewhat inchoate form, already embrace an approach more or less like this.

The liberal-conservative faction will not be dominant in enough states to ever—with rare exceptions—form a majority in the congressional party or get one of its adherents a presidential nomination. But if it is able to develop a genuinely distinctive, independent factional brand—such that voters do not think of themselves as supporting the dominant populist faction with their vote in congressional elections, and perhaps even in presidential ones—it could be powerful enough that the majority faction will have to negotiate with it.

The nationalizing trends in American politics will certainly make the creation of a distinct party factional brand challenging in ways that it has not been in the past. Voters are already becoming accustomed to casting ballots in state and local elections on the basis of their national party preferences, for instance.[3] The liberal-conservative wing of the party, however, will have some very impressive advantages with which to build a distinct brand. The nationalization of the media will play into the hands of the liberal-conservatives since its strongholds are in the country's media centers. And because it will be particularly attractive to wealthy business interests in technology and finance,[4] it will have more than adequate resources to build institutions, fund candidates, and engage in intra-partisan warfare for control of state parties. Because it will be especially attractive to the kinds of experts and thinkers who played such a key role in Never Trump, it will not lack for policies and well-developed public philosophies. These are impressive resources with which to engage in faction building.

Assuming the Democrats also move in a more factionalized direction, a Congress with durable, organized factions would look far different from the leadership-dominated one we have become accustomed to. In a world with more heterogeneous parties, neither party's majority leadership could organize either chamber of Congress without reaching a bargain with its minority faction.[5] What that minority faction would insist upon, in exchange for its support in organizing Congress, would be institutional rules that significantly weaken the majority party leadership's exclusive control of the legislative agenda. This would be especially important because, in particular on issues of national security, trade, and immigration, the Republicans' liberal-conservative faction would have more in common with the Democrats' moderate faction than with its own party majority, and it would want the opportunity to legislate with it.

A more factional party system is one in which the kinds of people associated with Never Trump do not disappear, but go from a position as the professional and ideological elite of a more or less unified Republican Party, to performing similar functions for a considerably smaller and more geographically compact faction within the party. This scenario may help explain one of the puzzles in the earlier chapters, which is why there has been so little organizational legacy from Never Trump so far, and why the activity that has occurred has been fairly underwhelming. The critics of the president responded to what they took to be an emergency created by his unfitness by building linkages across ideological lines. While most of them were deeply concerned about the ideological changes Trump imposed on the party, what concerned them most was the character of the man himself. They hoped that he might be defeated in the 2016 general election, and when that failed they put their hopes in the Mueller investigation, and then in the faint possibility of impeachment in the House and removal from office in the Senate. Yet the focus on Trump himself has dampened a recognition of the shifting tectonic plates under their feet, which have moved the bulk of the party in a populist-nationalist direction in which they will have a radically diminished role, even after Trump has departed the stage.

A factionalized Republican Party is one that will present some Never Trumpers with difficult choices. Some will choose to work with the bulk of the party, trying to de-racialize Trumpism and thus make it into the "Party of Sam's Club" that they have been trying to develop since the Bush administration. But most, we suspect, will attempt to build new organizations, with new kinds of social linkages, in the places where voters will be looking for an alternative to an increasingly left-wing—in some places openly socialist—Democratic Party. Many of the organizations that will be built for this purpose will also serve moderates in the Democratic Party. Almost all of the Republican foreign policy establishment will align with the liberal-conservative faction, bringing with them the cross-party linkages that they already have through organizations like the Council on Foreign Relations. Former Never Trumpers will find their future in building new institutions that will bridge the minority factions of both parties much as those created by the Progressives did in the early 20th century.

This will be a natural outgrowth of the increasingly bipartisan spirit and personal connections that many Never Trumpers acquired in their resistance to the president. Republican and Democratic donors terrified by Trump now meet regularly with various centrist activists through a network called Patriots and Pragmatists.[6] Billionaire donors like Kathryn Murdoch and Seth Klarman are already starting to target their giving on building up political infrastructure for the parts of the parties that are neither populist nor socialist. Those linkages will only become stronger, building on technology and finance's geographic base on the coasts, as donors in both parties choose to shift their support to their respective minority faction and away from the party as a whole. New magazines will form to provide ideas for the liberal-conservative faction of the Republican Party, which will provide an outlet for affiliated academics, writers, and think tanks like the Niskanen Center, one of the few organizations that emerged in the Trump era that was focused on providing an ideological direction for one part of a party. With the institutions of the national party largely out of their reach, former Never Trumpers will redirect their activity into capturing and then building up the GOP in places where it has desiccated, as a way to challenge the Democratic left for control of state government and to establish a power base for intra-party conflict. They will form new organizations of elected officials, along the lines of what the Democratic Leadership Council established in the 1980s, to create a political identity for aspiring officeholders distinct from the populist-nationalism of the national party. If they are successful, they will translate their custody of state government, at least on occasion, into electing factional supporters to Congress and will use their new institutions to coordinate their legislative efforts. The dominant populist faction of the Republican Party may not even resist the growth of the liberal-conservative faction, since it will operate in places where the Republican Party is all but extinct, and it may need the support of liberal-conservatives if it has any hope of controlling Congress in the future.

The experience of 2016 should have taught us all—professional political observers and citizens alike—to be careful with prognostication. What the rise and electoral success of Trump signaled was a profound shaking of the foundations of American politics. Things we all thought we knew about how American politics works may turn out to be wrong. Better, then, to abandon prediction-making and get into the scenario-building business. The scenario we sketch above is certainly not the only possibility, but it is internally consistent and makes sense of various pieces of activity and networks already in place.

Ultimately, the future is unwritten because it will be shaped by the choices of individuals, including many of those who have appeared in this book. Their ferment and entrepreneurial activity will create new institutions and make old institutions operate in new ways. It will make our parties look much different than they have in the recent past, and create new linkages across them and into civil society. It will change public policy, and with it the economy. New facts on the ground, including the country's shifting geopolitical position, will throw up new issues that will generate an altered political agenda. That agenda will flow through changed political institutions, which will be much less hierarchical in coming decades than they have been in the leadership-dominated recent past. With the parties less unified, it will be harder to operate our system of separation of powers like a parliament, and we could see a return of something like constitutional norms, as political change will be driven by shifting coalitions, legislative entrepreneurship, and deliberation.

In short, Never Trump will have failed comprehensively in its founding mission, which was to prevent the poison of Donald Trump from entering the nation's political bloodstream. But it is likely to be seen, in decades to come, as the first foray into a new era of American politics. If that comes to pass, the history books of tomorrow may tell a different story about Never Trump than the news feeds of today.

APPENDIX

List of Interviews

Jonathan Adler, December 2018

Kristen Soltis Anderson, January 2018

John Avalon, April 2018

Will Baude, July 2018

John Bellinger, May 2017 and September 2019

Sally Bradshaw, July 2018

Arthur Brooks, August 2019

David Brooks, February 2018

Mona Charen, April 2018

John Cochrane, July 2019

Eliot Cohen, July 2017 and September 2019

Tyler Cowen, July 2019

Ross Douthat, May 2018

Eric Edelman, February 2018

Erick Erickson, March 2018

Peter Feaver, September 2017

Mindy Finn, July 2017

David French, October 2018

David Frum, February 2018

Robert George, October 2017

Juleanna Glover, March 2018

Jonah Goldberg, July 2017

Michael Green, July 2017

Douglas Holtz-Eakin, July 2019

Glenn Hubbard, July 2019

Tim Kane, July 2019

Peter Keisler, September 2019

Orin Kerr, August 2019

William Kristol, May 2017 and May 2018

Matthew Kroenig, July 2017

Mark Laswell, March 2018

Yuval Levin, May 2017 and September 2019

Greg Mankiw, July 2019

Marisa Maleck, July 2018

Bryan McGrath, February 2018 and September 2019

Evan McMullin, July 2017

Lori Meyer, January 2019 and July 2019

Tim Miller, March 2019

Mike Murphy, June 2018

Charles Murray, August 2019

Tom Nichols, February 2019

Henry Olsen, March 2018

John Pitney, Jr., September 2017

Ramesh Ponnuru, February 2018

Jeremy Rabkin, January 2018

Russ Roberts, July 2019

Jennifer Rubin, July 2017

Patrick Ruffini, February 2018

Kori Schake, September 2017

Gabriel Schoenfeld, February 2018

Joel Searby, May 2018

Bret Stephens, October 2017

Stuart Stevens, July 2018

Michael Strain, July 2019

Charlie Sykes, January 2019

Peter Wehner, July 2017

Ed Whelan, June 2018

Adam White, June 2018

George Will, February 2018

Rick Wilson, October 2019

John Yoo, August 2017

Philp Zelikow, July 2017

NOTES

———◆———

Chapter 1

1. Throughout the book, we will refer to the movement as Never Trump, while reserving #nevertrump solely to refer to the Twitter hashtag.

2. David Azerrad, "The Never Trump Movement Is on Life Support," *Los Angeles Times* April 24, 2019; Henry Olsen, "The Never Trump Dilemma," *American Greatness* June 27, 2018; Liz Mair, "Has Republican Resistance to Trump Collapsed?," *New York Times* February 19, 2019.

3. "Ben Domench Interviews Pat Buchanan on Nixon, Culture Wars and Trumpism," *The Federalist* June 14, 2017, https://thefederalist.com/2017/06/14/ben-domenech-interviews-pat-buchanan-nixon-culture-wars-trumpism/.

4. Negative partisanship is a concept suggesting that partisan attachments are driven more by hatred of the other party than enthusiasm for one's own party. Alan I. Abramowitz and Steven W. Webster, "The Rise of Negative Partisanship and the Nationalization of U.S. Elections in the 21st Century," *Electoral Studies* 41 (2016), 12–22.

5. Andrew Abbott, *The System of Professions* (Chicago: University of Chicago Press, 1988).

6. Daniel Ziblatt, *Conservative Parties and the Birth of Democracy* (Cambridge: Cambridge University Press, 2017). Unlike Ziblatt, we think there's a parallel issue for parties on the left, for example when they are unable to exercise control over their followers' extreme demands for, as examples, mass expropriation of property or violations of rule of law in the economic sphere.

7.   Steven Levitsky and Daniel Ziblatt, *How Democracies Die* (New York: Crown, 2018).

8.   Milan Svolic, "When Partisanship Trumps Civic Virtue: Partisan Conflict and the Subversion of Democracy by Incumbents," https://papers.ssrn.com/sol3/papers.cfm?abstract_id=3243470; Matthew Graham and Milan Svolic, "Democracy in America? Partisanship, Polarization and the Robustness of Support for Democracy in the United States," https://papers.ssrn.com/sol3/papers.cfm?abstract_id=3354559.

9.   Frances E. Lee, *Insecure Majorities* (Chicago: University of Chicago Press, 2016).

10.   Part of the reason we do this is that we are well aware that we come to this story with our own priors. In addition to our primary academic homes, we are both fellows at the Niskanen Center, a think tank that has taken on a particularly important role as a home for Never Trumpers. Precisely because of that affiliation, we have largely left the role that the Niskanen Center has played in the resistance to Trump as a story for others, who did not participate directly in it, to tell. That should in no way be read as reflecting our own assessment of the Niskanen Center's significance, which we think has been considerable. But while we strive in the pages to come to give as neutral an account of Never Trump as we can, where Niskanen is concerned our objectivity necessarily reaches its limit. That said, whatever insight the reader finds in these pages is largely due to the access to members of Never Trump that we were able to glean by looking over the shoulders of the people involved.

Chapter 2

1.   Donald Trump, "Transcript: Donald Trump's Foreign Policy Speech," *The New York Times* Apr. 27, 2016, https://www.nytimes.com/2016/04/28/us/politics/transcript-trump-foreign-policy.html.

2.   Ibid.

3.   Michelle Ye Hee Lee, "Donald Trump's Baseless Claim That the Bush White House Tried to 'Silence' His Iraq War Opposition in 2003," *Washington Post* Oct. 21, 2015, https://www.washingtonpost.com/news/fact-checker/wp/2015/10/21/donald-trumps-baseless-claim-that-the-bush-white-house-tried-to-silence-his-iraq-war-opposition-in-2003/; Eugene Kiely, "Donald Trump and the Iraq War," FactCheck.org Feb. 19, 2016, https://www.factcheck.org/2016/02/donald-trump-and-the-iraq-war/.

4.   "Donald Trump Attacks George W. Bush on 9/11, Iraq," CBS News Feb. 13, 2016, https://www.cbsnews.com/video/donald-trump-attacks-george-w-bush-on-911-iraq/.

5.   An example of scholarly disagreement about the significance of the foreign policy establishment can be found in Patrick Porter, "Why America's Grand Strategy Has Not Changed: Power, Habit and the U.S. Foreign Policy Establishment," *International Security*, Spring

2018, 9–46, along with the response by Peter Feaver and Hal Brands, "Correspondence: The Establishment and U.S. Foreign Policy," *International Security*, Spring 2019, 197–204.

6. Jeffrey Goldberg, "The Obama Doctrine," *The Atlantic*, April 2016; David Samuels, "The Aspiring Novelist Who Became Obama's Foreign Policy Guru," *The New York Times* May 5, 2016.

7. The boundary lines between who's in and who's out of the foreign policy establishment aren't entirely clear, but the term is generally used to refer to the constellation of foreign policy experts who have served as political appointees in government—typically at the State Department, the Defense Department, or on the National Security Council—as well as prominent scholars and writers based at think tanks or universities. Technically, "foreign policy" is distinct from "defense," while "national security" is a term that encompasses both. But in practice, "foreign policy" as it's commonly employed in the phrase "foreign policy establishment" is often used synonymously with "national security," a practice we adopt here.

8. A critical account of the multiple roles played by what she calls "flexians" is Janine Wedel, *Shadow Elite: How the World's New Power Brokers Undermine Democracy, Government and the Free Market* (New York: Basic, 2009).

9. Bryan McGrath 2018 interview.

10. Tom Nichols interview.

11. Nichols interview.

12. Eliot A. Cohen, "A Really Bad Deal for America," *New York Times* May 17, 2016.

13. Cohen 2017 interview.

14. John Bellinger 2017 interview.

15. Cohen 2017 interview.

16. Matt Grossman and David A. Hopkins, *Asymmetric Politics: Ideological Republicans and Group Interest Democrats* (New York: Oxford University Press, 2016).

17. Mike Green interview.

18. Cohen 2017 interview.

19. Cohen and Bryan McGrath, "Open Letter on Donald Trump from GOP National Security Leaders," *War on the Rocks*, Mar. 3, 2016, https://warontherocks.com/2016/03/open-letter-on-donald-trump-from-gop-national-security-leaders/.

20. We were granted access to an email chain in which Republican foreign policy experts discussed the Cohen–McGrath letter detailed in Chapter 3. We were granted access to these emails with the understanding that we could quote from them as we wished in order to convey the contemporaneous thinking and dialogue within the Republican foreign policy network. However, we agreed that we would not divulge the names

of the participants. As such, we cite this batch of emails in footnotes simply as "Republican foreign policy network email chain."

21. Bellinger, "Statement by Former National Security Officials," August 8,. 2016, https://www.nytimes.com/interactive/2016/08/08/us/politics/national-security-letter-trump.html.

22. Green interview.

23. Green interview.

24. Eric Edelman interview.

25. Geoffrey Kabaservice, *Rule and Ruin: The Downfall of Moderation and the Destruction of the Republican Party, From Eisenhower to the Tea Party* (New York: Oxford University Press, 2012), 6–7.

26. Colin Dueck, *Hard Line: The Republican Party and US Foreign Policy Since World War II* (Princeton, NJ: Princeton University Press, 2010).

27. Philip Zelikow interview.

28. Cohen, "A Really Bad Deal for America.".

29. Edelman interview.

30. Nichols interview.

31. In fact, there is evidence that the Iraq and Afghanistan wars played a consequential role in Donald Trump's general election defeat of Hillary Clinton. Douglas Kriner and Francis Shen, "Battlefield Casualties and Ballot Box Defeat: Did the Bush-Obama Wars Cost Clinton the White House?" https://papers.ssrn.com/sol3/papers.cfm?abstract_id=2989040.

32. Samuel R. Berger, interview, Presidential Oral Histories: Bill Clinton Presidency, Miller Center of Public Affairs, Mar. 24–25, 2005, https://millercenter.org/the-presidency/presidential-oral-histories/samuel-r-berger-oral-history-deputy-assistant-president.

33. Berger. "Scoop Jackson Democrats" refers to admirers of Henry "Scoop" Jackson, the Democratic senator from Washington known for his hawkish foreign policy views.

34. Michael O. Leavitt, Christopher Liddell, Daniel Kroese, and Clark Campbell, *Romney Readiness Project 2012: Retrospective and Lessons Learned* (R2P, Inc., 2013).

35. Peter Feaver interview.

36. Feaver interview.

37. Feaver interview.

38. Feaver interview.

39. The John Hay Initiative, "About JHI," 2015, http://www.choosingtolead.net/about-jhi/.

40. Marco Rubio, "American Strength: Building 21st-Century Defense Capabilities," Sept. 17, 2014, https://www.rubio.senate.gov/public/index.cfm/press-releases?ID=C83FC52C-2B78-4615-A7F9-515B85FDE3CE; Kevin McCarthy, "House Majority Leader McCarthy on Foreign Policy," Sept. 28, 2015, https://www.c-span.org/video/?328408-1/house-majority-leader-kevin-mccarthy-foreign-policy.

41. The John Hay Initiative, *Choosing to Lead: American Foreign Policy for a Disordered World* (Washington: The John Hay Initiative, 2015); Peter Feaver, "What the Next President Should Learn from This One: Process Matters," *Foreign Policy* Sept. 30, 2015, http://foreignpolicy.com/2015/09/30/what-the-next-president-should-learn-from-this-one-process-matters/.

42. Cohen 2017 interview.

43. Feaver interview.

44. Edelman interview.

45. Feaver interview.

46. "Statement of Principles," June 3, 1997; Thomas Donnelly, *Rebuilding America's Defenses* (Washington: The Project for a New American Century, 2000); Robert Kagan and William Kristol, eds., *Present Dangers: Crisis and Opportunity in America's Foreign and Defense Policy* (New York: Encounter Books, 2000).

47. Right Web, "John Hay Initiative," Nov. 12, 2015, http://rightweb.irc-online.org/profile/john_hay_initiative/; Daniel Larison, "Romney's Foreign Policy Lives Again in the 2016 Field," *The American Conservative* Aug. 17, 2015, https://www.theamericanconservative.com/larison/romneys-foreign-policy-lives-again-in-the-2016-field/.

48. See, for instance, Jeffrey Steinberg, "The 'Ignoble Liars' Behind Bush's Deadly Iraq War," *Executive Intelligence Review* Apr. 18, 2003.

49. Green interview.

50. Anne Gearan, "Clinton Launching National Security Case Against Trump in California Speech," *Washington Post* June 1, 2016.

51. Zelikow interview.

52. Zelikow interview.

53. Zelikow interview.

54. Cohen 2017 interview.

55. Republican foreign policy network email chain.

56. Republican foreign policy network email chain.

57. Matthew Kroenig interview.

Chapter 3

1. We address these two letters because they were the most prominent and because they were signed by people who explicitly identified as Republicans or who had worked in previous Republican administrations. However, there were other anti-Trump letters. Many of the signatories to these letters also signed one or both of those we focus on. One of the other letters featured a bipartisan group of 53 foreign policy experts addressing how the military would have to respond if it were ordered to commit war crimes. They wrote: "One leading candidate, Donald Trump, has repeatedly insisted that he will direct the military to take steps that every reputable legal expert we know has deemed illegal: targeting the families of terrorists and other civilians not directly

involved in hostilities for lethal military strikes, and torturing suspected terrorists and their families. If Donald Trump becomes president and carries through with these campaign promises, the US military will be obliged to refuse these orders." Another letter was written by Asia experts who had worked in previous Republican administrations. They announced that they'd be voting for Clinton. A third letter was issued by 75 diplomats who worked in the Foreign Service or in foreign policy and security organizations. Many had served under both Republican and Democratic administrations, and most had not previously taken public political positions. All pledged their support for Hillary Clinton. Also of note: There was a pro-Trump letter signed by 88 high-ranking military officials, including three Army generals and one Navy admiral. See: "Defending the Honor of the U.S. Military from Donald Trump, *Foreign Policy* Mar. 4, 2016; "Preserving U.S. Credibility in Asia: An Open Letter," *Foreign Policy* Aug. 15, 2016; "Open Letter from Military Leaders," Sept. 6, 2016, https://assets.donaldjtrump.com/MILITARY_ LETTER.pdf; "Statement by Former Career Ambassadors and Senior State Department Officials" Sept. 21, 2016, http://apps.washingtonpost. com/g/documents/national/former-ambassadors-sign-a-letter-refusing-to-vote-for-donald-trump/2155/.

2. McGrath 2018 interview.
3. The disastrous exchange for Rubio featured Florida's junior senator repeatedly offering compelling evidence that he was, indeed, the programmed robot that Christie alleged. The back-and-forth began with Rubio making the point that the problem with Obama wasn't that he was incompetent—as some of his interlocuters had suggested—but that he was *exceedingly* competent in his "systematic effort to change America" from the "greatest nation in the world" to a horrific liberal dystopia. Christie responded by suggesting that, as a young, first-term senator, Rubio had no real-world experience of solving problems. Rubio oddly responded by repeating, nearly verbatim, his point about Obama's effectiveness at ruining America. Christie subsequently mocked Rubio's "memorized 25-second speech" implanted into his brain by his advisors. Bizarrely, Rubio then repeated that very speech yet again. The exchange continued with a few more heated salvos before mercifully drawing to a close. It was not a good look for Rubio, and it was the moment of the debate that garnered the most attention. See: https://www.youtube.com/watch?v=u9OZ8xHTX7c.
4. Eliot Cohen 2017 interview.
5. Cohen 2017 interview.
6. Cohen and McGrath, "Open Letter on Donald Trump from GOP National Security Leaders."
7. Republican foreign policy network email chain.

8. John Bellinger 2017 interview. For the blog post, see: Bellinger, "Donald Trump Is a Danger to Our National Security," *Lawfare*, Dec. 8, 2015.
9. Bellinger, "Statement by Former National Security Officials."
10. Bellinger, "Statement by Former National Security Officials."
11. Bellinger 2017 interview.
12. Republican foreign policy network email chain.
13. Republican foreign policy network email chain.
14. Zelikow interview.
15. Republican foreign policy network email chain.
16. Cohen 2017 interview.
17. Republican foreign policy network email chain.
18. Republican foreign policy network email chain.
19. Republican foreign policy network email chain.
20. Jacob Heilbrunn, "The Neocons vs. Donald Trump," *The New York Times* Mar. 10, 2016. See also, for instance: Heilbrunn, "Only One Man Can Heal Donald Trump's Rift with the Neocons," *The Spectator* May 14, 2016; Zaid Jilani, "Neoconservatives Declare War on Donald Trump," *The Intercept* 29 Feb. 2016.
21. Bellinger 2017 interview.
22. Republican foreign policy network email chain.
23. Republican foreign policy network email chain.
24. Republican foreign policy network email chain.
25. Bellinger 2017 interview.
26. Republican foreign policy network email chain.
27. Republican foreign policy network email chain.
28. Republican foreign policy network email chain.
29. Republican foreign policy network email chain.
30. Republican foreign policy network email chain.
31. Republican foreign policy network email chain.
32. Cohen and McGrath, "Open Letter on Donald Trump from GOP National Security Leaders."
33. Republican foreign policy network email chain.
34. Republican foreign policy network email chain.
35. Republican foreign policy network email chain.
36. Republican foreign policy network email chain.
37. Cohen 2017 interview.
38. Republican foreign policy network email chain.
39. Republican foreign policy network email chain.
40. Green interview.
41. Republican foreign policy network email chain.
42. John B. Judis and Ruy Teixeira, *The Emerging Democratic Majority* (New York: Scribner, 2002).
43. Kroenig interview.

44. Kroenig interview. The reference to the "party decides thesis" is the idea that even in the post-reform era of selecting presidential candidates—in which primaries have replaced "smoke-filled rooms"—party elites still play a decisive role in picking presidential nominees. See: Marty Cohen, David Karol, Hans Noel, and John Zaller, *The Party Decides: Presidential Nominations Before and After Reform* (Chicago: University of Chicago Press, 2008).
45. Kroenig interview.
46. Kroenig interview.
47. Kroenig interview.
48. Mark Mazzetti, Helene Cooper, and Eric Schmitt, "'NeverTrump' Becomes 'Maybe Trump' in Foreign Policy Sphere," *New York Times* Nov. 10, 2016.
49. Kroenig, "The Case for Trump's Foreign Policy: The Right People, the Right Positions," *Foreign Affairs* May/June 2017.
50. Kori Schake interview.
51. McGrath 2018 interview.
52. Cohen 2017 interview.
53. Cohen 2017 interview.
54. Republican foreign policy network email chain.
55. Republican foreign policy network email chain.
56. Republican foreign policy network email chain.
57. Republican foreign policy network email chain.
58. Republican foreign policy network email chain.
59. Republican foreign policy network email chain.
60. Schake interview.
61. Green interview.
62. Republican foreign policy network email chain.
63. Mitt Romney, "Transcript of Mitt Romney's Speech on Donald Trump," *New York Times* Mar. 3, 2016.
64. John McCain, "Statement by SASC Chairman John McCain on Current National Security Debate," Mar. 3, 2016.
65. Republican foreign policy network email chain.
66. Republican foreign policy network email chain.
67. Maureen Dowd, "Chickens, Home to Roost," *New York Times* Mar. 6, 2016.
68. Paul Krugman, "Clash of Republican Con Artists," *New York Times* Mar. 2, 2006.
69. Republican foreign policy network email chain.
70. Trump, "Statement on Politically Motivated Letter," Aug. 8, 2016, https://www.facebook.com/DonaldTrump/posts/10157461920570725.
71. Cohen 2019 interview; McGrath 2019 interview; Bellinger 2019 interview.
72. Bellinger 2019 interview.
73. Cohen 2019 interview.
74. McGrath interview; Cohen interview.

Chapter 4

1. The most prominent advocate of this strategy before the 2016 election was Sean Trende, who became famous for his "missing white voter hypothesis." This argument had considerable impact on the group known as "Reformocons," who will be discussed in Chapter 6, but was widely seen as directly in tension with the theory that informed the Autopsy. Sean Trende, *The Lost Majority* (New York: St. Martins, 2012).

2. For more on political operatives, see Adam Sheingate, *Building a Business of Politics: The Rise of Political Consulting and the Transformation of American Democracy* (New York: Oxford University Press, 2016).

3. Mike Murphy interview.

4. Stuart Stevens, "Drug Test," *Outside* Nov. 1, 2003.

5. Murphy interview.

6. Murphy interview

7. Stevens interview.

8. Ruffini interview.

9. Ruffini interview.

10. Ruffini interview.

11. Ted Cruz, Facebook post, Sept. 23, 2016.

12. Rebuild the Party, "A 20-Point Action Plan to Strengthen and Modernize the Republican Party," Nov. 6, 2008, http://www.rebuildtheparty.com/plan; Jose Antonio Vargas, "Seeking the GOP's Future on the Internet," *Washington Post* Nov. 25, 2008.

13. Mike Murphy, "For Republicans, the Ice Age Cometh," *TIME* Jun. 22, 2009.

14. Murphy, "For Republicans, the Ice Age Cometh."

15. Murphy interview.

16. John B. Judis and Ruy Teixeira, *The Emerging Democratic Majority* (New York: Scribner, 2002). Judis and Teixeira's account was more nuanced than the popular understanding of the trends they depicted.

17. Kristen Soltis Anderson interview.

18. Republican National Committee, "Growth and Opportunity Project," Mar. 18, 2013, 1.

19. Sally Bradshaw interview.

20. Tim Miller interview; Ruffini interview.

21. Republican National Committee, "Growth and Opportunity Project," 4, 6, 7.

22. Each of these groups, that is, except Indian Americans and Native Americans, which, despite their initial appearance on the "must focus" list, were oddly never mentioned again.

23. Republican National Committee, "Growth and Opportunity Project," 12.

24. Republican National Committee, "Growth and Opportunity Project," 8. See also 15–17, 76.

25. Bradshaw interview.
26. Bradshaw interview.
27. Miller interview.
28. Murphy interview.
29. Republican Debate, Houston, Texas, April 23, 1980, https://www.c-span. org/video/?c4608794/1980-republican-debate-tx.
30. Ronald Reagan, "Farewell Address to the Nation," Jan. 11, 1989.
31. Miller interview.
32. Miller interview.
33. Sara Murray and Ashley Killough, "Donald Trump's Unconventional Approach to Building a Ground Game," *CNN* June 10, 2016; David A. Graham, "There Is No Trump Campaign," *The Atlantic* June 9, 2016; Tina Nguyen, "Trump Campaign Staffers Quit After Not Getting Paid," *Vanity Fair* Sept. 9, 2016.
34. There were many other unconventional staffing episodes that fueled the impression that Trump was not a serious candidate. For instance, Trump hired John McLaughlin, the pollster who had earned notoriety for assuring then–Majority Leader Eric Cantor that he had nothing to worry about in his 2014 primary challenge from soon-to-be Congressman Dave Brat. The Cantor debacle came after a string of similar not-close McLaughlin prognostications in 2012. So much had McLaughlin's professional stock fallen that there was an organized Republican effort to warn the party's candidates to avoid hiring him. Yet after being introduced by mutual friend Dick Morris, the *National Enquirer's* "Chief Political Correspondent" most remembered for a prostitute scandal during his time as Bill Clinton's advisor, Trump tapped McLaughlin with the unusual task—particularly given how small Trump's staff was—of focusing exclusively on the candidate's low-probability effort to win solidly Democratic New York. In the end, the plan was unsuccessful; Hillary Clinton carried the Empire State by over 22 points. See: Cameron Joseph, "National GOP: Don't Use Cantor's Pollster," *The Hill* June 30, 2014.
35. Juleanna Glover interview; Ruffini interview.
36. Mindy Finn interview; Glover interview; Ruffini interview.
37. Ruffini interview.
38. Finn interview.
39. Murphy interview.
40. Ruffini interview; Murphy interview.
41. Murphy interview.
42. Murphy interview.
43. Christopher McKenna, *The World's Newest Profession: Management Consulting in the Twentieth Century* (New York: Oxford University Press, 2006).
44. Finn interview.

45. Finn interview; Ashley Young, "Ex-Mexican President Fox: Donald Trump Reminds Me of Hitler," *CNN* Feb. 27, 2016; Melissa Chan, "Donald Trump Refuses to Condemn KKK, Disavow David Duke Endorsement," *TIME* Feb. 28, 2016; Eli Stokes, "Sen. Jeff Sessions Endorses Trump," *Politico* Feb. 28, 2016; Michael Barbaro, Maggie Haberman, and Ashley Parker, "Chris Christie Endorses Donald Trump and Calls Marco Rubio 'Desperate,'" *New York Times* Feb. 26, 2016. Several days later, Trump disavowed Duke and the Klan.

46. Finn interview; Erick Erickson interview; Michael Cohen, "Top Political Hashtags of 2016," *Medium* Sept. 19, 2016; Jim Dalrymple II, "#NeverTrump Trends Worldwide in Revolt Against Donald Trump," *Buzz Feed*, Feb. 27, 2016.

47. Center for Responsive Politics, OpenSecrets.org, "Our Principles: Contributors, 2016 Cycle."

48. Our Principles PAC, "Mission Statement," https://web.archive.org/web/20160923041554/http://www.ourprinciplespac.com/.

49. Miller interview.

50. Miller interview.

51. Center for Responsive Politics, OpenSecrets.org, "Future 45: Contributors, 2016 Cycle," and "Future 45: Contributors, 2018 Cycle."

52. Miller interview.

53. Finn interview.

Chapter 5

1. Joel Searby interview; David French interview.

2. Searby interview.

3. Searby, "Condoleezza Rice for President," Mar. 10, 2016.

4. Searby interview.

5. See, for instance, John Podhoretz, "The Murder of the Weekly Standard," *Commentary* Dec. 14, 2018; David Brooks, "Who Killed the Weekly Standard?" *New York Times* Dec. 15, 2018.

6. Matt Dixon, "GOP Donors Pushing Condoleezza Rice to Run Independent Campaign," *Politico* Mar. 10, 2016. See also: Scott Bland, "Donors Ask GOP Consulting Firm to Research Independent Presidential Bid," *Politico* Feb. 26, 2016.

7. Searby interview.

8. James N. Mattis, "The Middle East at an Inflection Point," CSIS Apr. 22, 2016; William Kristol 2018 interview. For the record, we dissent from Kristol's assessment of the Beacon Hotel.

9. Searby interview; Kristol 2018 interview; Rick Wilson interview.

10. Kristol 2018 interview; Searby interview; Rick Wilson interview.

11. Kristol 2018 interview.

12. Wilson interview; Kristol 2018 interview; Searby interview.

13. Kristol 2018 interview; Alexander Burns, "James Mattis, Retired General, Decides Against Independent Presidential Bid," *New York Times* Apr. 29, 2016.

14. *The Hill* reported in May 2016 that Singer and Ricketts were still willing to support a third-party challenge, which adds credibility to the claim that Singer offered to support Sasse in this meeting. Jonathan Swan, "Third Party Effort Fizzling Out," *The Hill* May 13, 2016, https://thehill.com/blogs/ballot-box/presidential-races/279749-third-party-effort-fizzling-out.

15. Kristol 2018 interview; Robert Costa, "Mitt Romney Met Privately with William Kristol, Who is Leading the Effort to Draft an Independent Candidate, *Washington Post* May 6, 2016; Mitt Romney, Hinckley Institute speech, May 3, 2016.

16. Kristol 2018 interview.

17. Philip Klein, "'Dismayed' Romney Says He Doesn't Intend to Back Trump, Worried about 'Demagoguery and Populism,'" *Washington Examiner* May 5, 2016.

18. Kristol 2018 interview.

19. Kristol 2018 interview.

20. Searby interview.

21. Kristol 2018 interview.

22. Stuart Stevens interview.

23. French interview.

24. Kristol, Twitter, 3:00 PM May 29, 2016.

25. Donald J. Trump, Twitter, 5:02 PM May 29, 2016.

26. Mark Halperin and John Heilemann, "Kristol Eyes Conservative Lawyer David French for Independent Presidential Run," *Bloomberg* May 31, 2016.

27. French interview; Eliana Johnson, "Inside the #NeverTrump Candidacy That Almost Was," *National Review* June 7, 2016; Mark Halperin and John Heilemann, "Kristol Eyes Conservative Lawyer David French for Independent Presidential Run," https://www.bloomberg.com/news/articles/2016-05-31/kristol-eyes-conservative-lawyer-for-independent-presidential-run;Dylan Matthews, "Meet David French: The Random Dude off the Street That Bill Kristol Decided Will Save America from Trump," *Vox* May 31, 2016; Janell Ross, "Who, Exactly, Is David French, the 'NeverTrump' White Knight Candidate?," *Washington Post* June 1, 2016.

28. Tina Nguyen, "Bill Kristol's Secret Third-Party Pick to Challenge Trump Is . . . Some Random *National Review* Writer," *Vanity Fair* May 31, 2016.

29. Hanna Trudo, "Mitt Romney Praises Possible Independent Candidate David French," *Politico* May 31, 2016.

30. Searby interview; French interview.

31. Searby, "The Most Rejected Man in America," joelsearby.com Nov. 22, 2016; Searby interview.
32. French interview.
33. Searby interview; Kristol 2018 interview; Finn interview.
34. Searby interview.
35. Searby interview; Searby, "The Most Rejected Man in America."
36. Finn interview.
37. Evan McMullin interview.
38. McMullin interview; Wilson interview.
39. McMullin interview.
40. McMullin interview.
41. Wilson interview.
42. McMullin interview.
43. Murphy interview.
44. Erickson, "I Have Disinvited Donald Trump from the RedState Gathering," *RedState* Aug. 7, 2015; Erickson, "I Will Not Vote for Donald Trump. Ever.," *The Resurgent* Feb. 22, 2016.
45. Erickson interview.
46. NPR, "Vocal Critic Explains Why He Now Supports President Trump," *Morning Edition* Feb. 21, 2019.
47. Stevens interview.
48. Murphy interview.
49. Sally Bradshaw interview.
50. Murphy interview.
51. Murphy interview.
52. Wilson interview. Wilson, *Everything Trump Touches Dies: A Republican Strategist Gets Real About the Worst President Ever* (New York: Free Press, 2018).
53. Stevens interview.
54. Kristen Soltis Anderson interview.
55. Patrick Ruffini interview.
56. Tim Miller interview.
57. Miller interview.
58. Stevens interview.
59. Anderson interview.
60. Stevens interview.
61. Julie Kelly, "Never Trump's Billionaire Leftist Benefactors," *American Greatness* Nov. 14, 2018.
62. Stand Up Republic, "Our Work," https://standuprepublic.com/our-work/.
63. The New Center, "About Us," Nov. 12, 2018.
64. Murphy interview.
65. Murphy interview.

Chapter 6

1. *National Review*, "Conservatives Against Trump," Jan. 22, 2016, https://www.nationalreview.com/2016/01/donald-trump-conservatives-oppose-nomination/.

2. *National Review* (@NRO), Twitter Post, Feb. 1, 2016, 7:30 PM.

3. Some party leaders have even found themselves in hot water for their excessive interest in right-of-center thought. Paul Ryan and his attraction to Ayn Rand is just one of many possible examples. Rachel Weiner, "Paul Ryan and Ayn Rand," *Washington Post* Aug. 13, 2012, https://www.washingtonpost.com/blogs/the-fix/post/what-ayn-rand-says-about-paul-ryan/2012/08/13/fd40d574-e56d-11e1-8741-940e3f6dbf48_blog.html.

4. This reflects the argument of Daniel Ziblatt, *Conservative Parties and Birth of Democracy* (New York: Cambridge University Press, 2017), that we discuss in Chapter 1.

5. David Dagan and Steven Teles, *Prison Break* (New York: Oxford University Press, 2016).

6. Alan I. Abramowitz and Steven W. Webster, "The Rise of Negative Partisanship and the Nationalization of U.S. Elections in the 21st Century," *Electoral Studies* 41 (2016), 12–22.

7. A good, recent example of this is Jonah Goldberg, *Suicide of the West: How Tribalism, Populism, Nationalism and Identity Politics Is Destroying American Democracy* (New York: Crown Forum, 2018).

8. Alvin Felzenberg, "The Inside Story of William F. Buckley Jr.'s Crusade Against the John Birch Society," *National Review* June 20, 2017.

9. A long essay by Buckley in *National Review*, which took up the better part of an entire issue, was later published as William F. Buckley, Jr., *In Search of Anti-Semitism* (New York: Continuum, 1992).

10. George F. Will, "Donald Trump Is a Counterfeit Republican," *Washington Post* Feb. 12, 2015.

11. Jonah Goldberg, "No Movement That Embraces Trump Can Call Itself Conservative," G File, *National Review*, Sept. 5, 2018.

12. Goldberg interview.

13. Will, "Conservatism Is Soiled by Scowling Primitives," *Washington Post*, May 17, 2017; David Brooks interview.

14. James Q. Wilson, *Political Organizations* (Princeton: Princeton University Press, 1973).

15. Steven Teles, "The Eternal Return of Compassionate Conservatism," *National Affairs*, Fall 2009.

16. Amy Binder and Kate Wood, *Becoming Right* (Princeton: Princeton University Press, 2014).

17. Brooks interview.

18. Bret Stephens interview.

19. Douthat interview.

20. Levin 2019 interview.

21. Jennifer Rubin interview.
22. Goldberg interview.
23. Charlie J. Sykes, *Profscam: Professors and the Demise of Higher Education* (Washington: Regnery Publishing, 1988).
24. Sykes interview.
25. Rich Lowry interview.
26. Lowry interview; David French interview.
27. *National Review*, "Conservatives Against Trump," ; The Editors, "Against Trump," *National Review* Jan. 22, 2016.
28. *National Review*, "Conservatives Against Trump." See individual essays by Bozell, Podhoretz, and Medved.
29. Lowry interview.
30. Buckley, "In Search of Anti-Semitism," *National Review* Dec. 30, 1991. On Gingrich: "The Gingrich Editorial," *National Review* Dec. 15, 2011.
31. Lowry interview.
32. Ramesh Ponnuru interview.
33. Lowry, "The Quisling Establishment," *Politico* Jan. 27, 2016.
34. Reihan Salam and Ross Douthat are often credited with coining and popularizing the term. Salam explained that the moniker was appealing in that it "brings to mind a hitherto unknown faction of Transformers." Sometimes it appeared under the slightly different spelling, "Reformicon." In a low-stakes battle over the "i" or "o," Avik Roy noted that the "i" variant unpleasantly evoked "formication," the word describing the sensation of insects crawling on your skin. Also, the "o" form is consistent with traditional conservative branding conventions, the lineage of which can be traced back to such formidable identifiers as "neoconservative" ("neocon") and "paleoconservative" ("paleocon"). In any event, core members of the network clearly prefer the "o" spelling, so we adopt that usage here. Reihan Salam, "A New Kind of Republican: Is Jeb Bush a Reformocon? Also, What's a Reformocon?" *Slate* Feb. 6, 2015; Ben Zimmer, "For GOP Reformers, A Key Vowel," *Wall Street Journal* Feb. 14, 2015.
35. Ross Douthat and Salam, "The Party of Sam's Club," *The Weekly Standard* Nov. 14, 2005. For other early contributions in the reform conservative genre, see: Douthat and Salam, "The Buck Stops Here," *The Weekly Standard* Oct. 9, 2006; Douthat and Salam, "What Is the Matter with Kansas?" *The Weekly Standard* Nov. 20, 2006.
36. Douthat, "What Is Reform Conservatism?," Douthat, "Reform Conservatism and Immigration," *New York Times* June 23, 2014.
37. Ryan Cooper, "Reformish Conservatives," *Washington Monthly* May/June 2013.
38. Yuval Levin 2019 interview.
39. Ponurru interview.
40. David Frum interview.

41. Ashley Parker, "'Koch Primary' Tests Hopefuls in the G.O.P.," *New York Times* Jan. 20, 2015; Fredreka Schouten, "2016 GOP Hopefuls Gear Up for 'Koch' Primary," *USA Today* July 29, 2015.

42. Frum interview.

43. Salam, "Folks Before Kochs," *Slate* Feb. 29, 2016.

44. Douthat interview.

45. Douthat and Salam, "The Party of Sam's Club"; Ross Douthat and Reihan Salam, *Grand New Party : How Republicans Can Win the Working Class and Save the American Dream* (New York: Anchor Books, 2009), 123, 162, 164–165.

46. Frum interview.

47. Douthat interview.

48. Ziblatt, *Conservative Parties and the Birth of Democracy.*

49. Goldberg interview.

50. Lowry interview.

51. Brooks interview.

52. Jeffrey M. Berry and Sarah Sobieraj, *The Outrage Industry* (New York: Oxford University Press, 2013).

Chapter 7

1. Michael Anton, "The Flight 93 Election," *Claremont Review of Books* Sept 5, 2016, https://www.claremont.org/crb/basicpage/the-flight-93-election/.

2. Stephens, "The Flight 93 Election Crashes Again," *New York Times* May 17, 2017, https://www.nytimes.com/2017/05/17/opinion/flight-93-election-trump-conservatives.html.

3. James Kirchik, "The 'Flight 93 Election' Moment Is Now," *Daily Beast* Aug. 17, 2017, https://www.thedailybeast.com/the-flight-93-election-moment-is-now.

4. Nick Gass, "P.J. O'Rourke Hate-Endorses Hillary Clinton on NPR Quiz Show," *Politico* May 9, 2016, https://www.politico.com/story/2016/05/pj-orourke-endorses-hillary-clinton-222954.

5. Brooks interview.

6. Orin Kerr interview.

7. White interview.

8. Rabkin interview.

9. Robert George interview.

10. Goldberg interview.

11. Douthat interview.

12. Charles Murray interview.

13. William Kristol got his Ph.D. from Harvard under the tutelage of Straussian political theorist Harvey Mansfield, while Yuval Levin got his doctorate at the Committee on Social Thought at the University of Chicago, where he studied with the Straussians Leon Kass and Nathan Tarcov.

14. Thomas Pangle, *The Ennobling of Democracy: The Challenge of the Postmodern Age* (Baltimore: Johns Hopkins University Press, 1993).

15. James W. Ceaser, *Designing a Polity* (Lanham, MD: Rowman and Littlefield, 2010), 79.

16. Ceaser, *Presidential Selection* (Princeton: Princeton University Press, 1979).

17. The founder of West Coast Straussianism, Harry Jaffa, explains his differences with the more prestigious East Coast version in the essays included in *Crisis of the Strauss Divided* (Lanham, MD: Rowman and Littlefield, 2012). An extended discussion of Jaffa's thought can be found in Ken Kersch, *Conservatives and the Constitution* (New York: Cambridge University Press, 2019).

18. Charles Kesler, "Thinking About Trump," *Claremont Review of Books* May 7, 2018, https://www.claremont.org/crb/article/thinking-about-trump/.

19. Stephens interview.

20. Levin 2019 interview.

21. Frum interview.

22. Frum interview.

23. Frum interview.

24. Frum interview.

25. Murray interview.

26. Murray interview.

27. Stephens interview.

28. Mona Charen interview.

29. Peter Novick, *The Holocaust in American Life* (Boston: Houghton Mifflin, 1999).

30. Charen interview.

31. Kerr interview.

32. Kerr interview.

33. Eliot Cohen 2019 interview.

34. Stephens interview.

35. Gabe Schoenfeld interview.

36. Lowry interview.

37. Cohen 2019 interview.

38. Cohen 2019 interview.

39. Goldberg interview.

40. Levin 2019 interview.

41. David French, "The Price I've Paid for Opposing Trump," *National Review* October 21, 2016, https://www.nationalreview.com/2016/10/donald-trump-alt-right-internet-abuse-never-trump-movement/.

42. Goldberg interview.

43. Rubin interview.

44. Goldberg interview.

45. Schoenfeld interview.

46. Rubin interview.

47. Charen interview.
48. Stephens interview.
49. Rubin interview.
50. Charen interview.
51. Stephens interview.
52. Douthat interview.
53. George Will interview.
54. Brooks interview.
55. Charen interview.
56. Charen interview.
57. Levin 2019 interview.
58. Charen interview.
59. Lowry interview.
60. Ponnuru interview.
61. Stephens interview.
62. Stephens interview.
63. Rubin interview.
64. Sykes interview.
65. Sykes interview.
66. Murray interview.
67. Charen interview.
68. Sykes interview.
69. Frum interview.
70. Frum interview.
71. Frum interview.
72. Frum interview.

Chapter 8

1. Jonathan Swan, "Leonard Leo Attacks George Conway's 'Checks and Balances' Group," *Axios Sneak Peek*, https://www.axios.com/newsletters/axios-sneak-peek-5d299a4a-778b-48d6-b193-e06dce3cf43e.html.
2. Ken Kersch, *Conservatives and the Constitution* (New York: Cambridge University Press, 2019).
3. Steven Teles, *The Rise of the Conservative Legal Movement* (Princeton: Princeton University Press, 2008).
4. John Yoo interview.
5. Adam White interview.
6. White interview.
7. Yoo interview.
8. Yoo interview.
9. Marisa Maleck interview.
10. Will Baude interview.
11. Jeremy Rabkin interview.
12. White interview.

13. Jonathan Adler interview.
14. White interview.
15. Yoo interview.
16. Peter Keisler interview.
17. Kerr interview.
18. Email from Stephen Sachs, Sept. 27, 2019.
19. Antonin Scalia, *A Matter of Interpretation: Federal Courts and the Law* (Princeton: Princeton University Press, 1998). A good example of a more libertarian version of originalism is Randy Barnett, *Restoring the Lost Constitution* (Princeton: Princeton University Press, 2013).
20. Email from Sachs, July 5, 2018.
21. Baude interview.
22. Email from Sachs, July 5, 2018.
23. Maleck interview.
24. Baude interview.
25. The most important example of this is the emergence of "liberal originalism" in the legal academy, prominent examples of which are Jack Balkin, *Living Originalism* (Cambridge: Harvard University Press, 2014), and Akhil Amar, *The Bill of Rights* (New Haven: Yale University Press, 2000).
26. Baude interview.
27. "2016 Statement: Originalists Against Trump," https://originalistsagainsttrump.wordpress.com/2016-statement/.
28. White interview.
29. "Statement by Former US Department of Justice Officials," Oct. 10, 2016, http://online.wsj.com/public/resources/documents/DOJ_Letter_10.10.16.pdf.
30. Rabkin interview.
31. White interview.
32. Swan, "Leonard Leo Attacks George Conway's 'Checks and Balances' Group."
33. Maleck interview.
34. Baude interview.
35. Adam White interview.
36. Maleck interview.
37. On the power of the Federalist Society network, see Amanda Hollis-Brusky, "'It's the Network': The Federalist Society as Supplier of Intellectual Capital for the Supreme Court," *Studies in Law, Politics and Society*, April 2013.
38. Maleck interview.
39. Greg Price, "Trump Administration a 'Shitshow in a Dumpster Fire,' Says George Conway About Turning Down Justice Department Appointment," *Newsweek* Nov. 16, 2018, https://www.newsweek.com/trump-shitshow-dumpster-fire-conway-justice-1219567.

40. Lori Meyer interview.
41. Background interview.
42. Background interview.
43. Adler interview.
44. A further discussion of the Federalist Society's organizational model can be found in Teles, *The Rise of the Conservative Legal Movement*, Chapter Five.
45. Keisler interview.
46. Kerr interview.
47. Keisler interview.
48. Adler interview
49. Background interview.
50. This is a reference to an anonymous *New York Times* op-ed written by a "senior official in the Trump administration." The piece asserted that "many" administration officials, including the author, were secretly "working from within to frustrate parts of [Trump's] agenda and his worst inclinations." Anonymous, "I Am Part of the Resistance Inside the Trump Administration," *New York Times* Sept. 5, 2018, https://www.nytimes.com/2018/09/05/opinion/trump-white-house-anonymous-resistance.html.
51. Background interview.
52. Background interview.
53. Background interview.
54. John Bellinger 2019 interview.
55. Background interview.
56. Adler interview.
57. Ed Whelan interview.
58. Adler interview.

Chapter 9

1. Donald J. Trump, Inaugural Address, Jan. 20, 2017.
2. https://thehill.com/blogs/pundits-blog/presidential-campaign/297719-economists-have-a-message-clintons-policies-are.
3. Marion Fourcade, *Economists and Societies* (Princeton: Princeton University Press, 2009).
4. Derek Bok, "Government Personnel Policy in Comparative Perspective," in John Donahue and Joseph Nye, eds., *For the People: Can We Fix Public Service?* (Washington: Brookings Institution Press, 2003).
5. Benyamin Applebaum provides a highly critical perspective on this transformation in the role of economists in the modern state in *The Economists' Hour: False Prophets, Free Markets and the Fracture of Society* (New York: Little, Brown, 2019). An earlier and more appreciative examination of how the increasing role of economists changed the making of economic policy can be found in Martha Derthick and Paul

Quirk, *The Politics of Deregulation* (Washington: Brookings Institution Press, 1985).

6. Glenn Hubbard interview.

7. The obituaries for Feldstein, including by prominent economists, always mention his experience in government as an example of the kind of bravery the discipline admires. Consider, for example, Harvard Kennedy School economist Jeffrey Frankel's remarks on Feldstein's passing: "Guest Contribution: Remembering Martin Feldstein," *Econbrowser*, https://econbrowser.com/archives/2019/06/guest-contribution-remembering-martin-feldstein.

8. Neil Gross and Solon Simmons, "The Social and Political Views of American College and University Professors," in Gross and Simmons, eds., *Professors and Their Politics* (Baltimore: Johns Hopkins University Press, 2014), p.30. . See also Jon Shields and Joshua Dunn, *Passing on the Right: Conservative Professors in the Progressive University* (New York: Oxford University Press, 2016).

9. Hubbard interview.

10. Hubbard interview.

11. Hubbard interview.

12. John Cochrane interview.

13. Tim Kane interview.

14. Greg Mankiw interview.

15. Michael Strain interview.

16. Kane interview.

17. Louis Nelson, "Trump: I'm the King of Debt," *Politico* June 22, 2016, https://www.politico.com/story/2016/06/trump-king-of-debt-224642.

18. Strain interview.

19. Strain interview.

20. Kevin Williamson, "The White Ghetto," *National Review* Dec. 16, 2013.

21. "Open Letter: 794 Economists Oppose Trump," https://sites.google.com/site/economistsagainsttrump/; Catherine Rampell, "Analysis of Economists' Presidential Endorsements: Who Switched Teams Between 2012 and 2016?" *Washington Post* Nov. 2, 2016, https://www.washingtonpost.com/news/rampage/wp/2016/11/02/analysis-of-economists-presidential-endorsements-who-switched-teams-between-2012-and-2016/. A few generally conservative economists, like Robert Lucas and Edmund Phelps, signed a separate letter by Nobel Laureates endorsing Clinton, http://nobellaureatesforclinton.us/economics/.

22. Hubbard interview.

23. Mankiw interview.

24. Cochrane interview.

25. Strain interview.

26. Douglas Holtz-Eakin interview.

27. Holtz-Eakin interview.

28. Greg Mankiw, "My Take on Mr. Trump," *Greg Mankiw's Blog* Aug. 5, 2016, http://gregmankiw.blogspot.com/2016/08/my-take-on-mr-trump.html.
29. Michael R. Strain, "Donald Trump Isn't Funny Anymore, and We All Have to Stop Him," *Washington Post* Feb. 29, 2016, https://www.washingtonpost.com/posteverything/wp/2016/02/29/donald-trump-isnt-funny-anymore-and-we-all-have-to-stop-him/.
30. Strain interview.
31. Mankiw interview.
32. Strain interview.
33. Mankiw interview.
34. Holtz-Eakin interview.
35. Tyler Cowen interview.
36. Kane interview.
37. Russ Roberts interview.
38. Cowen interview.
39. Holtz-Eakin interview.
40. Strain interview.
41. Holtz-Eakin interview.
42. Hubbard interview.
43. Hubbard interview.
44. Strain interview.
45. Adam Davidson, "Boom, Bust or What?," *New York Times* May 2, 2013, https://www.nytimes.com/2013/05/05/magazine/larry-summers-and-glenn-hubbard-square-off-on-our-economic-future.html.
46. Hubbard interview.
47. Holtz-Eakin interview.
48. Kane interview.
49. Kane interview.
50. Roberts interview.
51. Cochrane interview.

Chapter 10
1. Steven Teles, *The Rise of the Conservative Legal Movement* (Princeton: Princeton University Press, 2008); Sidney Blumenthal, *The Rise of the Counter-Establishment: The Conservative Ascent to Political Power* (New York: Times Books, 1986).
2. On the role of factions in American political parties across history, see Daniel DiSalvo, *Engines of Change: Party Factions in American Politics, 1868–2010* (New York: Oxford University Press, 2010).
3. Dan Hopkins, *The Increasingly United States: How and Why American Political Behavior Nationalized* (Chicago: University of Chicago Press, 2018).

4. Evidence that technology entrepreneurs in particular are not an ideal fit for either party—but would be a very good fit for a liberal-conservative faction of the Republicans—can be found in David Broockman, Gregory Ferenstein, and Neil Malhotra, "Predispositions and the Political Behavior of American Economic Elites: Evidence from Technology Entrepreneurs," *American Journal of Political Science* (Jan. 2019), 212–233.

5. This argument draws on "conditional party government" theory, the most important examples of which are David Rhode, *Parties and Leaders in the Post-Reform House* (Chicago: University of Chicago Press, 1991), and John Aldrich, *Why Parties?* (Chicago: University of Chicago Press, 1995).

6. Kenneth Vogel, "Concerned by Trump, Some Republicans Quietly Align With Democrats," *New York Times* May 24, 2018.

INDEX

For the benefit of digital users, indexed terms that span two pages (e.g., 52–53) may, on occasion, appear on only one of those pages.